IN LENINGRAD

IN LENINGRAD

Joseph Wechsberg

DOUBLEDAY & COMPANY, INC.   GARDEN CITY, NEW YORK   1977

ISBN: 0-385-01563-1
Library of Congress Catalog Card Number 76–18372
Copyright © 1977 by Joseph Wechsberg
All Rights Reserved
Printed in the United States of America
First Edition

Illustration Acknowledgments

The author and publisher are grateful to the following for permission to reproduce photographs: The Granger Collection for Nos. 6, 12, 13; the Bettman Archive for Nos. 7, 8, 10; Culver Pictures, Inc. for Nos. 9, 11.

Photographs Nos. 1, 2, and 5 are by Lenore Loft.

All color photographs are by Ronny Jaques.

Interview by Ulrich Schiller with A. N. Yemelyanov, "Auf den Spuren der Revolution," taken from *Merian*, vol. 10/XXIV. Copyright © Hoffmann und Campe Verlag, Hamburg, 1971.

Grateful acknowledgment is made for use of material from *The 900 Days* by Harrison E. Salisbury: portions of entry in Vsevolod Vishnevsky's diary (p. 425) and poem by Daniel Leonidovich Andreyev (p. 483). Copyright © 1969 by Harrison E. Salisbury. By permission of Harper & Row, Publishers, Inc.

FOR INE

CONTENTS

BLACK AND WHITE ILLUSTRATIONS

Following page 108

Following page 132

COLOR ILLUSTRATIONS

Following page 60

St. Isaac's Cathedral

Interior of St. Isaac's Cathedral

The Bronze Horseman: Falconet's statue of Peter the Great, erected by Catherine the Great in 1782

The cruiser *Aurora* at anchor in the Neva

Along Nevsky Prospekt

Detail of the interior of Gostiny Dvor

The Church of the Savior on the Blood: detail of the exterior

The Church of the Savior on the Blood, built on the site of the assassination of Alexander II

Following page 180

Petrodvorets, formerly Peterhof, looking from the palace toward the Gulf of Finland

Petrodvorets

The gardens of Petrodvorets: one of the pavilions

Pushkin Palace (formerly the Ekaterininsky)

The Lyons Room in the Pushkin Palace. Designed by Charles Cameron, it was one of Catherine II's state apartments

The stage of the Kirov Theater, formerly the Maryinsky, during a Kirov Ballet performance

Palace Square, with Alexander's Column

The Ambassadors' Staircase in the Winter Palace. It is now the entrance to the Hermitage

THE TWO-FACED CITY

Leningrad is a noble upstart. When Peter the Great built his northern fortress in 1703, Moscow and Paris were already many centuries old, and New York's early houses had been there for nearly a century. The Czar named the new settlement Sankt Petersburg, after his patron saint. In 1914, after the start of the First World War, "St. Petersburg" sounded too "German" to the Russians and became Petrograd, "City of Peter." Not for long though. Five days after the death of Vladimir Ilyich Lenin, in 1924, the city was renamed after the Red czar. During the German siege of Leningrad in World War II, Hitler referred to the city by the secular half of its "German" name, Petersburg. Hitler had no use for saints.

The name changes reflect Leningrad's paradoxical history. The city was the capital of the czars, and the scene of Lenin's October Revolution, which finished off the czars. Most chapters in Russia's modern history begin or end there. The city reflects the nation's beauty and its brutality, the luxurious life of the rulers and the poverty of the serfs, the glory and the shame. In Leningrad, the cruelty of the despots was matched by the stoicism of their victims. The Leningraders survived even the nine hundred days of Hitler's siege. But later, many of the city's heroic defenders were purged by Stalin. Some were summoned to the Kremlin and went there, knowing that the summons meant their death sentence. No one protested or tried to escape.

The city's short, violent history is full of such contradictions.

Peter the Great considered himself a modernizer, but personally tortured his son Alexis. He westernized Russia, yet ordered his wife's lover executed and his head put into a jar of alcohol, which she had to keep in her bedroom. Catherine II—no one calls her "the Great" in Leningrad—corresponded with Voltaire and Diderot but didn't bother to improve the condition of Russia's serfs. She admired the enlightened ideas of her French friends but had no use for social critics at home; they were exiled to Siberia. Everything seems to have already happened in the city of Peter. The dissidents were there and the secret police, the powerful bureaucrats and the rebellious students, the writers declared "insane," the palace intrigues and power struggles. In Kronstadt, Leningrad's sea fortress, the sailors of the Russian Navy, whom Lenin called "the pride and glory of the Russian Revolution," revolted against him. Much of Leningrad's history remains inaccessible to present-day Russians.

Pushkin loved the city and the citizens now return his love. "I love you, child of Peter / I love you calm and stern," he wrote in *The Bronze Horseman*. Dostoyevsky, whose *Crime and Punishment* caught the atmosphere of St. Petersburg with brutal clarity, called it "the most abstract and artificial town in the world." He was not loved there and became an unperson during the Stalinist regime, but since 1957 he has been much read again by the young people. The city was always either loved or hated; no one was indifferent to it. The Duke of Wellington thought it was "the most beautiful town" on earth. The Marquis Astolphe de Custine, a keen observer with strong prejudices, wrote in 1839, ". . . a Greek city improvised for the Tartars as a theater set—a decor, magnificent though without taste, to serve as the scene of a real and terrible drama—this is what one perceives at first glance in St. Petersburg." Custine was often opinionated but rarely deceived. "European engineers came to tell the Muscovites how they should build and embellish a capital worthy of the admiration of Europe."

Despite its Western façade, St. Petersburg remained thoroughly Russian. Peter ordered the boyars (his nobles) to cut off their beards, and occasionally took pleasure in cutting them off himself, but they continued to think like Asiatics. The czars imported French architects, French fashions, and French cooks, but

not the ideas of the French Revolution. Catherine II was terrified
of "the seditious principles followed in France" and in 1790 ordered all Russians residing in France to return home. Westernization was a mixed blessing for Russia. The country was not ready
for Western thought. Peter created an abyss between the few
who accepted the new habits—aristocrats, liberals, writers, scientists, artists—and the many millions who remained untouched by
them. The Russians' atavistic distrust of all foreigners remained
part of their emotional makeup.

Today the Leningraders have a deep personal affection for
both Peter *and* Lenin. It makes little sense; the city often made
history but rarely sense. In Peter and Paul Cathedral, the burial
church of the czars, I saw two old women selling flowers, considered a luxury and expensive. Many Russian visitors bought
flowers and placed them on Peter's white marble sarcophagus
while several policemen looked on benevolently. For two centuries a stubborn myth has survived in the city. Peter is not dead;
he is asleep in his sarcophagus and comes out, unseen by mortals,
in time of danger. Actually, the sarcophagi are empty. Nicholas I
had them built over marble slabs in the floor where the dead are
buried. During the siege, some people claimed to have seen Peter
in the Summer Garden, where he loved to walk. Officially, the
despotic czar is now called "an early revolutionary" who roused
the country from its apathy.

"Peter was trying to do something for his people, not for himself," a middle-aged intellectual, no Party member, told me in
Leningrad. "He remains a living presence among the people—so
to speak, a member of the family. Contrarily, Catherine II does
not belong. She never did anything for the people. Everything
she did was to enhance her legality, to increase her power. Foreigners have compared her to a Medici, which is wrong. Florence
was a small city-state with a quite different background. She was
a ruthless killer. When Marie Antoinette was told that the people
had no bread, she asked, 'Why don't they eat cake?' Catherine
had no such illusions. She *knew* that the Russian people had neither bread nor cake."

Anna Akhmatova, "the queen of Russian poetry," who grew up
near the gardens of Tsarskoye Selo (now called Pushkin), wrote
beautifully about "the city of Peter, the city of Lenin, the city of

Pushkin, of Dostoyevsky and Blok, the city of great culture and great achievement." (Stalin was not pleased. Akhmatova was expelled from the Leningrad Union of Writers, by order of the Kremlin.) To the people, their beloved city remained the magical metropolis, the city of baroque palaces and noble squares. It was also the inferno of hungry serfs and underpaid laborers, of slum dwellers and prostitutes, of decadence and suffering. The despair of the women of Petrograd, standing for hours in line in front of the bakeries, led to the spontaneous rebellion on March 8, 1917 (February 23 by the old Julian Russian calendar). No one had plotted it, in a city that had a long record of conspiracy. The March Revolution just happened. And it destroyed Nicholas II, the last czar.

In the late evening of April 16, Lenin arrived at Petrograd's small Finland Station. (Vladimir Ilyich Ulyanov had signed himself "Ilyin" or "Tulin," and in 1901 adopted the pen name "Lenin.") He spoke briefly in front of the station on what is now hallowed ground. Alexander Kerensky and his Provisional Government were too "moderate." Lenin was not moderate in *his* demands: all power to the *soviets* (the workers' councils), no deals with Kerensky. No deals with *anyone*. The true Bolshevik Revolution. Lenin's demands terrified Kerensky, and also Stalin and Molotov, who had stayed in Russia while Lenin was abroad. Lenin left nothing ambiguous; it was all black or white. His was the most far-reaching revolution in modern history and the least violent. Only six people were killed in Petrograd in November 1917.

In March 1918, when the Germans were dangerously close to the city, Lenin moved the Soviet Government to Moscow. Temporarily at first but, as it turned out, permanently. As long as he lived, nothing happened to the city he loved, but after his death the struggle began between Leningrad and Moscow which reached a macabre climax in 1946.

In Leningrad were the artists, the musicians, the writers, the scientists, many of them Western-minded, all of them deeply committed Russian patriots. In Moscow were the violently orthodox clergy, the peasants who had become nouveau riche, the tough merchants who disliked the West—France, Europe—and its very symbol, the former St. Petersburg. Stalin's purge of the heroes of Leningrad remains the most terrifying chapter in Russian history since Ivan the Terrible. Hitler had hoped to destroy "Petersburg," "the very soul of Bolshevism." Stalin wanted to break the power of Russia's "cosmopolitan" second city. Both failed.

Leningrad survives, a glorious paradox. Located at the northern fringe of the Soviet Union, it became one of the country's great industrial centers. At latitude 60 degrees, it is the world's northernmost metropolis, with a population of almost four million people. It has no cultural hinterland but became the birthplace of much of Russia's modern literature, of Russia's science, of Russia's new national music, of the Russian ballet, which is the almost perfect blend of Asiatic traditions and Western styles. Within a short time Catherine II created one of the world's great collections of paintings in St. Petersburg. Not because she loved paintings; she simply didn't want her royal competitors, especially Frederick the Great, to get hold of them. Her motives were dubious and her methods were scandalous, but today Leningrad has the Hermitage, with twenty-eight authenticated Rembrandts. And the Elektrosila Works that assembled the first Sputnik.

The city knows its precise birthday. On May 16, 1703 (May 5 by the old Russian calendar), Peter, standing on a small island on the north bank of the Neva, cut two pieces of turf and placed them cross-wise. According to legend he had a casket with the relics of St. Andrew buried in the ground, which was blessed and sprinkled with holy water. His vision and courage though, are fact, not legend. The island was a swamp in the cold, gray river, "designed rather as a lair for wolves and bears than for the dwellings of men," Voltaire later wrote, with his customary tendency toward *plaisanterie* and disdain for veracity. (On another occasion he wrote that "the united magnificence of all the cities of Europe could but equal St. Petersburg." How did he know? He had never been there.)

Peter's original idea was not to create a new capital. He needed a fortress against the Swedes, who had defeated him at Narva in 1700. Their ships were still in the Neva. The town was born under the guns and later survived in spite of the guns. Peter and Paul Fortress was a primitive citadel with walls made of earth, later of wood, and finally of stone. The town that was built in the rear of the citadel was an afterthought. Peter believed it was easier "to stop an attack when you fight between houses rather than in the open plain." Winston Churchill repeated this almost verbatim in 1940. After work began on the fortress, Peter gave orders to build a dockyard where the Admiralty now stands. He had studied shipbuilding, his great passion, in Holland. He told his people to pronounce the name of the new settlement "Pitersburch," in Dutch. On old maps one also reads "Petersburgh" and "Petersburch," but the citizens still affectionately call it "Piter."

The construction of the fortress and the town remains an engineering masterpiece. All buildings had to be erected on wooden piles driven with primitive means into the marshy ground. Modern experts admit that they cannot explain how many things could be done. The Neva remains frozen from early November to March. An old chronicle reports 104 days of rain and 74 days of snow during an average year. There were frequent storms, and the fog rising from the marshes carried the germs of pestilence and fever. When the ice melted, there were devastating floods. Peter built the fortress with forced labor. Forty thousand workers were levied from the provinces, and the governors were told to send more, or else. Thousands died from sickness and cold, and from Peter's atrocious demands. He was ruthless toward everyone. When stones were needed, he forbade the use of stones throughout Russia. Every cart entering St. Petersburg had to deposit several large rocks at the gates. Barges paid a landing fee of twenty boulders. It was forbidden to put up new buildings in Moscow while all efforts were being concentrated in St. Petersburg. They built in such haste that Count Algarotti, courtier and jester, remarked that "ruins make themselves in other places but they were built St. Petersburg."

During the early years the Czar lived in a modest blockhouse, only two rooms and a cabinet, near the construction site. He knew he had to stay close to the men to make sure they were working. Catherine II later built a stone shell around the blockhouse, creating a relic containing the Czar's wooden chair and workbench. Nicholas I converted the bedroom into a Chapel of the Redeemer: Peter had always carried a "wonder-working" picture of the Redeemer on his person.

Getting people to live in the new town was almost as difficult as building it. In 1712 the Czar made St. Petersburg the capital of Russia by official decree. His family and the court were moved from Moscow though they didn't like it. Every nobleman owning thirty families of serfs was ordered to build, at his own expense, a house in St. Petersburg. The site was given to him, according to his rank, and the style of the building was exactly prescribed. St. Petersburg was truly the creation of one man. Heavy new taxes were introduced to pay for it; even the poor were taxed. Soon it was said that Moscow was built by centuries, St. Petersburg by millions of rubles. History, traditions, and economic considerations were all in favor of Moscow, the natural heart and geographic center of Russia. St. Petersburg was far away—from the labor force, from the food supplies, from the lines of communication. Everything had to be brought there over long distances. Yet somehow Peter found time to continue the war against the Swedes. In 1709 his troops defeated them and he got his revenge for Narva. "By God's blessing and the bravery of my troops I have just obtained a complete and unexpected victory," he wrote. "P.S. Thank God the foundations of Petersburg are firmly laid."

Peter had visualized a Dutch-style town, New Amsterdam on the Neva. Dutch orderliness is still visible on Vasilevsky Island, with rectangular blocks and regular streets, somewhat like Manhattan. But genius is never dogmatic. With unerring instinct, the Czar hired Italian architects who would bring the beauty and exultation of the Italian baroque to the cool northern skies. Domenico Trezzini of Lugano was summoned to Moscow and from there to the Peter and Paul Fortress. Carlo Bartolomeo Rastrelli, a noted sculptor, was hired in Paris, mainly to perpetuate the glory of Peter, of whom he made several busts. Later, other Italian architects were hired: Matarnovi, Chiaveri, Cipriani, Michetti—but Trezzini's influence on the Czar remained strong. In 1710 he designed the inconspicuous Summer Palace for the Czar, with Dutch-style interiors (Peter was relatively modest in his personal tastes). The beautiful outside reliefs were done by the great Andreas Schlüter from Berlin, who worked only one year in St.

Petersburg before he died. Trezzini also started building a palace for Alexander Menshikov, Peter's favorite, in Italianate style, blue and white. It was later finished by the German architect Gottfried Schädel and became the most elegant residence in St. Petersburg. When Peter wanted a beautiful garden designed around his Summer Palace he summoned a Frenchman; he knew that no one could surpass the French in garden design. Alexandre Leblond was the pupil of the great André Le Nôtre, who had created the magnificent parks of Versailles, Vaux, and Chantilly. Leblond had trees and shrubs imported from France, and put up lovely marble statues bought in Italy, Holland, and England, portraying the subjects of Aesop's fables. Peter wanted the people to visit the Summer Garden "to cultivate the mind," but he turned down Leblond's suggestion to place books on the benches. The Czar didn't believe in books. He did, however, set up a chamber of curiosities, the Kunstkammer, and promised a glass of vodka to every visitor. The Kunstkammer later become the Academy of Science.

Though always concerned with the future, Peter did not ignore the past. He had the relics of the thirteenth-century Grand Duke Vladimir Alexander brought from Vladimir to the spot where the Grand Duke (whom Peter worshiped) had defeated the Swedes and Knights of the Teutonic Order in 1241, and there Trezzini built the Alexander Nevsky ("of the Neva") Monastery and laid out the Great Perspective. Now Nevsky Prospekt, the city's most famous avenue, it links the Admiralty with the Alexander Monastery and leads into the Moscow highway.

While the grand design of the new town was beginning to take shape, Peter listened to his architectural advisors, but ultimately he always made his own decisions. Some wanted the town to grow around the fortress, on the northern bank of the Neva, but Peter knew that it must be on the southern bank, on the mainland, and there he had the first Winter Palace built in 1711. The great squares, the palaces, and the prospekts (avenues) are there, and the three parallel main canals of the Neva—the Moika, the Griboyedev, the Fontanka. Peter clearly realized the dominance of the Neva. His town was built only a few steps above sea level; there is water everywhere. The Neva forms the estuary islands of Vasilevsky and Petrograd; its sixty canals are spanned by some six hundred bridges, more than in Venice or Amsterdam, many of them built by Peter. Comparisons with Amsterdam or Venice are inappropriate, however, in many respects. The lagoons of Venice are deep blue. The Neva is rarely blue. Russian poets call her waters "silvery," and often a fine mist hovers above them.

In the Soviet Union, history may be shaped to fit the ideology, even architectural history. St. Petersburg remains the personal creation of Peter the Great, but few of its original buildings survive. Today's Winter Palace, the fifth, hardly resembles the first that Peter built. Only Peter and Paul Fortress, the nucleus and his original idea, has kept some of the early atmosphere—the cobblestone squares and streets, the low red buildings, the damp prison cells. In its first years, St. Petersburg was a rough pioneer town; in wintertime wolves came into the outskirts. There were criminals and drunks, fights and fears. People would lie down in the street when the Czar passed them in his carriage, and he had to make a law to end the practice. He was not much interested in imperial conventions; he simply wanted to get things done. He was already ahead of his new town; he wanted to push it farther out into the sea so it would fulfill its maritime mission. The anchor spot was the island of Kotlin, where he built shipyards and fortifications. Large vessels, unable to pass through the shallow waters to St. Petersburg, would stop at Kronstadt, as the trading port was named in 1723, and their goods would be transferred to smaller boats. Peter foresaw lively trade with the West, and again he was right. At the time of his death in 1725, about a hundred vessels a year would use the quais of the Neva; fifty years later, there were ten times as many.

Until the 1960s, when suburban skyscraper developments in the south and southeast began forming inhabited high walls around the historical center, Leningrad was flat and low, almost monotonous in its basic design. A hundred years ago, Turgenev wrote about St. Petersburg, ". . . these empty, wide, gray streets, these gray-white, yellow-gray, gray-pink peeling plaster houses with their deep-set windows—that is our northern Palmyra. Everything visible from all sides, everything frighteningly sharp and clear, and all sadly sleeping." Palmyra was a city of ruins in the

Syrian desert, but the poet's vision was right. One is always aware
of the horizon in Leningrad, of the clearness, and often of the
stillness. The extravagant men and women who ruled Russia after
Peter I continued his vision in their own ways, often rebuilding
the palaces left by their predecessors. All of them saw St. Petersburg as an imperial city, not unlike Paris or Berlin, with wide
vistas and monumental perspectives, and broad avenues that
might be used as parade grounds. There was nothing small or
petty bourgeois about the noble city.

The monotony was relieved by the art of the great architects,
reflecting the tastes of the rulers for whom they worked. The
rococo and baroque exuberance of Bartolomeo Francesco Rastrelli—the son of the sculptor—expressed the preferences of the
Empress Elizabeth, Peter's daughter, for luxury, pleasures, and
good-looking men. The severe classicism that still dominates
some façades in the city reflected the strictly classical education
of the German-born Czarina Catherine (the Great). Czar Nicholas I decreed that all buildings in St. Petersburg, except
churches, must be six feet lower than his Winter Palace. That not
only proves his despotism but helped to preserve the architectural unity of the city. To a large extent it is really his St.
Petersburg that we now admire in Leningrad. His greatest architect was Carlo Rossi, born in 1775 in Florence. From his Russian
father he had inherited a vivid imagination, from his Italian
mother, a ballerina, a sense of classical beauty.

Rossi studied in Italy and in 1812 came to St. Petersburg,
where he worked on the Winter Palace. Across from the Winter
Palace he designed the General Staff Building, with two rounded
wings and a triumphal arch in the center, dedicated to the Russian victory over Napoleon. It gives the large Palace Square an
almost intimate character. In the middle of the square is Alexander's Column, the world's tallest monolith at one hundred and
fifty-eight feet, erected in 1832 by two thousand soldiers with a
bird's nest of pulleys. It was not Rossi's idea. But for the Czar's
brother, the Grand Duke Mikhail, he designed Mikhailovsky Palace, a classically beautiful building with two symmetrical wings,
Corinthian pillars, and a huge eight-columned portico, painted
yellow and white. It is now the great Russian Museum, with
Rossi's classically uniform façade overlooking Arts Square.

And across Nevsky Prospekt Rossi built the Alexandrinsky (now Pushkin) Theater, elegantly cream-colored, with a six-column loggia and a frieze of garlands and masks. Behind the theater he created the most beautiful short street in the city. It is one block long, with an unbroken row of classical façades on each side; tall arches divided by regular columns. The height of the buildings equals the width of the street. The colors are yellow and white, and there is a wonderful style and elegance about the street. One side is occupied by municipal offices, the other by the Central Theater Museum and the Kirov Ballet School. After Rossi, only one beautiful building was put up in St. Petersburg, in 1860: the Maryinsky (now the Kirov) Theater that replaced the former Bolshoi.

By that time St. Petersburg had become a city built of Finnish granite, mostly heavy and gray, as Turgenev said, but the great architects managed to create fantasies by using colors that are strangely translucent in the mild northern light. "Towards the evening it can be very beautiful," Somerset Maugham wrote in *A Writer's Notebook*. "Though you may be reminded of Venice and Amsterdam, it is only to mark the difference. The colors are pale and soft. They have the quality of a pastel and there is a tenderness in them that painting can seldom reach." Some of the colors are bright though, almost like colors used by small children who try to paint. The Admiralty has the yellow hue of peasant butter. The Smolny Cathedral is light blue, almost like the sky in a Paolo Veronese painting. The Winter Palace is white and apple green. And there is a profusion of gold. The golden dome of St. Isaac's Cathedral, the golden bell tower of the St. Nicholas Cathedral, the gilded tower of the Admiralty, the gilded arch in Rossi's Palace Square.

Fifty years after its foundation, St. Petersburg was already being compared to Paris, which had developed organically over the centuries. The Russian Court was said to be the most elegant in Europe; at least its members thought so. Most members of the nobility had moved from Moscow, a large village with narrow streets and wooden houses, to St. Petersburg, enjoying the new elegant style of life. Peter the Great had seen his new capital as a bridge between Asia and Europe, between the conservative part of his vast empire and the progressive promise of Western civilization. The experiment did not succeed. St. Petersburg did not become a bridge; at best it was a "window toward the West." (Court jester Algarotti, not Peter, had created the expression.) The rich aristocrats commuted between their palaces in St. Petersburg and their town houses in Paris, but they were a tiny minority. The people of Russia never crossed the bridge. They remained Russians even though they accepted, superficially, some Western habits and inventions; the strong Russian folk character was never diluted by westernization. The Russians have always remained what they were, with their great qualities of kindness and humanity, imagination and love of life, and with their eternal burdens of suspicion, cruelty, fear.

Under Peter's successors St. Petersburg became more beautiful than its founder might ever have hoped. The foreigners and diplomats were in St. Petersburg. But the legends, the traditions, the church and the economy remained in Moscow, the true capital in the hearts of the Russian people. In Moscow the cost of living was lower. Everything was more expensive in St. Petersburg. The less wealthy members of the aristocracy were often ruined there, which was fine with the wealthy ones, who felt they were among themselves in the "exclusive" capital. They became closely attached to the court, removed from the problems of their estates and their tenants.

Among the poorer classes there was continual movement. In summer many artisans, carpenters, and masons came to work in St. Petersburg, but they returned home before the beginning of the winter. Then came the ice cutters, very poor peasants who had no home and slept in cellars or in the timber barks on the Neva. St. Petersburg tried hard but somehow it always remained on the outside, a sort of living museum; it never became a deeply integrated part of Russia's life. It was always compared, with pride or derision, to Western models. After being Peter's "New Amsterdam," it became Catherine's "Eastern Paris" and Alexander's "Northern Venice." Napoleon well understood this when he took the longer route to Moscow, where he hoped to cut the life arteries of Russia. Peter's successors knew it too. They held court in St. Petersburg and were buried next to Peter in Peter and Paul Cathedral, in the very middle of Peter's fortress. But they were crowned at the Kremlin.

The artists, the artisans, the architects, the tailors, the cooks, and the gardeners were still brought in from France, Italy, Holland, Germany. Foreigners became an important element in St. Petersburg's Western façade. First came the Dutch, then the Germans, and then the British, as merchants, seamen, naval engineers. There were even two British-born admirals, Greig and Elphinstone, as well as many British doctors. Dr. John Rogerson, of Dumfries, was appointed in 1766 as Catherine's court physician. Two years later, Dr. Thomas Dinsdale came to teach his Russian colleagues all he knew about smallpox vaccination.

Toward the end of the last century, there were English, German, and Dutch factory owners; French tailors and restaurateurs; German private schools; Lutheran, Anglican, and Episcopalian churches. To find employment, one had to speak at least two foreign languages. The foreign-owned shops in Nevsky Prospekt were the best and the most expensive. E. M. Almedingen, the British writer who grew up in St. Petersburg prior to World War I, heard about a cabinet minister's wife "who spent the whole of her husband's salary one morning by visiting only three shops." There was Alexandre's, "a twin to Tiffany and Asprey," Druce's (Harris tweeds), Cabassue's (French gloves), and Wolff's Bookshop, selling books and magazines in seven languages. There were splendors at Fabergé's, French perfumes at Brocard's, delicatessen at Abrikossov's, French confections at Aux Gourmets. The Russians shopped at Gostiny Dvor ("Merchants' Yard"), which is now the city's big department store. People still go to the Café Sever, said to be the best pastry shop in the Soviet Union. It was once called the Café Nord, but that sounded too French, too "cosmopolitan." Fortunately the change didn't affect the quality of the pastry.

The House of Books, always crowded with people, was once the Russian headquarters of the Singer Sewing Machine Company. The Americans put up a brash, vulgar structure that was to go higher than any other building in Nevsky Prospekt—eleven stories. The city authorities forbade the excessive height. "The company had to content itself with a building of modest height," the official Leningrad guidebook says. "It was adorned with a pretentious décor in bad taste, which included a tower with a dome, topped by a glass sphere, the whole thing completely out of harmony with the sober lines of Nevsky Prospekt. In the evening, a light would appear inside the globe, and the name of the firm would sparkle round the metal ring."

Time, the great healer, has given the former Singer Building a patina of period elegance, and today it doesn't stick out like a capitalist monstrosity in Nevsky Prospekt. It wasn't the only one. Many foreign banks and international concerns had their branch offices there. People got quite used to them. The horses' hooves would make clapping sounds on the dark, wooden pavement. Taxis were not respectable at the turn of the century. People would hire a droshky, drawn by a single horse, after bargaining with *vanki*, the coachman, or an elegant *likhach*, two well-fed horses and no bargaining. The writer Johannes von Guenther, who lived there at that time, wrote, "There was hardly a novelist who didn't write about Nevsky Prospekt." The exception was Dostoyevsky. He disliked and ignored the elegant avenue. In his minute description of the city, Nevsky Prospekt doesn't exist. But Gogol wrote, "There is nothing finer than Nevsky Prospekt, not in St. Petersburg, at any rate."

> One cannot believe though everything Gogol wrote [Guenther says] for he saw everywhere his unfathomably real mysteries. The Nevsky was a turbulent business street and at the same time the avenue of elegant women wearing expensive furs, the boulevard of frivolous officers of the guard and of serious businessmen with briefcases under the arm. When they passed the Cathedral of Our Lady of Kazan [now a museum of atheism] they would lift their hat and the women would cross themselves. The cathedral was so overwhelming that it made even nonbelievers pay tribute to it. After the years of liberal professors and temperamental lawyers one "wore" again religion, and there were more arguments about the problems of the Orthodox Church than about *Das Kapital* by Marx. St. Petersburg affected every writer living there. Sinaida Hippius, the religious wife of Merezhkovsky, and Innokenty Annensky wrote bitter, beautiful poems about the city. . . .

Today Nevsky Prospekt is always crowded, though not with Leningraders. It is known as a shopping street all over the Soviet

Union, and people come from far away to spend their money there. I spoke to a woman from Tashkent, the capital of the Uzbek S.S.R., who had come to buy an Uzbek rug that she could not get at home. Many shoppers are Estonians, who have the reputation of working hard and saving their money. The Leningraders claim they have neither the money nor the time to do their shopping in Nevsky Prospekt.

Until 1850—the city was almost a hundred and fifty years old—it was considered impossible to build a permanent bridge across the Neva. People would cross the river by boat, and many drowned until a pontoon bridge was built of rafts near the Winter Palace. In winter "roads" were marked on the ice by small fir trees. A streetcar would cross the frozen river on temporary rails. The rich went skating and sledging. When the first permanent bridge was under construction—now named after Lieutenant Schmidt, the commander of the battleship *Potemkin*—Czar Nicholas I promoted the chief engineer one rank in the nobility after the completion of each span. Today Leningrad has four permanent bridges linking the mainland with the islands. At night, their central parts are raised to let the ships go through.

Late in June and throughout July the Arctic sun never moves low beyond the horizon. Even at midnight there is a pale, silvery light, magically transforming the cold stone façades, making them shimmer softly and become strangely alive. Pushkin loved "the white nights" when "I can read and write without a candle / With a dawn breaking through a sunset." The light plays tricks with the colors of the city. The dusk, reflected by the golden cupolas of the churches, creates a sort of fata morgana. There is something eerie and unreal about the butter-yellow and cream-colored façades. Alexandre Dumas called the white nights "the poetry of God." Unfortunately much of the magic has been spoiled by commercialism since the white nights were advertised by Intourist as a major tourist attraction.

The young people love them though. A young girl said they were waiting for the white nights, talking about them in advance, making plans. This is the time of official laisser faire. Students are permitted to return late to their dormitories; bedtime is postponed; the police won't interfere with the young people playing the guitar and singing on the Neva embankments. Lovers disappear between the trees of the parks and wander around Yelagin Ostrov, now a public recreation center, once the private island of Prince I. P. Yelagin, with a beautiful neoclassical palace built—of course—by Rossi. It is a time of mild abandon and fun, the most romantic time in Russia's most romantic city, Pushkin's city:

> Clear dusk and moonless glimmer
> When in my room I write
> And read without a lamp,
> And in the empty streets
> The huge buildings doze. . . .

Another scene comes back to my mind. I had been at a ballet performance at the Kirov. It was a fine white night, and I thought I would walk back to my hotel, along the Moika Canal. It was half past ten but the streets were empty. There was an unchanging dusk in the sky. A pale shimmer on the gray façades of the old houses and small palaces was reflected in the still, dark water. After the brilliantly painted sets on the stage of the Kirov the silent palaces were just as unreal. Turgenev's northern Palmyra was not only "sadly sleeping." It seemed quite dead. There would be people along the Neva, enjoying the moment, aware of its evanescence, but here, only minutes away from the river, there was no life, not even the memory of the past. Suddenly I wanted to get away. I was glad when I saw the golden dome of St. Isaac's Cathedral, my beacon in Leningrad, across from my hotel.

I heard the story (possibly apocryphal) about the old man who was born in St. Petersburg, went to school in Petrograd, was married in Leningrad, and, if he had the choice, would like to live again in St. Petersburg. This doesn't mean that there are secret monarchists in Leningrad today. If one meets a fragile old lady or one of the last courteous octogenarians who remember the days prior to World War I, they admit, perhaps with some reluctance, that czarism exhausted itself because the rulers were poor leaders and remained totally removed from their people. The last czarists long ago left for Paris and New York, Palm

Beach and Hollywood, where some of them attempted to relive
their past, sometimes pathetically as extras on movie sets.

They would talk wistfully about "St. Petersburg" but they
would not admit that it was really Lenin who saved its beauty,
when he ruled that nothing must be touched. Lenin's orders were
not forgotten after the Second World War, when many great palaces were burned-out shells. Everything of historical interest was
re-created, and the effort and cost be damned. Leningrad is the
greatest restoration job in modern history, dwarfing such ambitious projects as Warsaw or Dresden. One sees it today as it was a
hundred years ago, a great city comparable to certain parts of
Paris, Rome, or Vienna. It cost billions of rubles that might have
been used to raise the standard of living, but the citizens of the
Soviet Union enthusiastically approved of the expense, even people who are often critical of the regime. Apparently the restoration of their great monuments gives them a sense of identity with
their history. The restoration drive is stronger in the Communist
countries than in the Western world, where much beauty of the
past is neglected and ruined because people take it for granted;
there was no violent break in history as in the Communist world.
And the Communist leaders now feel so confident about the future that they can afford to let their people enjoy the past.

The Leningraders have an almost personal, proprietory feeling
about the palaces that were built by despots and exploiters who
wouldn't even permit the people to stand outside and look in.
Today they consider themselves joint owners of the Winter Palace and of Tsarskoye Selo. Young people accept this as a matter
of course, but their elders still walk through the outrageously
sumptuous palaces with an incredulous feeling, as though they
can't believe that they may now enter the rooms where once the
czars lived. It is only 115 years since Alexander II published his
Emancipation Manifesto freeing the peasants.

Leningraders have a superior feeling about their city. It isn't
just local patriotism. The Leningraders' feelings were distilled by
history and tested during the siege. They are honestly convinced
that their city is unique, and they are probably right. They let
the Muscovites boast about their metro; they know that Leningrad's subway is *unique*. It was said it would be impossible to
build one, owing to the marshy ground, but after several years

the geologists found some veins of clay and hard stone going through the low swampy strata. The tracks were laid along these veins, at a very great depth. The exact depth is a military secret; no one will talk about it. Fast-moving escalators take you down to the stations, which are less flamboyant but in far better taste than Moscow's. This is Leningrad, where everybody seems to have a sense of beauty. There are statues, mosaics, soft colors, indirect lighting. Each station has a sort of leitmotif. The Baltic Station is lined with sea-blue marble. The Pushkin Station is dominated by a statue of the poet. The trains are fast and comfortable; the people are quiet and reserved. Noisy passengers are immediately known as "visitors from Moscow and other less developed places." Local snobbism is as strong as a sense of self-confidence, a residue from having survived the siege and saved the city that was all but lost.

The duality of St. Petersburg and Leningrad remains. The two live side by side but not with each other. They are not even on speaking terms, having nothing in common. Old St. Petersburg remains a beautiful stage set, visited by millions of people from Russia and all over the world. That is the city every Russian wants to see once, but to the Russians it is not what Rome is to the Italians or Paris to the French. The decisions are made in the Kremlin. The city of Peter remains a museum, open from 8:00 A.M. to 5:00 P.M.

And there is Leningrad, alive and viable, with a style of its own, quite different from Moscow, with no trace of the decadence sometimes claimed in Moscow. Leningrad's strength is its intellect. It was the mind and the will, not the body, that enabled the Leningraders to survive the hardship and horror of the nine hundred days.

Once in a while the borderline between St. Petersburg and Leningrad becomes blurred. The other evening I walked through Peter's Summer Garden, where he had his Dutch mansion, and where his great admirer Pushkin loved to walk. Walking between the lovely marble statues, I suddenly had an acute sense of *déjà vu, déjà entendu*. And then, just as suddenly, I remembered: the first scene in Pushkin's and Tchaikovsky's *Queen of Spades*.

THE ROMANOVS

HOW IT BEGAN

Russia emerged from the dawn of history in A.D. 862 when, after centuries of wars and massacres, a Viking chief named Rurik settled in Novgorod, becoming first prince of Russia and the founder of the country's first two dynasties. His successors moved south and after the capture of Kiev about 880 established their residence there, as dukes of Kiev. In 988 Vladimir adopted Christianity, the Byzantine-Greek faith. It was a political decision, and so was his marriage to a daughter of the Byzantine emperor. Russia was moving south, as she was later to move toward the north and finally the east.

The dukes of Kiev ruled until 1169, when Andrew Bogolubsky captured Kiev and established the dynasty of the grand dukes of Vladimir. In 1223 the Mongols under Genghis Khan invaded Russia. The country never quite recovered from this disaster. The Mongols overran Moscow, Vladimir, and Kiev, and pushed toward Silesia and Hungary. The "Golden Horde" under Batu, the grandson of Genghis Khan, reached the shores of the Adriatic before going back to the Lower Volga. In 1380 Tamerlane of Samarkand led his Tatars from the south, defeated the Mongols and went back again. For a long time, the Tatars and the Mongols devastated Russia, ruined the country's culture, and established a system characterized by despotism, cruelty, suspicion, and poverty.

The power of Kiev was ruined. Prince Vladimir Alexander, now known as Alexander Nevsky, defeated the invaders from the north and established a new dynasty, the grand dukes of Muscovy (Moscow). In 1380 Dmitri Donskoi defeated the Tatars and called himself grand duke of all Russia. A hundred years later Ivan III (the Great) established independence at last, and made Moscow his capital. He was called "czar" by the powerful Church and married Sofia, a niece of the last Byzantine emperor. His grandson, Ivan IV (the Terrible), was crowned in Moscow as czar of all the Russias in 1547. Moscow was a grandiose and sinister place of icons and torture chambers. Ivan's father died early; when he was eight, his mother died. The boy grew up amid the wild fights and intrigues of the boyars. He amused himself by throwing live dogs over the walls of the Kremlin.

When he wanted to get married, he was shown dozens of girls, and selected Anastasia Romanovna. He adored her; they had a son. But when Moscow burned down soon afterwards the baby died, and after him Anastasia. Ivan became deranged; it was said that his wife had been poisoned. In his moments of madness he would order people tortured and killed; he was driven by his suspicion and once had three quarters of the population of Novgorod executed for suspected treachery, never proven. There were moments of self-pity and prayer, drunken orgies and more tortures. Once again, the Tatars came from the south and burned Moscow to the ground. The Czar felt lost and frightened; he had no friends. Once he became annoyed at the French ambassador and ordered the unfortunate diplomat's hat nailed to his head, with fatal consequences. He tried to marry Lady Mary Hastings, and even sought refuge in England, where he would be safe. Queen Elizabeth promised he would "be friendly received." At fifty he said he was hopelessly sick. "The cords of my soul have been stretched too tight . . . no doctor can heal me." Yet he was a mysteriously paradoxical man. He made Russia larger and more powerful, extending the country's eastern borders far into Siberia, but cut off contacts with the West.

In 1582 in a sudden rage he killed his older son (he had remarried). Three years later he died, leaving his country in chaos, "the Time of Trouble." The surviving son, Feodor, weak and frightened, was dominated by Boris Godunov, the ambitious boyar immortalized (and somewhat romanticized) by Pushkin and Mussorgsky. After the death of Feodor, Boris became czar;

the dynasty died out. There were invasions by the Swedes and by the Poles, who marched into Moscow. The Russians never forgave them and later took terrible revenge.

There was complete anarchy after the Cossacks besieged the Poles and drove them out of the Kremlin. Western ambassadors were frightened to go there, where they were "treated like convicts." Conniving boyars and fanatical priests fought for power. And then, in 1613, an assembly of the Church decided to elect another ruler, Michael Feodorovich, a boy of sixteen whom no one had ever seen. Eventually they found him living with his mother in the Ipatiev abbey near Kostromo.

Michael had a certain claim to the throne: he was the grand-nephew of the first wife of Ivan the Terrible. He became the first ruler of the Romanov dynasty in 1613. Three hundred and five years later Czar Nicholas II, the last Romanov, and his family were murdered in Ekaterinburg, strangely also in an Ipatiev house.

Not interested in power, Michael was a quiet, melancholy man who let his father, the Patriarch Philaret, become the most powerful man in Moscow. After thirty-two years of relative stability, except for a constant struggle to get rid of the Poles and the Swedes, Michael was followed by his son Alexis, who also became czar at the age of sixteen. He is described as a handsome man of good will, but not an effective ruler. Though some Russian historians call him "gentle and amiable," he showed moments of the terrifying Romanov wrath. In 1662 the gentle Czar sentenced seven thousand people to death because they had dared send him a petition in which they asked for better living conditions. They were certainly justified: there was corruption, the currency was almost worthless, and the people were starving. But the gentle ruler wasn't satisfied with the blood bath; he ordered fifteen thousand more people seized in the villages. They had their arms and legs cut off.

Alexis's first wife, Maria Miloslavskaya, bore him thirteen children. Only two of the sons survived—Feodor, weak and sickly, and Ivan, mentally retarded. It looked like the end of the Romanovs, but Alexis decided to marry again. Russian women at that time enjoyed no rights. They were, in fact, not treated like human beings but were the property of their men, who might do to them anything they liked except strike them "in the eye or under the breast." If they made a scene, they were severely punished; if they tried to murder their husbands, for which they might have had good reason, they would be buried up to their neck and left for days, until they died. No wonder even the female members of the imperial family preferred not to marry. They were doomed to a life of boredom in the *terem*, their own quarters, surrounded by women servants, doing needlework and gossiping, seeing no men. When their doctor visited them, he felt their pulse through a curtain. When they traveled in their elegant carriages drawn by a dozen horses, the curtains were drawn, and their faces were veiled.

After the Czar announced his decision to marry again, preparations were made for two hundred attractive girls to be "inspected" by His Majesty. But the inspection never took place. At a dinner party in the house of the Czar's prime minister, Artamon Matveyev, His Majesty met Natalia Naryshkina, seventeen and pretty, the ward of Matveyev and his Scottish-born wife. Madame Matveyevna, born Hamilton, had no use for the poor veiled ladies in their seraglios. In her house, the finest in Moscow, no one was veiled and all women were treated like ladies. Doubtless she had something to do with the introduction. Natalia's father was Cyril Naryshkin, a minor nobleman of Tatar origin. Naryshkin's brother had married a niece of Madame Matveyevna, also a former Miss Hamilton.

At the end of the dinner party, the Czar is said to have said to Natalia, "Little pigeon, I will find thee a suitable mate." He was in one of his gentle moods. He soon told his prime minister that he was going to marry Natalia. Matveyev was not overjoyed. He would have preferred that the Czar go through the motions of "inspecting" and "selecting" Natalia; he feared the wrath of the influential family of Alexis's first wife. Soon there were rumors in Moscow that Matveyev had used black magic on Natalia so she would bewitch the Czar. There were so many difficulties that the marriage had to be postponed. By the time it took place, it was no secret that Natalia was five months pregnant. A few months later, a healthy boy was born and christened Peter. He is now known as Peter the Great.

Czar Alexis shocked Moscow society when he took his bride

everywhere, even when he went hunting. She was present at the performance of plays at Preobrazhensky Palace. She didn't mingle with the guests, but she could watch them, and they knew she was there. Young Peter had a few happy years. When his mother rode in her coach, drawn by twelve snow-white horses, she was followed by a small gilded carriage drawn by four ponies. The little boy was inside. The gilded carriage had been a gift from the prime minister.

In 1676—Peter was four—his father died, and Feodor, the weak, sick boy, was made czar. He was under the sinister influence of his sister Sophia, who had long ago made up her mind that the dynasty should continue through Alexis's first wife and Feodor, and that Natalia and Peter must disappear. A fine imperial family situation; unfortunately there was no Shakespeare in Moscow. Sophia, whom some historians called beautiful, was, according to the French diplomat Adrien de la Neuville, who often saw her, ". . . monstrously fat, broad, coarse in person." He also admitted that she was "acute and shrewd" and that "although she had never read Macchiavelli . . . all his maxims came naturally to her."

Sophia soon established her position as her brother's dominating influence. She took part in all decisions. The boyars had to accept her, and one of them, Prince Vasily Galitzin, became her lover. The first thing Sophia did was to get rid of Matveyev. At her orders, Czar Feodor dismissed the former prime minister and sent him to Siberia—as governor of Verkhoturye. By the time he got there, he had lost his title and his job and was treated like a criminal.

Feodor died in 1682. Sophia's other brother, Ivan, was considered unfit to rule, being mentally retarded. Peter, ten years old, was proclaimed czar. The crisis was fast approaching. Sophia conspired to place her brother Ivan on the throne. She and Prince Galitzin had the powerful support of the *streltsy* musketeers of the palace guard.

Matveyev had survived the exile in Siberia and returned. He was with Natalia and Peter when the soldiers came into the Kremlin. Natalia asked for his life. The soldiers cut off Matveyev's hands and feet and killed him; they then killed many members of Natalia's family. Historians claim that Peter, aged ten, saw the terrible things, and that the soldiers "put his feet into the blood of the Naryshkins" to make sure the boy knew what was going on. When it was all over, the *streltsy* musketeers were given ten rubles each, and the Assembly was forced to recognize Peter and Ivan as joint czars, and Sophia as regent.

PETER: THE SCHIZOPHRENIC GENIUS

The bizarre genius who admired Western technology, personally executed people he didn't like, and created St. Petersburg in the middle of nowhere, on marshland, was born in Moscow's Kremlin on May 30 O.S., 1672. Benevolent historians have tried to explain that Peter's early life "in the dark labyrinths of the Kremlin" inspired him to build a new capital that would have plenty of "space and light." Nonsense. Peter needed a military basis in his expansionist policy against the Swedes, who were then the dominating power in the Baltic.

He was a giant, six feet eight inches tall, with a terrible Romanov temper, a wild drinker, "very brutal in his passions." Gilbert Burnett, the Bishop of Salisbury, who saw Peter in Moscow, wrote that the Czar had "convulsive motions all over his body." He was badly handicapped by heredity *and* environment. His traumatic experience at the age of ten never wore off, and left him emotionally unbalanced. All his life he suffered from nightmares and convulsions.

In 1697, when he was twenty-five, he traveled in Western Europe with a staff of two hundred and fifty people, "the Great Embassy." He shocked everybody with his terrible manners, dressing like a sailor and belching, "especially in the company of foreign ambassadors." At official banquets the Czar amused himself, dressed up as a servant, by standing behind the chair of his friend François Lefort, a Swiss adventurer who was officially introduced as "head of mission." Lefort's main achievement was his ability to outdrink Peter. The "mission" consisted mostly of lackeys, musicians, and court dwarfs, all having diplomatic status, but there were twenty boyars and thirty-five young men, known as "volunteers," who took part in alcoholic and sexual "divertissements." An Austrian diplomat named Pleyer reported to Vienna that the Great Embassy's aim was "to divert the Czar a little." Peter traveled "incognito" as "Mynheer Peter Mikhailov" and pretended to pay no attention when he was addressed "Your Majesty," but he expected foreign dignitaries to treat him as emperor. When the Swedish governor of Riga called him "Mynheer," sticking to the fiction of Peter's incognito, the Czar was furious and swore he would later start a war against the hated Swedes—and he did.

Voltaire wrote that Peter went abroad "to learn better how to govern his dominions," but the true purpose of Peter's travels was to study shipbuilding and Western techniques in general, and to hire foreign experts. He planned to create a Black Sea fleet for his expansionist policies against the Turks; he wanted the Crimea. And he wanted to westernize Russia in a hurry, defying the normal pace of history. His intellectual curiosity was enormous and covered engineering, botany, carpentry, mechanics, navigation, even dentistry, which he practiced by pulling out the teeth of courtiers who had made the mistake of complaining of a toothache.

The Great Embassy visited Königsberg and Pillau, and went to Holland. Peter took his friend Alexander Menshikov and six of the "volunteers" to Zaandam, where he became a ship's carpenter at Lynst Rogge's shipyard. He lived with a pretty Dutch girl in a small house, worked twelve hours a day, and created big problems for the local authorities by his erratic behavior. He didn't want to be recognized as the Czar but complained when people didn't treat him deferentially. After a short time he and his retinue moved to Amsterdam, where he worked four months at the yards of the East India Company. He met a professor of medicine, a Dr. Ruysch, and visited the dissecting rooms. One of Peter's "volunteers" fainted at the sight of cut-up bodies. Peter had the wretched man revived and forced him to bite into the corpse. He spent six months in Holland, and ever since, Russian tourists have gone to Holland to visit the places where Peter lived.

In London he visited King William III, who gave the Czar his new private yacht, *The Transport Royal*. Peter sailed in the North Sea, returned to London, was rowed past the Tower, and was put up by the King in a large house in Norfolk Street. He later repaid the King's hospitality by sending him an enormous diamond, suitably wrapped in cheap brown paper. Once he received the King of England in his shirt sleeves. It was common knowledge in London that the King had almost fainted from the stench in the small room where the Czar of Russia was sleeping with four other men. But a czar can do no wrong. At Oxford, Peter was given the degree of Doctor of Law. When too many curious people kept bothering him in London, he moved to Deptford, where the English court arranged for the Czar to live at Sayes Court in a house belonging to John Evelyn. He would get up at four in the morning and work all day at the docks. Dinner was at ten in the morning, supper at six in the evening, and then the Russians went to bed, which "much astonished the Englishmen," according to the reports of foreign diplomats.

After a while Peter found Miss Cross, an attractive English actress who became his mistress. There were parties almost every night. The butler wrote to Evelyn, "There is a house full of people, and right nasty," which much distressed the diarist. The Russian guests showed their enthusiasm for Evelyn's paintings by shooting at them; obviously they made fine targets. (After the Second World War, the Soviet troops who "liberated" Vienna continued the practice in some Viennese houses.) Everything was ruined—curtains, carpets, glassware, china. One day Peter discovered a most fascinating contraption, a wheelbarrow, which he happily drove back and forth through the holly hedge, the diarist's great pride. Evelyn later got his house back in terrible condition; the Treasury gave him 150 pounds for repairs.

The Great Embassy was traveling in Austria when Peter was informed that the *streltsy* musketeers had started a rebellion in Moscow. By the time he returned, the rebellion was over, several hundred musketeers had been executed, and seventeen hundred were imprisoned in various monasteries. The reason for the mutiny was the miserable living conditions of the musketeers fighting at the port of Azov against the khan of the Crimea. Peter had not forgotten what the musketeers had done to his mother's family when he was a child; he had his revenge, in Romanov style. The seventeen hundred prisoners were tortured and "roasted alive" at his estate at Preobrazhensky; some who survived were publicly executed in Moscow. A chronicler wrote, "Finding the executioner too slow, Peter picked up the axe himself, and sent his subjects' heads rolling to the dust." The massacre lasted six months. People said it was worse than at the time of Ivan the Terrible.

Life at Peter's court was strenuous. There were wild orgies, and next day Peter would lecture his boyars on how to become more "civilized." No one was permitted to wear Russian clothes except priests and peasants. The Czar got up at four in the morning and held a government meeting at five. Ambassadors had to present their credentials at dawn, without ceremony. Peter would say they were accredited to him and not to his palace. The Prussian ambassador had to come aboard a ship and was ordered by the Czar to join him by climbing up into the maintop. The Prussian admitted he was unable to do it, which amused the Czar no end. He shouted obscenities at the envoy and was still convulsed with laughter when he came down to the quarterdeck to meet the ambassador. Not surprisingly, diplomatic service in St. Petersburg was considered harsh punishment among Western diplomats.

The Czar's idea of good fun was to get everybody wildly drunk. At official banquets, some unfortunate courtiers had to drink large bumpers of brandy without stopping while Peter watched them. He was pleased when some died after the ordeal. Foreign dignitaries were not exempted. The Danish minister Juel once had to kneel before the Czar and drink "half a dozen bumpers of wine," while the Czar knelt down next to him. By the time the minister had drunk the wine and was permitted to get up, he was unable to do so. Juel reported that on his way home from the banquets he saw the frozen Neva covered with the bodies of drunken men and women sleeping there, "like the slain on the battlefield." Many froze to death.

Peter himself drank more than anybody else except Lefort; when he got drunk, he was dangerous. Once he attacked the

Dutch minister with his fists, another time the representative of the Duke of Holstein with his sword. Even his favorites, Lefort and Menshikov, were sent "reeling across the room." The Czar loved to start a brawl among his guests by the ingenious device of providing only a hundred chairs for two or three hundred guests. Dr. Birch, a scholar and an original trustee of the British Museum, who often talked to British diplomats returning from Russia, reports there was "such scuffling and fighting for chairs that nothing more scandalous can be seen in any company." Even dignified foreign ambassadors were obliged "to follow the Russian fashion in defending the possession of their chairs, by cuffing and boxing their opposer." Foreigners were also shocked to see that "carpenters and shipwrights sit next to the Czar. . . . senators, ministers, generals, priests, sailors, buffoons, sit pell-mell, without any distinction." Dr. Birch, quite scandalized, wrote that there was such a noise that one couldn't even hear the music, "consisting of a sort of trumpets and cornets, for the Czar hates violins, and with this revelling noise and uproar the Czar is extremely diverted, particularly if the guests get bloody noses." He continues,

> Each person of the company has but one plate for dinner, so if some Russian does not care to mix the sauces of the different dishes together, he pours the soup that is left in his plate either into the dish or into his neighbor's plate, or even under the table after which he licks his plate clean with his fingers and last of all wipes it with the tablecloth.

The Czar loved to have his dignitaries put on strange costumes and ride through the streets in carts drawn by goats and swine. At Christmastide he and his nobles dressed up as popes and cardinals, holding a "drunken synod composed of the most dissolute men in Moscow." A venerable patriarch, Matthew Golovin, refused to join the procession dressed as a devil. Peter ordered him seized and stripped naked, and he had to sit on the ice of the Neva. A few days afterward Golovin died of pneumonia.

More serious was Peter's interest in executions and torture. Yet Johann Korb, an Austrian diplomat who wrote about some terrible excesses he had witnessed in his *Diary of an Austrian Secre-*

tary of Legation at the Court of Czar Peter the Great, published in Vienna in 1700, also realized that the Czar's aims would benefit backward Russia:

[The Czar] labored to introduce into Muscovy those polite arts that had for ages been proscribed there. . . . He made his reasons to the boyars. They all commended the monarch's prudence but insinuated that such immense good, however desirable it might be, was unattainable, that the genius of the Muscovites was unsuited to such pursuits. The Czar was indignant at these sayings, worthy of the profound ignorance of those that gave utterance to them . . . for they liked their benighted darkness. "Are we then born less blest than other nations that the divinity should have infused inept minds into our bodies? Have we not hands? Have we not eyes? Why should we alone be left out as unworthy of the glory of human science? By Hercules! we have the same minds, we can do like other folk if we only will. We are all born to all these things; when the stimulus is applied, all those properties of the soul that have been, as it were, sleeping, shall be awakened."

The Austrian diplomat sums up, somewhat reluctantly, that "the greatest things may be expected from such a prince." Captain John Perry, a hydraulic engineer who worked fourteen years under the Czar, was often shocked by Peter's brutality but impressed by Peter's social reforms. Marriages, for instance, had always been arranged by the parents on both sides. The young people were not asked for their consent; often they were not even permitted to meet. The Czar didn't like this "unacceptable way of joining young people together without their own approbation." He knew that it was "a thing common in Russia to beat the wives in a most barbarous manner, very often so inhumanly that they die with the blows." Such murder was not punished, "being interpreted by the law to be done by way of correction." The Czar decreed that "no young people should be married together, without their own free liking and consent, and that all persons should be admitted to visit each other at least six weeks before they were married together."

Peter's dual personality was apparent in everything he did. He might be wearing Russian clothes, but the boyars "and people whatsoever that came near his court" would have "to equip them-

selves with handsome cloaths made after the English fashion."
Women who until then had not been permitted "into the sight or
conversation with men" would now attend weddings and "other
publick entertainment." Peter would often attend weddings "of
any distinction amongst the foreigners" and would give a present
to the bride. His reforms were, naturally, hotly debated and not
accepted by everybody. A famous popular print showing the funeral procession of Peter the Great, was captioned "The Mice
Bury the Cat," and sometimes "The Mice Bury the Rat."

Peter's private life was equally complex and bizarre. He had
sexual relations with Alexander Menshikov, whom he addressed
"My heart" in his letters, but he often fined him for disobedience
and said that Menshikov, "born in sin, will end his life as a rascal
and a cheat." Nevertheless he was charmed by the rascal and
cheat. At Peter's request, Emperor Charles VI of Austria made
Menshikov a Prince of the Holy Roman Empire. It must have
been a great joke among Vienna's aristocrats. Peter and Menshikov also shared their women as befits close friends. Peter dispatched his wife Eudoxia to a convent and lived with Menshikov's former mistress, Martha Skavronskaya. She was a Lithuanian
peasant girl who had been brought to Russia as a slave by General B. P. Sheremetev. He lived with her—she was seventeen—until Menshikov saw her and claimed her for himself. Then Peter
saw Martha in Menshikov's palace and asked his friend to send
her over. Peter had lived several years with Anna Mons, a pretty
woman, the daughter of a German wine merchant. Peter refused
to marry Anna but he became furious when the Prussian ambassador, Keyserling, fell in love with her and wanted to marry her.
Peter refused to permit the marriage and placed the Mons family
under house arrest for two years.

Martha Skavronskaya was luckier than Anna, who finally married Keyserling in 1711 only to lose him during the honeymoon.
Peter kept Martha, made her take on the Greek Orthodox faith,
and changed her name to Catherine. They had three children. In
1707 Peter married her, simply ignoring Eudoxia. Catherine was
not attractive, much too plump for Western taste but just what
the Muscovites liked. Peter appreciated her ability to drink and
swear like a man. Catherine (who later became Empress Catherine I) was no fool, however: she and Menshikov remained

good friends and would help each other when the Czar fell into one of his rages.

Peter had started the promised war against the Swedes, who were led by King Charles XII, a boy of eighteen. At Narva Peter lost ten thousand troops and ten generals, but not his courage. New taxes were proclaimed, church bells were melted down and made into guns, eighty per cent of the national income was allotted to war. One year after the defeat he had a stronger army than before; now he needed a fortress for the attack against the shore of the Baltic. And that is how he looked at the islands in the Neva estuary, one day in May, 1703. A few Finnish fishermen lived there. It was an unlikely place to build a new town but that was the beginning of St. Petersburg.

> On a lonely windswept shore
> He stood, filled with lofty visions
> And gazed afar. . . .
>
> "Here the Swedes we will threaten
> Here a city we shall found
> To defy our proud neighbors.
> Nature has destined us
> To open a window into Europe. . . ."
>
> (Pushkin, *The Bronze Horseman,* 1833)

The poet glorifies the visionary, not the despot. As an organizer and supercontractor, Peter was a genius. He approved the overall planning. Construction jobs were given to private builders submitting their bids. Some were early entrepreneurs; others were artisans, and there were a few bonded peasants among them. Peter set up a strict control system. Subcontractors who didn't deliver or tried to swindle the state were severely punished. In the beginning they built with primitive methods and few tools, but that soon changed. The Great Embassy expedition was paying off. Peter had brought to Russia more than five hundred technicians and a great many books, plans, blueprints, and new techniques. He imported windmills from Holland, pumps from Prussia, and his beloved wheelbarrows from England. He knew how much had been acccomplished in Asia by primitive methods, with an almost unlimited supply of labor. Over a hundred and fifty houses were built in the first five years, though many burned down. In 1710, seven years after work had started, there were eight thousand permanent inhabitants despite the brutality of life in Peter's new "paradise." There were no bridges; people moved around in small boats. Once the Czar almost drowned. People were not permitted to use oars and had to learn to sail. Wood was allotted for shipbuilding but not for fuel. Everybody hated to live in the cold, swampy town. Only Catherine and Menshikov pretended to like it.

The sacrifices were terrific. F. C. Weber from Hannover, who worked as secretary in the English embassy in St. Petersburg, wrote that no one came to St. Petersburg unless he was forced to. "Many Swedes, Finlanders and Livonians, not being able to subsist in their towns and villages, which were ruined and many destroyed by fire, not knowing where else to go, were obliged by necessity. All sorts of artificers, mechanicks, and seamen with their families were drawn to Petersburg. Many labourers being Russians, Tartars and Calmucks, having served the time prefixed by their sovereign, and being unwilling to return home, engaged with the *boyars* who were building houses; some thousands of them even built houses for themselves and settled at Petersburg. All those circumstances together contributed to the sudden peopling of Petersburg."

After his defeat, the young King of Sweden went to Turkey and concluded an alliance with the Sultan. Peter led his army down the Danube, hoping to get the support of the Christian Slavs in the Balkans. At the Prut, his army was surrounded by the forces of the Grand Vizier. Peter had to sue for peace, agreeing to accept all conditions "except slavery." The conditions were surprisingly lenient: Peter was to give up his Black Sea fleet and the port of Azov, which he'd taken from the Turks in 1700. The Turks demanded nothing for their Swedish allies, and it was rumored that "the Grand Vizier had been bribed by Catherine, who gave him her jewels and carts of gold collected from the troops." The story is too good to be true but doubtless Catherine stood by Peter while he went through the worst crisis of his life, and he never forgot it.

In 1717 he took her on a state visit to Berlin. Princess Wilhelmina, the eight-year-old daughter of the king of Prussia (and the sister of Frederick, later known as the Great) wrote in her diary,

> The Czarina has a stumpy little body, neither air nor grace. . . . her dress, you would have said, had been bought at a secondhand shop. All was out of fashion, loaded with silver and greasy dirt. All along the facings of her gown were orders and little things of metal, so that when she walked, it was with a jingling, as if you heard a mule with bells to its harness. . . .

The little girl also noticed that the Czar was suffering "a sort of convulsion, like Tic or St. Vitus." Doubtless he was a sick man. But between wars and building his new capital he had the imagination to simplify the Russian alphabet, found the Academy of Sciences, establish a small art museum, remodel the calendar, improve the roads, publish the first Russian newspaper, make the people grow potatoes and vines, appoint a government of nine departments, and install the Senate. (Senators were expected to fall in line; in 1711 two were publicly flogged for protesting.) The Czar created a table of ranks and a social scale of fourteen grades that survived for a long time. He did nothing for the peasants who made up ninety per cent of the country's population. They had to work, pay taxes, and fight his wars; they were serfs, forbidden to leave their owners.

After the death of Charles XII of Sweden in 1718, Peter concluded a peace treaty with the Swedes that gave Russia hegemony in the Baltic. He was triumphantly received in St. Petersburg, and the members of the Senate (who had learned their lesson) awarded him the title "Father of the Fatherland, Peter the Great, Emperor of all Russia."

The Czar had been angry for years with his official heir, Alexis, his and Eudoxia's son. The boy was sensitive and frail, the very opposite of his father. Peter had tried to remake the Czarevitch in his image when he sent him to the front as a soldier, and to the yards to build ships, forcing him to study military science and engineering. Alexis became terrified of his father and would faint when he was summoned. After the death of his wife, a German princess, the Czarevitch wrote a letter to his father renouncing his right to the throne. He would rather go to a monastery than become czar. The letter was signed, "Your slave and useless son, Alexis."

Peter was furious and ordered Alexis to join him at the front, at once. Instead, Alexis went to Vienna, acccompanied by Afrosinya, a Finnish girl he'd come to love, and asked the Emperor for political asylum. Peter sent his senior diplomat, Count Peter Tolstoy, to Vienna to persuade Alexis to return. Tolstoy spent several months convincing the Czarevitch that he had nothing to fear, but Alexis returned only after he'd received a handwritten letter from his father. The Czar swore "before God" that Alexis would be "cherished like a son" and be allowed to marry Afrosinya.

Alexis returned to St. Petersburg, and was immediately arrested, and interrogated by his father and Count Tolstoy. The Czar told his intimates that the Czarevitch was "involved in a plot to depose his father." Alexis was innocent of any conspiracy; but he was loved by millions of people—members of the clergy and the nobility, and especially the peasant serfs—who hated the Czar. Alexis admitted, "I know that many people here love me."

Alexis's friends were arrested and tortured. Afrosinya was made to "confess." Yes, the Czarevitch "hated" his father and hoped to make Moscow again the capital of Russia. Her confession sounds strangely familiar these days. Alexis was sentenced to twenty-five strokes of the knout; somehow he survived. On June 21 O.S., 1718, the members of the High Court, at the Czar's demand, "sentenced the Czarevitch to death for having desired the death of the sovereign . . . with the aid of foreign arms." On June 26, according to the records of the guard at the Trubetzkoy Bastion, "torture was applied in the presence of the Czar." Alexis died at 6:00 P.M. Officially, his death was attributed to "apoplexy" but no one in St. Petersburg believed it. Alexis was rumored to have been killed with the axe. Only the Czar and the six men who had accompanied him to the prison knew the truth, and they were not talking. Peter ordered his son to be buried underneath a stairway at the rear of the church. The bell ringer mounted the steps each day, and Alexis's grave would be daily "disgraced" by the man's plebeian feet. The following night Peter attended a banquet at Menshikov's palace, "celebrating the victory of Poltava."

Earlier, Peter had astonished the rulers of Europe by having his wife crowned as empress at the Kremlin. Catherine wore a crown studded with thousands of stones, the most precious a ruby as large as a pigeon's egg, which had been bought in Peking for sixty thousand rubles.

Six months later, Catherine and Menshikov were afraid of being executed. The Czar had accidentally discovered that William Mons, one of Catherine's courtiers and the brother of Peter's former mistress, had been taking bribes, and that both Catherine and Prince Menshikov had known about it. Peter was absolutely furious; he had never tolerated corruption though he had not always been able to prevent it. Mons was executed after Peter discovered that he'd had an affair with Catherine. Menshikov was in disgrace, but not for long. Peter forgave him and after a few weeks he even made up with Catherine. He needed them both. Late in January he began suffering from an acute kidney ailment, and on January 28 O.S., 1725, he died.

Few people were sorry. Peter had tried to take Russia, a backward country, out of the Dark Ages and directly into a new, technological age. But though he'd had many human, almost liberal ideas, he had no respect for simple human dignity. People were "animals whom I have dressed to look like men." He bought progress at a high price for the Russian people. They learned about Western fashions and Western dress but not about Western morality. Diderot wrote, "The Russians as fashioned by Peter were rotten before they were ripe."

But the reality remains—and today's successors of Peter I are realists—that he made Russia a political and military power. When he ascended the throne, his country had no diplomatic representatives. At his death Russia had twenty-one permanent diplomatic missions. He remains remembered as Peter the Great, but in many ways he resembles Ivan the Terrible, whom he had always admired.

INTERLUDE

During the thirty-seven years between Peter's death and the reign of Catherine II (the Great), Russia had six rulers. St. Petersburg was the scene of considerable confusion. Peter's widow, Catherine I, and his grandson, Peter II, ruled only a short time and were succeeded by the Empress Anna. Her father, the feeble-minded Czar Ivan, had once shared the throne with Peter. Anna was said to be "dull, coarse, fat, harsh, spiteful." She was also stingy, having lived for nineteen years in poverty in the Duchy of Courland, where she had been "known to count the apples on a tree for fear that her gardener would cheat her," according to a Baltic baron.

All this changed when Anna became empress. Her lover, Ernst Biren, "the grandson of a stable boy," was given a palace in St. Petersburg, but he loved only horses. It was said that when Biren spoke of horses he talked like a man but when he spoke of men he talked like a horse. Two other powerful men at Anna's court were Count A. I. Ostermann and Field Marshal von Münnich. Biren established the Secret Chancellery, a precursor of the infamous Third Section. A vast network of spies and informers was organized. "Life or death depended on Biren's smile or frown," wrote the Russian historian, V. O. Kluchevsky. Biren, Ostermann, and Münnich were called "the German party" in Russia. They were hated, as were all foreigners.

Biren liked luxury and in order to please him Empress Anna created an elegant court. She gave orders to rebuild the Winter

Palace. The Empress didn't like members of the court to wear the same costume twice at her balls, and foreign ministers wrote home asking for larger allowances. The British minister, Rondeau, wrote, "I cannot imagine that this magnificence will last, for if it should, it must ruin most part of the Russian nobility. Several families are obliged to sell their estates to buy fine clothes." Other diplomats commented about the vulgar aspects of Anna's court. She liked ugly handkerchiefs tied round her head, and all the women had to wear them too. She made matters worse by fighting for the Polish succession, unsuccessfully, and against the Turks in the Crimea, which cost the lives of thousands of Russian soldiers.

People were beginning to say that Russia could be saved only by Peter the Great's surviving daughter, Elizabeth, who was living quietly in a country house near Moscow, surrounded by Biren's spies and informers. She was vain and voluptuous, but also generous and popular. And she liked men. A handsome young Cossack shepherd, Alexis Rasumovsky, became a member of her household, where even Biren's spies could not report on the affair.

Anna died in 1740 and was succeeded by Ivan VI, a four-month-old baby. Biren, Ostermann, and Münnich tried to remain regents but were arrested, one after the other. With the help of the French ambassador, La Chétardie, a coup was arranged that made Elizabeth Russia's Empress in 1741. She was thirty-two and full of life, but politics didn't interest her. She wanted luxury and pleasures that cost money, and the peasants were taxed more heavily than ever before. On her regular journeys between St. Petersburg and Moscow, the Czarina was surrounded by a retinue of thousands of people. Wooden palaces were put up, then dismantled when they were no longer needed.

She still loved Alexis Rasumovsky, married him secretly, and made him a count. He didn't care for power but loved money and elegance, or what he thought was elegant; he was seen striding around with diamond buttons and epaulets decorated with diamonds. Elizabeth gave several balls a week, often dressed as a sailor. Men were ordered to dress as women; she had inherited her father's bizarre taste. The Chevalier d'Éon, Louis XV's bril-

liant secret agent (himself a transvestite), called her "a ravenous
bacchante whose skin sweats lasciviousness." Her passion for
Rasumovsky didn't prevent her from having two other lovers,
Shuvalov and Beketov; both were young enough to be her sons.
Life at her court was not very amusing. Half the people couldn't
read or write. The Empress discouraged reading as "bad for the
health."

She cared little about affairs of state, leaving them to her chan-
cellor, Count Alexis Bestuzhev-Ryumin, who had been a protégé
of Biren but now became a friend of Rasumovsky. But she had
her moments of rage and might send people she didn't like to
prison or to the torture chambers. Meanwhile she would be
drinking and playing cards all night. She was, in short, very much
her father's daughter. Around 1750 she became much influenced
by Peter and Alexander Shuvalov, the uncles of her youthful
lover Ivan Shuvalov. Peter ran Russia's financial policies, established savings banks, reformed the currency, and in the proc-
ess became quite rich. His brother Alexander became chief inquisitor of the Secret Chancellery; people were terrified to
whisper his name. The only pleasant Shuvalov was young Ivan,
who liked artists and writers, corresponded with Voltaire, and
convinced Elizabeth to found the University of Moscow and the
Academy of Arts in St. Petersburg—quite an accomplishment
since she was still convinced that reading was unhealthy.

Elizabeth was concerned about her succession; in that respect
she was different from her father. At the advice of Frederick the
Great she finally selected a young German princess, Sophia
("Figgy") Augusta Frederika of Anhalt-Zerbst, to become the
wife of her nephew and heir, Karl Peter Ulrich, duke of Holstein-
Gottorp. His mother had been Elizabeth's sister, and she had
loved her very much. In spite of his German title, Grand Duke
Peter was a real Romanov—decadent, high voiced, more interested in toy soldiers than in the fate of his people. He lived in a
dream world. Sometimes he would stay in his room for days,
leading toy troops in mysterious battles, ordering servants to
join his war games.

When Elizabeth wasn't putting on a new dress—she was said to
change her clothes ten times a day—she effected bizarre ideas.

She ordered the wooden Winter Palace pulled down and told Francesco Rastrelli to build a new one, of stone. Above all, she looked after Sophia, who had arrived in St. Petersburg accompanied by her mama. Sophia was only fifteen; her fiancé, Peter, was sixteen. Sophia was ordered to renounce her Lutheran faith, and was taken into the Russian-Orthodox Church as Catherine Alexeyevna. Today she is better known as Catherine the Great. We know most about her from her own memoirs:

> . . . the Grand Duke showed himself very assiduous for the first ten days. I became aware that he was not greatly enamoured of the nation over which he was destined to reign; he was a convinced Lutheran, did not like his entourage, and was very childish. I kept silent and listened, which helped to gain his confidence. . . . he confided that he was in love with one of the Empress's ladies-in-waiting. He would have liked to marry her but had resigned himself to marrying me as his aunt wished it.

It wasn't exactly a propitious beginning for a good marriage between teenagers, but they did get married. Catherine was quite philosophical about it. "I did not care about Peter but I did care about the Crown." She wasn't surprised when her new husband never came close to her. "His Imperial Highness came to bed after supper and said how amused the servants would be to find us in bed together. . . . My maid questioned us the next day about our marital experiences but she was quite disappointed in her hopes." She wasn't depressed; she knew what she wanted, and went about it with Teutonic thoroughness, winning the affection of the Empress. The Chevalier d'Éon wrote to Paris,

> The Grand Duchess is romantic, ardent, passionate. Her eyes are brilliant, fascinating, glassy, the expression of a wild beast. . . . if I am not mistaken, a long and terrifying future is written on them. But when she comes close to me I instinctively recoil for she frightens me.

A brilliant assessment. Catherine accompanied the Empress on her exhausting travels, which was no fun, and discussed with her the latest building projects. Elizabeth ordered two large wings added to the palace in Tsarskoye Selo which Catherine I had started, but after seven years she didn't like what had been done and ordered Rastrelli to start all over. Rastrelli designed a colossal palace in blue and white, with enormous caryatids and moldings in gold. The borderline between the splendid and the vulgar is somewhat blurred. Ekaterininsky Palace is now named for Pushkin, who deserves a monument in better taste.

Nine years after her marriage, Catherine had a son. In her memoirs she states that the father was not her husband but her lover, Sergei Saltykov. That would mean that Elizabeth was the last Romanov, but most historians are doubtful about Catherine's admission. She is not an objective witness and her memoirs contain more poetry than truth. Her son, Paul, turned into what seemed a genuine Romanov, with his terrifying temper, his brutality, and his moments of stark madness. But Catherine never cared for her son, and Paul was brought up by Empress Elizabeth. Catherine was happy with her lover, and Grand Duke Peter was very happy with his mistress, Elizabeth Vorontsova, who played soldiers with him all the time. It was an almost ideal *ménage à quatre*, while it lasted.

Peter's great hero was Frederick the Great, the finest soldier in Europe. Unfortunately this was the time of the Seven Years' War and Frederick's Prussian soldiers were fighting against the Continental coalition of Austria, Sweden, France, Saxony, Poland—and Russia. While Russian soldiers were killed on the battlefield, the heir to the throne of Russia proclaimed his admiration for the leader of the enemy forces and celebrated Frederick's victories and Russia's defeats. This was bad enough, but matters were made worse because the Empress, usually not interested in fighting wars, hated Frederick, whose jokes about her love life were repeated in all the chancelleries of Europe.

At the beginning of January 1762, Frederick's situation was desperate. The Russians had overrun East Prussia and much of Pomerania. The Austrians had occupied much of Saxony. Berlin was badly damaged. Frederick was considering suicide, the honorable way out, when he was told that Elizabeth had died and been succeeded by his great admirer who became Czar Peter III. The young czar decided to end the war at once. Frederick was grateful and he had good reason. He wrote to Peter:

While all the rest of Europe is persecuting me, I find a friend who has truly a German heart, a friend who would never suffer Germany to become the slave of the House of Austria. In you I place all my trust, and I vow to you a loyal and eternal friendship.

From St. Petersburg Czar Peter III wrote back, "I recognize in Your Majesty one of the greatest heroes the world has ever seen." St. Petersburg was shocked. The Saxon Minister was heard to remark, "Here in St. Petersburg the King of Prussia is the Emperor." When Frederick sent a draft of the peace treaty to Peter, the Czar signed it without showing it to anybody or changing a word. The treaty returned to Prussia all territories that Russia had won during five years of bitter war. It was said that Peter the Great must be turning in his grave. The Czar astonished the foreign diplomats in St. Petersburg by calling the King of Prussia "my Master."

Peter III achieved some good reforms. He abolished the dreaded Secret Chancellery, changed the system of police patrols, outlawed the knout. He established street lighting in St. Petersburg, reducing crime, and transferred the shipyards to Kronstadt. He also made the mistake of Prussianizing the Russian army, appointing Prince Georg of Holstein as a field marshal, and replacing the Preobrazhensky Regiment, the palace guard, with a regiment of Holstein grenadiers. He created a scandal when he forbade the traditional Easter procession and talked of installing a Protestant chapel in the Winter Palace, "to be used by the Lutheran domestics." Peter didn't know that a conspiracy was building up around him with the purpose of making Catherine the ruler of Russia. He didn't improve matters by living openly with Elizabeth Vorontsova and insulting his wife at state banquets.

Count Gregory Orlov, an elegant guards' officer, was Catherine's new lover; she had a child by him. He had four brothers, all army officers. The Orlovs organized a conspiracy among fellow army officers, and they were joined by Princess Catherine Dashkova, a sister of Elizabeth Vorontsova. On June 28 O.S., 1762, Catherine was taken by Gregory Orlov to the headquarters of the Ismailovsky Guards who swore to her a solemn oath of allegiance. The Semenovsky Regiment did the same. At the Kazan

Cathedral the Archbishop of Novgorod proclaimed Catherine sovereign and her son Paul her successor. At the Winter Palace, the Senate and the Holy Synod officially confirmed her succession. With her Teutonic sense of orderliness, Catherine wanted everything to be strictly "legitimate," including the assassination of her husband.

When Peter III found out what had happened, it was too late. He offered in a letter to abdicate if Catherine would spare his life and permit Elizabeth and him to go into exile in Holstein. At Catherine's demand he signed a document of formal abdication. Nevertheless, on June 30, 1762, Peter, called "Duke of Holstein," was taken to Peterhof and imprisoned. Elizabeth was not allowed to join him. But he couldn't stay there as a prisoner indefinitely. And Catherine didn't want him to go to Holstein, where he would certainly meet with Frederick the Great.

At Peterhof Peter asked for his violin, his poodle, his servant, and his German doctor. The next day, he was found dead, "his face black, his body badly bruised." No one knew exactly what had happened. Alexis Orlov, one of Gregory's brothers, knew but wouldn't talk. Though no proof exists, there is virtually no doubt that Catherine was an accessory to her husband's murder. The assassins were pardoned and it was officially announced that Czar Peter III had died of a fit of colic.

CATHERINE, NO LONGER THE GREAT

Catherine's image in history is strictly black or white. Some German historians call her the greatest woman of her epoch. Prince Adam Czartoryski, the ardent Polish patriot and historian, wrote in his memoirs, "The Empress Catherine, who possessed neither virtue nor the decorum which befits a woman, nevertheless succeeded in winning inside her country, especially within her capital, the veneration, even the love of her servants and subjects." Others agree with Virginia Cowles: "Not only was she a murderess but a usurper, not only a usurper but a whore." Poets called her the Semiramis (or the Messalina) of the North.

She became empress at thirty-three, describing her appearance as "very attractive." Her French secretary, Favier, remembers her "ungraceful walk, her long face, deep-set mouth, a slightly aquiline nose, small eyes." Her painted portraits seem to confirm this.

Her private life was dominated by the confession, "I cannot be a day without love." She rewarded her lovers shamelessly with money, position, diamonds, estates, and serfs. Gregory Orlov was named her adjutant-general and made a count, received Catherine's portrait set in diamonds, and had an apartment in the Winter Palace next to the Czarina's. The French chargé d'affaires wrote to Paris that Orlov "lacks nothing but the title of Emperor." Count Orlov wore a suit with a million pounds worth of diamonds sewn on it. She gave him an annual salary of 150,000 rubles, six thousand serfs, and china worth a quarter of a million rubles. He gave her the solitaire known as the Orlov diamond, at that time the most famous stone on earth. Catherine had it mounted in her scepter, possibly to demonstrate that she owed the crown to the Orlovs. Gregory was the father of one of her children, Alexis Bobrinsky, but she refused to marry him. The little German ex-princess knew that "Madame Orlov could never remain Empress of Russia." In 1772 Catherine decided to fire Orlov and install handsome Alexander Vasilchikov in his apartment at the Winter Palace. Vasilchikov received 100,000 rubles and was named aide-de-camp, but he wasn't happy, complaining that he was

> nothing more than a kept woman and treated as such. I was not allowed to receive guests or go out. If I made a request for anyone else, I received no answer.

No one can tell how many handsome men she slept with; they were simply sent to guard her apartments but their duties were not restricted to standing watch. Only a few who were installed in a special apartment next to hers remain known: Vasilchikov, Zavadovsky, Zorich, Korsakov, Lanskoy, Yermolov, Mamonov, Zubov. Almost all of them were chosen by Gregory Potemkin, undoubtedly the great passion of her life. The Prince de Ligne called him "the most extraordinary man I ever met."

Potemkin, a Ukrainian, was no beauty but he was fascinating. He was said to be morose, with dirty hair and an interestingly ugly face. He had lost an eye (perhaps after being beaten up by the Orlov brothers), which made him even more interesting. He had moments of depression followed by stretches of wild exhilaration. Sir Robert Gunning, the British ambassador, wrote, "Potemkin is of gigantic height . . . and his appearance in general is far from pleasing." The French minister called him a "Tartar." Catherine knew better, of course. He was a wonderful lover, and the only one among her lovers with a brilliant mind. "He has done more than anyone to end the Turkish war and is as amusing as the Devil." Potemkin wrote songs and ballads, among them the famous song composed when he was fighting the Turkish war. It ends:

Cruel Gods, why have you given her such charms?
Or why did you exhalt her so high?
  Why did you destine me to love her and her alone
The one whose sacred name will never pass my lips
Whose charming image will never quit my heart?

Catherine's love letters (357 of them published) reveal her to
have been completely in his power. "My beloved little pigeon, I
love you greatly. You are handsome, intelligent, amusing. In your
company I forget the whole world. Never have I been so happy. I
often try to hide my feelings, but my heart betrays my passion. . . ." She was around fifty, ten years older than Potemkin,
whom she called "my beloved husband" in a number of letters
and presented with 900,000 rubles on his fortieth birthday. Many
historians believe that she married him secretly, late in 1774.
They often quarreled because Potemkin's moments of mysticism
would spoil their lovemaking. He was terribly restless and often
away, traveling in the style befitting a great general and a prince
of the Holy Roman Empire. (Catherine arranged this honor
through her influence with the Austrian Emperor.) When he was
away, he would select an ersatz lover for her. The candidate was
examined by Dr. Thomas Dinsdale, the court physician, and
"tried out" by two ladies-in-waiting known as *éprouveuses,*
Countess Bruce and Countess Protasova, who reported their
findings to Her Majesty with clinical detachment. There must be
order. When Potemkin died of a heart attack, "worn out by loose
living and gluttony at the age of fifty-six," Catherine was desperate.

Catherine's reign lasted thirty-four years and is full of contradictions. She admired Peter the Great and continued the westernization of Russia and her hero's expansionist policies. At the end
of her life she had won the Crimea, the Black Sea steppe between
the Bug and the Dnieper, and freedom of navigation in the Black
Sea. She failed to reach and control Constantinople. But after
making her former lover Stanislas Poniatowski king of Poland in
1764, she presided over several partitions of Poland that added
large territories to Russia—the lands between the Dwina and
Dnieper rivers, much of Lithuania, White Russia, and the
Ukraine, the Duchy of Courland, the rest of Lithuania, and

Vilna. She doubled her army to 458,000 men by 1796, at the end
of her reign. Peter the Great had made Russia an important naval
power. Catherine expanded the Russian navy. After Catherine's
brilliant victories, Russia was feared by Prussia and Austria for
her army, and by England and France on the seas.

Because she was German-born, she tried to be more Russian
than the Russians. She studied Russian and spoke it quite well.
She ordered a continual census of the population, and sent out
expeditions to survey the frontiers of a country so vast that she
didn't know where it ended. At the beginning of her reign, she
gave the appearance of a benevolent despot. She studied the
ideas of the Age of Reason, but it is doubtful that she understood
them, though she had carefully read the works of the *philosophes*, and corresponded with Voltaire (the first who called her
"the Great") and Diderot. She always sacrificed her "liberal
ideas" when they collided with the harsh facts of Russian life.
For five years she worked on her "Instructions." Though the
opening statement said, "Christian law teaches people to do good
to another," she continues:

> The Sovereign is absolute: for there is no other authority but that
> which centers in a single person. The true end of the monarchy is
> . . . not to deprive the people of their natural liberty but to correct
> their actions in order to attain the supreme good. . . . We are
> obliged to alleviate the situation of the subjects as much as sound
> reason will permit, and therefore to shun all occasions of reducing
> people to slavery except when the utmost necessity should inevita-
> bly oblige us to do it.

Once she wrote to Diderot that in a country "mainly composed
of illiterate slaves" the only possible form of ruling was abso-
lutism. Diderot called her "a despot . . . since whatever the true
end of her government, it makes all liberty and property depend-
ent on one Person." (He knew that she had copied parts of her
"Instructions" from the works of Locke, Montesquieu, Beccaria.)
Voltaire wasn't ashamed to write about her "Instructions," "I consider it the finest monument of the century. . . . Your genius
conceived it, your pretty hand wrote it."

Catherine didn't really care about reforms. She hoped they

would be taken at face value in the West and increase her prestige, and they were. Even Frederick the Great couldn't help making her a member of the Berlin Academy. Yet at the end of her regime, the number of serfs had increased by one million. She enslaved the Ukrainians, who had been free before her rule. When General Rumyantsev claimed that his troops had killed five thousand Turks, Catherine gave him five thousand serfs as a gift. Freedom had no meaning for nine tenths of her population, and she was well aware of it. So were many intelligent foreigners who were not fooled by her "liberal" ideas. The French ambassador, the Comte de Ségur, wrote,

Catherine's imagination was never able to rest. Moreover, her plans were more precipitous than mature; this precipitation stifled at birth part of the creations of her genius. She wanted at one and the same time to form a third estate, attract foreign trade, establish manufactures, extend agriculture, found credit, increase paper money, raise the rate of exchange, lower the interest on money, build towns, create academies, populate the deserts, annihilate the Tartars, invade Persia, continue her conquest of the Turks, enchain Poland, extend her influence all over Europe. This was a great deal to undertake. . . . More success would have been obtained if fewer objects had been embraced at the same time. . . .

Catherine remained completely isolated from the people of her country. Otherwise she couldn't have written, "In Russia every peasant has his turkey in the pot every Sunday" or "Men have died of overeating but never of hunger." (It's also possible, though, that she knew the awful truth.) When she went to Moscow in winter, she rode in a silver sledge drawn by twenty-four horses, with glass windows installed, and hot-water pans placed on the floor. In 1787 she went to Kiev and down the Dnieper with the ambassadors of Austria, Britain, and France. There were French chefs, musicians, and dancers in her entourage, and she slept in large tents made of silk. At Kaidak, Emperor Joseph II of Austria met Catherine. They visited a Cossack's house, suitably redecorated. After her visit to Ekaterinoslav, the Comte de Ségur wrote ironically, "She has laid the foundation of a capital she will never inhabit." In Potemkin's cardboard villages she was cheered by hastily dressed-up peas-

ants who were afterwards ordered to return to their villages
(many died on the way). At the same time, Sir James Harris, the
British minister, reports macao games, with hundreds of diamonds distributed among the winners. "Great luxury and little
morality seem to run through every rank. . . . their entertain-
ments, their apartments, and the number of their domestics are
quite Asiatic." Potemkin inaugurated for her the new port of
Sevastopol with a triumphal arch at the mouth of the Bug,
inscribed, "This is the way to Constantinople."

Catherine had no use for Moscow, ". . . full of symbols of fa-
naticism, churches, miraculous icons, priests, and convents . . .
devout hypocrites, beggars, thieves." In St. Petersburg "the inhabitants are more docile and polite, less superstitious, more accus-
tomed to foreigners from contact with whom they always acquire
something valuable."

French became the official court language because Catherine
loved it and used it in her correspondence. Russian was "the language of the servants." Many nobles spoke it badly. Russian
writers were encouraged to translate Molière, Racine, Corneille,
Montesquieu, Voltaire. Literary ideas were discussed; social ideas
were taboo. Francomania led to bizarre extremes. Nikolai Ivanovich Novikov wrote that French adventurers arrived in St. Petersburg to teach French; many had phony titles and had been in
trouble with the police in France. French etiquette was practiced
more strictly than in Paris. People in high society couldn't afford
to spit on the floor, eat with their fingers, or beat their wives; life
was no longer fun. They wore their new Easter dresses though
they were shivering in the cold—because it was the fashion in
Paris. But Frenchification remained superficial. Martha Wilmot,
an Irish girl who was a friend of the rich Princess Dashkova,
called life in St. Petersburg "a superstructure from France, the
monkey rampant on the bear's back."

The French Revolution terrified Catherine and cooled her enthusiasm. She had never really liked France itself. In 1790, when
she no longer pretended to be "liberal," some people in the West
remembered that she had stopped being an "enlightened" despot
seventeen years earlier. In 1773 Emelyan Pugachev, a Cossack
soldier from the Don, had organized an army of Cossacks and
Kirghiz tribesmen. Pugachev was a colorful black-bearded man,

almost an operatic character with great charisma. He mystified his critics and mesmerized his followers, claiming to be Peter III (the murdered husband of Catherine) returned to save his people. He may have come to believe it himself. He created his own court, assigned ladies-in-waiting to his Cossack wife, the "Czarina," and surrounded himself with colorful bodyguards. People who had never seen the real Peter III believed in the reincarnation of "Little Father of all the Russias." Little Father promised to abolish serfdom and to distribute the land among the peasants. "When we have destroyed the guilty nobles, each man will be able to enjoy a life of peace." He was a clever demagogue, an Old Believer, who said, "We shall make the true faith prevail and take over the land for ourselves." The story has happened before and will happen again, as long as humans are willing to believe in a Little Father, or a Big Brother.

Pugachev's movement became a revolt and finally a popular uprising as millions of people joined the rebels. Landowners were killed or managed to escape to Moscow, where they told stories of horror. Late in 1773 Pugachev's army, fifteen thousand men, was only 120 miles from Moscow. Many regular troops joined the insurgents, and the clergy of Moscow seemed to side with the Old Believer. After Pugachev's army stormed and burned down Kazan, there were rumors that Catherine might abdicate.

Catherine never even thought of abdicating, never lost her nerve. She ordered her military leaders to end the war against the Turks. After the peace treaty was signed in July 1774 (it gave Catherine the northern Caucasus and access to the Black Sea), she directed General Suvorov to finish off the "Marquis de Pugachev," as she called the Little Father. Pugachev was betrayed by his underlings, who handed him over after secret negotiations with Catherine's emissaries in return for being pardoned. Pugachev was brought to Moscow in a cage, and Catherine wrote to Voltaire, "There is not the least indication that he was the tool of a foreign power. . . . M. Pugachev is simply a robber baron and not the servant of any living soul. . . . If he had offended only myself I should pardon him, but this cause is the Empire's and that has its own laws." Pugachev was executed; torture had been outlawed. Catherine ordered scaffolds to be erected in all villages, and Pugachev's followers were hanged, thousands of them. The size of Pugachev's revolt convinced her that Russia was no place for enlightened despotism. In these years, long before the French Revolution, she gave up all pretense of liberalism. There was no need to keep up a façade of enlightenment for the Western world. She was firmly established as the successful ruler of a powerful nation, and she didn't have to justify herself.

When Alexander Radishchev published his impressions, *A Journey from St. Petersburg to Moscow*, about the dreadful conditions of the serfs, the Empress called him "tainted with the French madness," though Radishchev's book may now seem merely the travel notes of a thoughtful man with a social conscience. Catherine and her police chief, Stepan Sheshkovsky, considered it a manifesto calling for revolution. (Sheshkovsky was said to begin an interrogation by knocking out the victim's teeth with his stick. Torture was outlawed but cruelty was practiced.) Radishchev said, quite rightly, that his book had not been written for the peasants since most of them hadn't learned to read. Its very small edition—only 650 copies were printed—was intended for the authorities, to give them the facts and the author's conclusion that reforms were absolutely necessary. The Czarina, who had learned to read, said that he was "a rebel worse than Pugachev," and had him sentenced to death by the High Criminal Court on fictitious charges—"harming the Sovereign's health . . . and mutinously attacking military installations." Later, she commuted the sentence to ten years in Siberia, which was slow death. Radishchev was reprieved after Catherine's death in 1796, but he was a broken man and committed suicide six years later.

Catherine spent the last years of her regime trying to prevent "the French madness" from spreading in Russia. A new Secret Chancellery was set up "to pursue all those poisoned with the pernicious venom of liberal thought." In 1791 Catherine announced that French diplomats would no longer be received at her court; two years later she broke off diplomatic relations with France and banned ships flying the French flag from Russian ports. French royalist émigrés were given asylum in Russia, and St. Petersburg became a center of counterrevolutionary activities. Russian citizens were forbidden to import French products, including French newspapers. She had come a long way from her early days, when French fashion and French conventions had been *de rigueur* at her court and Martha Wilmot had written, "The land is overrun with French as with locusts."

Catherine couldn't prevent people from dancing in the streets of St. Petersburg when the fall of the Bastille became known there. Pamphlets were smuggled in, translated, and secretly circulated. But she succeeded in keeping revolutionary fever out of Russia without trying to improve the social conditions that were the root of the evil. Apparently she failed to understand that the French Revolution had occurred because the *ancien régime* had lost its credibility with and hold on the people. (Her last successor, Czar Nicholas II, suffered from a similar delusion after the 1905 revolt in St. Petersburg.)

She was now in her sixties and still active in every way, though she could hardly walk, had lost her teeth, and looked spent and old. Her sexual needs, as strong as ever, were satisfied by young Platon Zubov. In 1793 and 1795 she was involved in the second and third partitions of Poland. And in 1796, shortly before her death, she decided to take advantage of Peter the Great's Succession Act of 1722, giving her the right to name her own heir. She planned to discard her son Paul and select her oldest grandson, the nineteen-year-old Alexander. Catherine had heard rumors that Paul was going mad: for once, the rumors later proved correct. But Catherine was more bothered by Paul's telling everyone that his mother had been involved in the murder of his father. She didn't understand that Paul was frightened of being murdered himself. He lived at Gachina, a country palace his mother had built for Gregory Orlov, and spent four years and a fortune turning it into a fortress. He summoned architects, engineers, even ballistics experts from Berlin. (He had inherited his father's admiration for Prussia, especially the Prussian Army.) "His Imperial Highness's Battalion," several companies dressed in Prussian uniforms, were stationed in large barracks near his castle and drilled every day.

In October 1796 Catherine summoned her daughter-in-law, Maria Feodorovna, and told her to a sign a paper demanding Paul's renunciation of the succession. Maria refused. She didn't tell Paul about her talk with the Czarina, nor about the rumors she'd heard that Catherine wanted Alexander to be the next czar. Maria was worried that the news might affect her husband, who suffered from nightmares and felt persecuted in his dreams. Once he had dreamed of the day his mother had been acclaimed the new ruler after his father's assassination. Paul saw himself taken to the Winter Palace but then the dream switched and he was taken to a scaffold in Senate Square. In another dream he was followed by Peter the Great, who stared at him, saying, "Paul, poor Paul." And poor Paul began to cry.

Catherine remains complex and ambiguous. Modern science understands the psychological contradiction between her masculine style of ruling, her brutality and utter ruthlessness, and her intensely feminine intimate life. She might give orders to execute someone who had displeased her and an hour later would break into tears at discovering that a lover had betrayed her with another woman. They all betrayed her when they thought they no longer needed her. "The office of lover to the Empress became almost an official position," writes Miriam Kochan. The official lover of the moment had his salary, his title, his apartment close to Catherine's own, his seat at the table next to her, at the royal mistress's right hand, and there would be country palaces, serfs, estates, diamonds.

But it was not an easy life. Catherine would get up at five or six in the morning, and the official lover had to be ready for duty at that time. Business until ten, breakfast, and prayers. Dinner at two, another summons for the young man, tea at five, and afterwards the social life. A theater, a masquerade, playing cards, listening to gossip that was often meaningful, mixing pleasure and business. She was said to be a good whist player. Sometimes she would take a coach ride in the countryside, without attendants. She liked small suppers with a few intimates, who were forbidden to rise when she entered a room. Her "Regulations to all who enter therein" said, "They will leave their dignity at the door together with their hats and swords." But Prince Adam Czartoryski wrote, ". . . the prosperous reign of Catherine confirmed the Russians in their servility. . . . Thus the whole nation is in no way scandalized at the depravity, the crimes, and the murders committed by their sovereign. Everything was permitted, and no one dreamed of criticizing her debauchery. It was thus that the pagans respected the crimes and obscenities of the gods of Olympus and of the Caesars of Rome."

Her vanity was almost proverbial in Europe. Emperor Joseph II wrote, "Vanity is her idol. Luck and exaggerated compliments have spoiled her." In 1785 Catherine in a special charter recognized the nobles as a separate estate with rights and privileges, and made nobility a hereditary institution. They no longer paid taxes and were exempted from military service, while the serfs paid higher taxes than before.

The abyss between her and her only legitimate son widened. The Empress did not permit Paul to sit in on the state councils. Officially, he didn't exist. He was encouraged to travel, and when he was away from her court and got drunk, he would say terrible things (which were promptly reported to his mother). In Vienna he was heard to say that he would dismiss his mother's advisors the moment he became czar. In Paris he once said, "If I had a faithful dog, my mother would have it drowned." He hated her and publicly called her a whore. Catherine responded in kind: she took his oldest two sons away from him and insisted on bringing them up as her own children. She told everybody that Alexander, aged seven, "is the delight of myself. . . . The child loves me instinctively."

Count Alexander Vorontsov, who later became the advisor of Czar Alexander I, wrote in 1801, "Immoderate luxury, indulgence in all forms of corruption, the avidity of self-enrichment, and the ill-gotten gains by the perpetrators of all these evils led people almost to long for a rapid change in 1796." Empress and sensualist, a great executive and a weak woman, buying some great paintings sight unseen, and, perhaps an hour later, having people tortured and killed—that was Catherine, the onetime fairy-tale princess who had come to believe anything her courtiers told her. The Empress remains a doubtful, disturbing major character in history; but no matter what she did, she did it in imperial style, and she was never dull.

She was never the same after Potemkin died of a heart attack in 1791. She cried for weeks and said, "I have no one left on whom I can rely." She died of a stroke on November 6, 1796. The day before, she had awakened at six in the morning, her usual

hour, had summoned her current lover, Platon Zubov, for his customary duty, and had drunk several cups of black coffee. She had
attended to the business of ruling the nation that during her regime had increased from eighteen to thirty million people. She
had added to the Russian Empire, as left by Peter the Great, the
territories of the Crimea, the northern Caucasus, the Ukraine,
much of Poland, and the Duchy of Courland. And she had found
time to write the inscription for her own tombstone:

Here lies Catherine II. . . . She went to Russia in 1744 to marry
Peter III. At the age of fourteen she made the triple resolution to
please her husband, Elizabeth, and the nation. She neglected nothing in trying to achieve this. Eighteen years of ennui and solitude
gave her the opportunity to read many books. Enthroned in Russia,
she desired nothing but the best for her country and tried to
procure for her subjects happiness, liberty, and wealth.

She forgave easily and hated no one. Tolerant, undemanding, of a
gay disposition, she had a republican spirit and a kind heart. She
made good friends.

PAUL I AND ALEXANDER I

The inscription was not placed on Catherine's tomb. Her son and successor, Czar Paul I, didn't permit it. He started his reign by ordering the coffin of his father, Peter III, taken from the Alexander Nevsky Monastery, and arranging "the joint funeral of Their Imperial Majesties." The stolid Russian people were ordered to mourn for a czar who had been murdered thirty-four years earlier. Paul ruled that the murderers of his father should bear the regalia through the streets of St. Petersburg. Count Alexis Orlov had to carry the crown. Peter III and his wife, who had almost certainly been involved in his murder, were buried in a single grave.

By that time everybody in St. Petersburg said that the Czar was mad. He methodically reversed his mother's policies, stopped the war with Persia, made an alliance with the Turks she'd fought against, offended the King of Prussia, and apologized to the Poles for the partitions his mother had engineered—without, however, returning the territories Russia had taken from Poland. His maniacal moments were terrible. The British ambassador reported home: "The fact is . . . that the Emperor is literally . . . not in his senses."

He freed his mother's prisoners and filled the prisons with his own enemies. He dictated decrees at night doing away with the few liberties that had been left. Foreign books were forbidden, censorship became strict, people were not allowed to travel abroad. He determined the shape of hats to be worn, the cut of

collars. Everybody had to bow when the Czar passed by in the
street. Even ladies had to get out of their carriages and curtsy.
He treated his son Alexander, the Czarevitch, with brutality,
making him a private in the army and keeping him busy with
trivial duties. Paul hated his mother's Winter Palace and turned
it into an army barracks; he ordered Brenna to build him a new
palace, dark and gloomy, which was surrounded by a moat and
ramparts and guarded by his own regiments. (It is now Engineers' Castle, not one of Leningrad's beauty spots.)

The most influential man at his court was a former prisoner of
war, Ivan Kutaisov, who became Paul's barber and was made a
count. An early Rasputin with sinister power, he intrigued against
the Czar's wife and his long-time mistress, Catherine Nelidova.
Catherine was exiled from St. Petersburg, and Paul installed a
new lady next to his apartments, while his wife was seen crying.
In true Romanov style, Paul turned his wrath against his sons.
Alexander wrote secretly to his tutor Frédéric César de La Harpe,
who had gone back to Switzerland, that there was chaos in Russia, and he had to perform duties "which might easily be discharged by any sergeant. . . . If and when my own turn comes, I
shall dedicate myself to my country, which must never become
again a toy in a madman's hand."

The madman next decided to conquer India and instructed
General Orlov of the Don Cossacks, "Your business is solely
against the British. . . . You must assure [the natives] of Russia's
friendly disposition toward them. . . . Make straight for the
Indus and the Ganges." Orlov left with twenty thousand Cossacks, came up against spring floods and lack of supplies, and the
campaign was over; thousands of Cossacks perished.

When Count Peter von der Pahlen heard of a conspiracy
against the Czar, he came to see Paul's son Alexander. Pahlen,
the governor-general of St. Petersburg, in charge of the police,
persuaded Alexander that his father must abdicate and that the
Czar's life would be spared. Pahlen selected sixty conspirators, all
of them officers from the Semenovsky Guards and loyal to Alexander. Paul had made many enemies among the officers of the
guards. (He said their colors reminded him of his mother's petti-
coats.) He made other enemies among the upper classes when he

decreed that the peasants would have to work only six days a week.

One night in 1801, two weeks after the Czar had moved into his new, "safe" palace, a group of conspirators approached the palace, where the Semenovsky Regiment had taken over the guard. Platon Zubov and Count Levin von Bennigsen overpowered two sentries and a valet and entered the Czar's bedroom. He stood there terrified, a nightcap on his head, staring at them. The lifelong nightmare had become truth. Other conspirators, most of them drunk, came in and moved against the Czar. He begged them to let him say his prayers, but they picked up a heavy malachite paperweight from the desk, and one pressed it against Paul's neck. In the morning it was announced that Czar Paul I had died of apoplexy.

At the coronation in the Kremlin of Paul's son, Alexander I, it was noticed that his entourage included men who had murdered his grandfather and some who had probably helped to kill his father. Perhaps there were also a few who would have liked to kill Alexander. He turned out to be a different sort of Romanov, however. He was charming and educated, disliked ostentatious pomp, and wore no jewelry. He abolished the bizarre laws his father had introduced. People were permitted to read foreign books and travel abroad. He was haunted by his father's assassination, for which he had not been prepared, and tried to escape into mysticism.

Alexander's private life was complicated; it was the Romanov pattern all over again. He was deeply in love with Marie Naryshkina, a Polish lady both beautiful and unfaithful. She gave him two children and much unhappiness. In public he was always extremely polite to his wife, the Empress Elizabeth. A miniature portrait shows a beautiful woman, but Martha Wilmot speaks of "the dreadful scurvy in her face." Alexander thought a great deal about the terrible condition of the serfs, particularly under the enlightened influence of his Swiss former tutor, La Harpe, and of Michael Speransky, the brilliant son of a village priest. Speransky drafted a plan for modernizing and streamlining the government, but the only idea that was carried out was the Council of State, a body of eminent advisors of the sovereign. Nothing else was done because of Napoleon Bonaparte.

Alexander's personal tragedy was his great antagonist, Napoleon. After the disastrous defeats of Austerlitz and Friedland the Czar sued for an armistice. A "treaty of friendship" was signed in 1807, on a raft in the Niemen River near Tilsit. It made Alexander extremely unpopular among his own people, who still remembered the victories of Catherine II. By 1811, however, he had convinced them that he would not give in to the French. He refused to uphold the Continental Blockade; his secret emissaries were trying to win Poland, Austria, and Prussia away from France. Many observers in the West thought Alexander was mad. It was common knowledge that the Russian army was poorly equipped and badly trained. An English visitor to an arms factory in Tula reported that the Russian muskets "missfire five times out of six and are liable to burst whenever discharged."

Early in 1812 the Treaty of Niemen was not worth the parchment it had been signed on. Like dictators before and after him, Napoleon was unavoidably set on his fatal collision course. On June 22, during a ball in a mansion near St. Petersburg, Czar Alexander was told of Napoleon's invasion. The military experts agreed that the campaign would be decisive and short. The Emperor's *grande armée* was said to have 600,000 well-trained men. Actually, one third of them were German conscripts whose loyalty was doubtful.

Napoleon began in blitzkrieg style, crossing the Niemen and occupying Vilna four days after the invasion. Alexander sent a letter to Vilna asking Napoleon to stop. Napoleon's answer sounds familiar. "Even God could not now undo what has been started." The blasphemic statement seemed to fill Alexander with unexpected strength. He was cheered by a message from Count E. V. Rostopchin, the Governor of Moscow, who made the bold prediction that Napoleon's invasion would fail in the end. "Your Empire, Sire," wrote Rostopchin, "has two powerful defenders— space and climate." In Vienna, Metternich declared, somewhat prematurely, "Russia has ceased to exist as a European power."

Not quite. Napoleon took Smolensk and continued toward Moscow. Bowing to widespread popular demand, Alexander appointed Prince Mikhail Kutuzov, a sixty-seven-year-old professional soldier, as supreme commander of the Russian forces. Personally, the Czar had no faith in Kutuzov, who was fat and lazy, couldn't even mount a horse, and spent his days lying, when he wasn't in bed. He peered with his one eye (he'd lost the other in a battle) at the maps and seemed hopelessly old-fashioned, a character from another century. Alexander couldn't understand why so many high-ranking officers had implicit belief in Kutuzov. The Czar didn't know that behind his mask of laziness Kutuzov was a man with a brilliant mind, cunning and very patient, truly a great military leader.

Even Kutuzov's admirers were shocked, though, when he did almost nothing to stop Napoleon's advance toward Moscow. Alexander was told that one of his closest friends, Prince Alexander Galitzin, was building a new palace "in which he would entertain Napoleon." The Czar didn't believe it but he was troubled and went to see Galitzin. The Prince denied the rumors and was ready to swear his loyalty on the Bible. He reached out for the Holy Scriptures. The Bible fell down, and opened on Psalm 91. ". . . I will say of the Lord, He is my refuge and my fortress: my God; in Him will I trust." Galitzin convinced the Czar that this was no accident but a "message." Alexander, like so many Romanovs with his strong streak of mysticism, was unable to speak. He took the Bible home and began reading it.

Napoleon, meanwhile, continued his advance. At the village of Borodino he was stopped by Kutuzov's forces. The battle lasted fifteen hours and cost the lives of eighty thousand men; each side claimed victory. Kutuzov, however, decided to retreat. One week later the *grande armée* marched into Moscow.

A few days later the Czar and his wife attended the Te Deum at the Kazan Cathedral in St. Petersburg to celebrate the anniversary of his coronation. People in the overcrowded cathedral were silent and hostile. The Empress later wrote she had worried for her husband's life. News reached St. Petersburg that Moscow —then a city of wooden houses—was burning. Russian historians claim that the Russians had started the fire in order that the enemy should occupy nothing but the burned earth. Count Rostopchin, the governor, set fire to his palace with his own hands. It was a desperate, heroic effort and it paid off. The thought of Russia's old capital burning did something to the people. For the first time in Russia's history they were united—serfs and nobles, priests and liberals. Alexander too found himself at last and declared he would not negotiate with Napoleon "as long as one enemy soldier remains on Russian soil." The entire nation supported him in this sentiment. The constitutional crisis had passed. "More than ever before, my people and I stand together," the Czar wrote to Bernadotte, crown prince of Sweden and a former general of Napoleon's who was now supporting Russia's cause against France.

Napoleon, no fool, knew he was trapped in Moscow. He tried to sue for an armistice, but now Alexander turned him down. Kutuzov and his staff considered Napoleon as good as beaten. After five weeks in Moscow and mounting problems of logistics, Napoleon decided to retreat toward the West. But he had waited too long. As Count Rostopchin had predicted, Napoleon was defeated by space and climate, and by the brilliantly dilatory tactics of Marshal Kutuzov. (Awakened at night and told that Napoleon was getting out of Moscow, the old marshal crossed himself and quietly went back to sleep.)

Napoleon's retreat remains one of the great military tragedies in history. Sir Robert Wilson, a British general attached to the staff of Marshal Kutuzov, wrote of

the naked masses of dead and dying men; the mangled carcasses of ten thousand horses, in some cases cut for food before life had ceased, the craving of famine at other points forming groups of cannibals; the air enveloped in flame and smoke. . . .

And the terrible winter. The *grande armée* no longer existed and Kutuzov refused to attack what was left of it, while Alexander had dreams of pursuing Napoleon all the way to Paris. Kutuzov suddenly died, and now Alexander himself took over and the war went on.

At the Battle of Nations, at Leipzig in October 1813, Napoleon was decisively beaten by the combined forces of Russia, Austria, Prussia, and Sweden. He no longer fought for his throne but for his very life. He abdicated in April 1814, and was exiled to Elba. Louis XVIII returned to Paris from his exile in England.

Czar Alexander made a triumphal entry into Paris surrounded

by his allies, the King of Prussia, and Prince Schwarzenberg, representing the Emperor of Austria. The exhilaration was followed by the Congress of Vienna. The Allied Powers, who had kept together under deadly pressure, immediately began bickering. At one point, Britain, Austria, and France signed a secret treaty. Some diplomats began talking of starting a war against Russia. Fortunately for the alliance, Napoleon escaped from Elba and went to Paris to try a comeback. Louis XVIII took refuge in Lille. On his desk Napoleon found the secret treaty. He sent it to the Czar to make the Russian emperor leave the alliance. But Alexander still wanted no part of such a deal. He summoned Prince Metternich, showed him the not-so-secret treaty, threw it into the fire, and told the Austrian diplomat that "the alliance must now be stronger than ever before."

After Napoleon's final defeat at Waterloo (Alexander's forces were too late to join the battle) the Czar went to Heilbronn in Germany. Shortly thereafter he met Baroness Barbara Juliana von Krüdener, fifty and still beautiful. She told the Czar "to seek salvation at the foot of the Cross." The Czar saw her every day, and when he went to Paris, she accompanied him. During a parade of the Russian troops in the Champs-Élysées, Madame de Krüdener was standing next to him. Charles Augustin Sainte-Beuve wrote, "Not even the homage which Louis XIV paid to Madame de Maintenon at the camp of Compiègne exceeded the veneration shown by the conqueror toward Madame de Krüdener." Probably under her strong influence, the Czar asked the states of Europe to sign the Treaty of the Holy Alliance, which Metternich, the skeptic, called "a piece of sublime mysticism and nonsense." Austria and Prussia signed, mostly in order to please Alexander; the British refused. But the Allies signed a Treaty of Alliance late in 1815 which contained no mystical clauses.

Alexander returned to St. Petersburg, more involved than ever in mysticism. In this frame of mind he came under the sinister influence of a former police official named Alexis Arakcheyev. Pushkin described Arakcheyev as "a man of little culture, reeking of malice and spitefulness . . . a vampire," and called him Alexander's "black angel." Today he seems like another precursor of Rasputin. Arakcheyev took clever advantage of having been at the palace the night Alexander's father was murdered, and of the sense of guilt that underlay the Czar's mysticism. He considered himself an instrument of God. He ignored corruption and the wretched conditions of the serfs. "Within a stone's throw of the Winter Palace, at the City Hall, human flesh was being put up for sale with permission of the authorities," wrote Turgenev. Censorship became very strict; the Security Police were everywhere.

Young Pushkin, whose poems were read surreptitiously all over Russia, wrote in his *Ode to Liberty*:

> O tyrants of the world, beware!
> And you, good men, take heart and dare
> Arise, fallen slaves

and was exiled by Alexander to the south of Russia.

When Alexander set up a Ministry of Spiritual Affairs and talked of going into a monastery, groups of officers and noblemen began plotting his abdication. The Czar talked of abdicating "to live a life of meditation." His brother Constantine was next in line of succession. He had a touch of the Romanov madness, was viceroy of Poland, had his marriage to Princess Julie of Coburg annulled, and married his beautiful Polish mistress, Joanna Grudzinska. Because of this, people said he was unfit to reign in Russia. Next in succession was the other brother, Nicholas, eleven years younger than Alexander. He too had married a beautiful German princess, Charlotte, the daughter of the King of Prussia, who took the name Alexandra. His passion for "Mouffy," as he called her, and later his affection for their children were his only endearing human qualities. The Czar had a secret document drawn up, in which Constantine renounced the throne.

Czar Alexander I died suddenly in Taganrog on the Sea of Azov on November 19 O.S., 1825. The news did not reach St. Petersburg until two weeks later and many people refused to believe it. It was whispered that the Czar had retreated to a monastery "to meditate." When one Feodor Kuzmich, a pious hermit, appeared in Siberia, he was said to be Alexander. Many Russians believed it, but the story was never confirmed.

THE DECEMBRISTS

St. Petersburg was the scene of a strange tragicomedy after the death of Alexander. Constantine had already refused the throne; and now his younger brother, Nicholas, also refused, though Prince Alexander Galitzin, the friend of the late czar, showed him the secret document. Nicholas knew he was very unpopular with the army because of his mania for discipline. (He remained a despot all his life. When he visited England in 1841, Queen Victoria noticed that he talked only of political and military matters, and she wrote that "his mind is an uncivilized one." Countess Nesselrode, a lady-in-waiting, wrote, "Nicholas is severe, vindictive and mean.")

When Nicholas refused to become czar, the army officers began plotting again. Most were aristocrats, members of the Northern Secret Society, in favor of constitutional monarchy. Some had joined the Southern Secret Society; they wanted Russia to become a republic. During the campaign against Napoleon, many Russian soldiers had been exposed to contacts in the West. "The army, from general to private, upon its return did nothing but discuss how good it is in foreign lands," wrote Bestuzhev-Ryumin, a member of the Southern Society. "Why should it not be so in our own lands?"

The plot was betrayed. Nicholas at last realized that the monarchy was in danger. At a dramatic midnight session of the Imperial Council he reluctantly accepted the succession. But things had gone too far. At the same hour the members of the conspiracy held a fateful meeting in the house of Conrad Ryleyev, a poet. Prince Trubetskoy was elected as the leader of a future Russian "democracy." The conspirators were inefficient amateurs though, and had mobilized neither the army nor the people. They talked romantically of "liberty" and of asking Constantine to accept the crown, but they lacked organized support; they hoped the Good Lord was on their side and would help them.

The revolutionaries met in Senate Square, on December 14 O.S., 1825. A few hundred soldiers from the Moscow Regiment were there. Later some workers who were employed at the construction of the nearby St. Isaac's Cathedral joined them. There was confusion. Prince Trubetskoy was not present and could not be found. A man named Kakhovsky who had sworn to kill Nicholas was running all over the square, brandishing two pistols. When he didn't see Nicholas, he shot and killed Gregory Miloradovich, the governor-general of St. Petersburg.

Nicholas was implored by his generals not to appear, but he shook his head. "If I am only czar for one day, I shall prove to the world that I am worthy." He put on his splendid dress uniform— white breeches, green tunic, a plumed hat—and rode into the square. Somebody shouted "Long live Constantine!" and somebody else yelled, "Long live Constitution!" Some people in the crowd believed that Constitution was the wife of Constantine. Pushkin later called the affair "a real Russian riot without reason or pity." Actually, it was closer to a tragicomedy. Three thousand loyal cavalry soldiers faced the insurgents. All day long, the rebels, joined by the Naval Guards, and the loyalist troops—the Horse Guards, the Preobrazhensky Guards, the Pavlovsky Guards —stood there, staring at one another. Loyalties switched; the Grenadier Guards joined the rebels.

Nicholas hesitated to bring guns into the square. Though he was a disciplinarian he didn't want to start his reign with a blood bath. At last, General Count Carl von Toll said, "Sire, sweep the square with gunfire or abdicate." Nicholas gave a hardly perceptible nod. There was a salvo, and more than sixty rebels were lying dead in the red-streaked snow. Hundreds fled, many were injured and some drowned trying to escape across the Neva. Thus ended the earliest revolution in St. Petersburg. Today Senate Square is known as Decembrists' Square.

Five leaders of the rebellion were executed, among them

Kakhovsky, who had not been able to kill the Czar. Nicholas ordered a bizarre religious service held in Senate Square "to commemorate the executions." Local society "celebrated" by attending a gala and ball given by Prince Victor Kochubey, an intimate of the imperial family, at his beautiful Fontanka Palace. While the elegant guests drove up in their coaches, they almost collided with the carts, escorted by gendarmes, in which the rebels were taken to Siberia. The aristocratic revolutionaries had put on their gala uniforms, and their wives wore their finest evening gowns. As they passed the brilliantly illuminated palace, they defiantly raised their arms, in spite of their chains. It was a romantic, Pushkinesque scene in the revolutionary history of St. Petersburg, often retold by Russian historians, who fail to mention that the Decembrists were rather inept beginners in the art of revolution.

Nicholas I never quite recovered from the shock. He set up a brutal system of thought police and censorship. His motto was "orthodoxy, autocracy, nationality." The Czar had no use for civilians, politicians, or foreigners. Students and professors had to wear uniforms. Visitors at the Hermitage were ordered to put on evening clothes, even in the morning, as though they were ambassadors presenting their credentials. Count Alexander Benckendorff, in charge of the feared Third Section, specialized in persecuting writers and intellectuals. Pushkin was often in trouble with the Third Section. The Czar read his new play *The Comedy of Boris Godunov* and asked the poet to rewrite it. Pushkin refused. "Only the devil could have thought of having me born in Russia with a mind and talent," he wrote to his wife.

In 1830, A. I. Herzen wrote, "I found here (in St. Petersburg) a silent bureaucracy, Cossacks with whips, policemen always ready to use their fists, half the city's population in uniform, the other half watchful and worried, and the whole city obsequious." Torture and third-degree interrogations took place in the damp prisons of the Peter and Paul Fortress, where Peter the Great had originated these methods with his own son. Some of Russia's great writers, from Radishchev to Dostoyevsky and Gorky, were sent there for the treatment.

In 1837 the Winter Palace burned down, and Nicholas ordered that a new palace, looking exactly like the old one, be ready for occupancy within a year. The Marquis de Custine reported that six thousand workers were employed during the terribly cold winter. Many died every day "and were instantly replaced by other champions brought forward to perish . . . in order to gratify the caprices of one man." The new Winter Palace was ready on time. Paradoxically, the Czar was austere in his private life, sleeping on a camp bed in a small room. Custine noticed that the ladies never washed and that the nobles didn't sleep on beds but lay down on the floor, wrapped in rugs, because the beds and sofas were full of vermin. The court physician, Dr. Martin Mandt, a German, reported that cows were kept at the top of the Winter Palace near the rooms of the maids of honor to supply the kitchen's milk needs.

There was no middle class in Russia, no Russian apothecary, only a few Russian doctors; the engineers and merchants were foreigners. The bureaucracy, however, was Russian. It took weeks to get a passport, and one had to bribe the officials. The first railroad was built between St. Petersburg and Tsarskoye Selo in 1838. Nicholas was pleased, drew a straight line with a ruler between St. Petersburg and Moscow, four hundred miles away, and told his engineers to build the tracks without a curve. They did.

The Czar did have some thoughts about social conditions though, saying, "The nobility must help me to gradually change the state of the serf so as to forestall a radical upheaval." But the landowners refused to co-operate and after several attempts the Czar gave up. "I had to stop; it was the hand of Providence."

The Revolution of 1848 had repercussions though the Czar ordered the borders closed "to stop the deadly virus." He dispatched a Russian expeditionary force to help the eighteen-year-old Emperor Franz Joseph I of Austria against the Hungarian insurrectionists. The Hungarians were beaten at Világos by the Austrian-Russian coalition. Nicholas put the universities in Russia under police control, banned public meetings, and prohibited travel abroad. The works of Pushkin, Turgenev, and Gogol were placed on the Index. Russian music, which had just found its national idiom, was censored by a special commission for "conspirational" sounds. Even mathematics textbooks were searched with magnifying glasses "for secret codes."

Toward the end of his life, the Czar continued the expansionist policies of Catherine II, sending his troops into Moldavia and Wallachia. The Russians sank the Turkish fleet off Sinop, but in 1854 Britain and France declared war on Russia and the Austrian Emperor promised the Allies "diplomatic support." Nicholas was shocked. "Do you intend to make common cause with the Turks? Does your conscience permit you, the Apostolic Emperor, to do so?" The Crimean war went badly for Russia. Supplies did not reach the front, there being no railroads in the Crimea. Food, water, medical supplies were needed. Leo Tolstoy, as war correspondent, wrote about the heroic defense of Sevastopol and the courage of the Russian soldiers. But the military leadership was corrupt, the bureaucracy was inefficient, and in St. Petersburg the Czar carried on his senseless routine, inspecting the guards and talking about discipline. During a parade in February 1855 he caught pneumonia. The Emperor asked Dr. Mandt whether he was going to die.

"Yes, Your Majesty," Mandt said.

People arrived with despatches. The Emperor, lying in his bedroom in the Winter Palace, covered with two blankets and a military coat, told them to go away. He was no longer interested in earthly affairs. "I now belong wholly to God." A few hours later he was dead.

THE ORIGINAL TERRORISTS

The coronation of Alexander II at the Kremlin was a magnificent affair but the young Czar knew this was only a façade. His father had told him on his deathbed, "I hand over to you my command —unfortunately not in such order as I wish." Alexander managed to get Russia out of the war at the expense of Bessarabia, which was given to the Turks. Next, he relaxed internal security, permitting people to travel abroad, limiting censorship, and giving more rights to students, who were permitted to organize and hold meetings. Then he decided to free the forty million serfs in Russia, despite strong opposition by the landowners and the nobility.

"It is better to abolish serfdom from above than to wait for the time when it will begin to abolish itself from below," the Czar told his nobles in Moscow. "Gentlemen, I ask you to consider my words. . . ."

The "consideration" lasted five years. The landowners were dead set against emancipation, which, they said, would create anarchy. Both sides misunderstood the situation. The landowners were afraid of chaos to come. The peasants expected a wonderful free life, without much work. In March 1861 the Emancipation Manifesto was published and read in all churches of Russia. In St. Petersburg the Czar was cheered. "No pen could describe the rapture of the people as the Czar rode past," wrote General E. A. Cherbachev. The Czar thought it was the happiest day of his life. But the problems persisted. The peasants had personal freedom but economically they were worse off than before. They had to pay higher taxes and make annual payments to redeem their land. Their poverty increased. Some peasants became desperate and murdered officials and landowners.

The unrest in the countryside was followed by disturbances at Russia's eight universities. Most students, sons of petty bureaucrats and of lesser landowners, were so poor they couldn't afford enough food to keep body and soul together. The malaise was spreading. The students saw what had happened to the peasants. Now they were told of slow and steady progress, but they didn't believe it. In the autumn of 1861 the first student riots broke out in St. Petersburg. The police acted with brutality, and many young boys were wounded. Others were arrested. But the rebellion went on. P. G. Zaichnevsky wrote a pamphlet demanding "nationalization and a ruthless revolution." Another student, D. I. Pisarev, preached that "everything that can be smashed must be smashed." His charisma was great and his theories swept through all the universities. Young men wore their hair long, and young girls cut theirs short. There was fiery talk of emancipation and free love, and of breaking down the social values of the Establishment. In 1862 Ivan Turgenev wrote about the new credo of total destruction in *Fathers and Sons* and established a new term: "Bazarov is a nihilist . . . a nihilist is a person who does not take any principle for granted, however much that principle may be revered."

Curiously, everybody attacked Turgenev after the novel's publication. The radicals said he had not gone far enough and besides made Bazarov "a caricature." The students accused Turgenev of being wishy-washy. And the conservatives accused him of encouraging nihilism and making Bazarov "too sympathetic." When fires broke out in St. Petersburg, they were said to be started by the partisans of "Bazarov." Everybody blamed "nihilism" for all ills. "A friend I met on the Nevsky Prospekt said to me, 'Look what your nihilists are doing!'" Turgenev wrote.

In Poland, the people rebelled once more against the Russian occupation. It was one of the most tragic chapters in the country's long, unhappy history. The Poles were encouraged because for a while they hoped England and France might help them. They murdered some Russian peasants and their families, whereupon the Russian soldiers reacted with terrifying brutality, publicly executing many hundreds of people. The casualties were enormous on both sides. It was rumored that perhaps a hundred thousand Poles were sent to Siberia. Though there was unrest in St. Petersburg, the court and the nobility pretended to take no notice. The police would take care of the troublemakers. Night after night there were balls and banquets and festivities. The happy few were getting drunk in order to forget the misery of the many.

Lord Frederick Hamilton, a British diplomat who had always thought of St. Petersburg "as a second Paris . . . conceived on an infinitely more grandiose scale than the French capital" was shocked when he came there:

> The atrociously uneven pavements, the general untidiness, the broad thoroughfares empty except for a lumbering cart or two, the low cotton-wool sky all gave the effect of unutterable dreariness. And this was the golden city of my dreams! This place of leprous fronted houses, of vast open spaces full of drifting snow flakes, and of immense emptiness. I never was so disappointed in my life.

The Czar would give "intimate" *bals de palmiers*, for perhaps only a couple of hundred people, grouped in small circles around palm trees that were brought from hothouses in Tsarskoye Selo to the Winter Palace. Sir Horace Rumbold, an English visitor, felt guilty about leaving his coachman outside in the cold Palace Square while he spent the night in pseudotropical warmth:

> That terrible cold! In the squares adjoining the Winter Palace immense fires are kept all night long for the coachmen and sledge drivers. . . . But once the Imperial threshold has been passed . . . the effect of the immense room is that of a tropical grove in some gorgeous fairy scene. . . .

The "Czar Liberator," whom many considered the most glamorous sovereign in Europe, instituted many reforms—a new education act, local self-government, a promotion system in the army permitting soldiers to rise to the rank of officers, a regular budget, the opening of the conservatories in St. Petersburg and Moscow. He did so many things that some people began to forget even the massacre in Poland. But in 1866 a student dismissed from St. Petersburg University tried to shoot the Czar and failed. He was not a member of a conspiracy but had wanted to draw attention to the misery of the peasants. The police accepted his explanation but the Czar became convinced that something must be wrong with his ideas of "modern" education. He named D. A. Tolstoy, a violent reactionary, to be the new Minister of Education, and decreed that "in all schools the open and secret teaching of those destructive conceptions which are hostile to the moral and material well-being of the people will be forbidden." Tolstoy changed the curriculum. The study of subjects "stimulating independent thought"—history, science, modern languages—was restricted, and the students were told to concentrate on Latin, Greek, pure mathematics, and Church Slavonic.

Many students went abroad, particularly to Switzerland, where the aristocratic anarchist Mikhail Bakunin published the periodical *The Cause of the People*. Bakunin preached straight revolution and abolition of religion and marriage, and denied all forms of compulsion. In Russia he was surpassed by S. G. Nechayev, a young schoolteacher who stated that revolution can be achieved only through strict discipline—conspiracy through complete ruthlessness. Lenin studied Nechayev's "Revolutionary Catechism," and historians have called him the first of the Bolsheviks. ("For the dedicated revolutionary everything is immoral and criminal that stands in his way.") Nechayev escaped to Switzerland but was arrested in Zurich and sent back to St. Petersburg, where he was imprisoned in a cell not far from the one Dostoyevsky had occupied. Dostoyevsky immortalized Nechayev in *The Possessed*.

The trend toward violence could no longer be checked. In 1878 Vera Zasulich tried to shoot General F. F. Trepov, the governor-general of St. Petersburg, "because he had ordered a political prisoner to be flogged"—a punishment no longer permitted by law. She wounded Trepov and was acquitted by the jury; later she escaped to England. Leo Tolstoy, very famous after the publication of *War and Peace*, wrote to a friend, "The Zasulich business is no joking matter. . . . These are the first signs of something not yet clear to us; but it is serious."

There were other assassination attempts. General Mezentsev, in charge of the St. Petersburg police, was fatally stabbed; a schoolmaster fired four shots at the Czar but missed; a terrorist group, Narodnaya Volya ("Will of the People"), threatened to assassinate the Czar. There was talk of creating a "Federation of

Village Communes" all over Russia. Narodnaya Volya had been organized by A. I. Zhelyabov, a fanatic young peasant studying at Odessa University. The terrorists of the 1870s no longer called themselves nihilists. They considered nihilism, "the fight for absolute individualism," outdated and spoke vaguely of a new concept of society. Their job was to prepare the new system by destroying despotism. Then the liberals would have to carry out the political reforms. Zhelyabov decided that first priority must be given to the assassination of the Czar. Guns and knives were considered old-fashioned; only bombs and mines would be used. Nikolai Kibalchich, the son of a priest, an engineer and expert chemist, created the bombs and mines. The group blew up what they believed to be the imperial train at Moscow's Kursky Station, but it was the baggage train, which looked exactly like the Czar's. Alexander was at the Kremlin when he heard the news. He was shocked. "Am I such a wild beast that they must hound me to death?"

Alexander's life was not made easier by his political and private problems. Since the Crimean War the Russian troops had steadily advanced in Central Asia. The expansionist policies of Peter the Great and Catherine II were revived slowly and steadily, as the Russians moved toward Afghanistan and India. There was growing concern in London, and much talk about the dangers of Pan-Slavism. General F. A. Fadeyev and Nikolai Danilevsky had published books about a Slavic Federation under Russia as the future goal; the capital would be in Constantinople. Many members of the Russian nobility became fanatic followers of Pan-Slavism. The Czar was worried when he heard his own brother, the Grand Duke Nicholas, talk about Constantinople, as Russia's "rightful capital." Alexander hated war but in the end he bowed to the fanatics and in 1877 declared war on Turkey. It lasted nine months and was cruel and senseless. The Emperor's nephew wrote from the front, "We live among blood and corpses. . . . Our officers are disgusted with the war and would rather go home."

The Russians occupied Adrianople, only sixty miles from Constantinople. Queen Victoria was so bitter that she threatened to abdicate. "It is the question of Russian or British supremacy in the world. . . . the Queen will not be a party to the humiliation of England," she wrote to Disraeli, her prime minister. "Oh! that

Englishmen were now what they were," she wrote to her daughter, whereupon the Cabinet ordered Admiral Sir Geoffrey Hornby to take his six ironclads through the Dardanelles to the Prinkipo Islands, near Constantinople. The Russians continued their advance toward San Stefano, six miles from Constantinople. Indian troops were ordered to Malta. But there was no confrontation. At the Congress of Berlin, Russia was given indirect control of half of Bulgaria but did not get access to the Mediterranean. The Pan-Slavists were shattered and blamed the Czar for the debacle. Some also blamed his mistress, Princess Catherine Dolgorukaya.

Alexander had fallen in love with the beautiful princess in 1865. She came from one of the most distinguished families in Russia; her father had been his close friend, and when Prince Dolgoruky died bankrupt, the Czar financed the education of his children. The Czar met Catherine, then eighteen, at the Smolny Institute. She refused to become his mistress until the student in St. Petersburg tried to shoot him in 1866. She knew then that she loved him and would devote her life to him. She was not ambitious or interested in power, and lived quietly in the houses in St. Petersburg and Tsarskoye Selo that the Czar had set up for her.

The Empress knew about the affair but didn't take it too seriously in the beginning. She remembered how Alexander had fallen madly in love with her when she was fifteen and married her two years later; and she knew about the love life of earlier Romanovs. She was ailing—the doctors later said it was tuberculosis—spending much of her time at Livadia, near Yalta. But she became deeply concerned when Princess Dolgorukaya had a son in 1872 and a daughter the next year. The Czar had sent a secret order to the Senate, giving the children the titles Prince and Princess Yurievsky. The Empress was heartbroken and escaped into religion, attending mass twice a day. The Czar was deeply regretful but still spent considerable time with Catherine. She was in her twenties, and he was sixty at the end of the disastrous Constantinople campaign. He looked older than his age, and people said it was the fault of his passionate mistress.

The situation played into the hands of Zhelyabov and his terrorists. After the unsuccessful attempt to kill the Czar in his train, they decided on a more ambitious plan. They were going to blow up the dining room at the Winter Palace while the imperial family was there for dinner. Zhelyabov's mistress, Sophia Perovskaya, the daughter of a former governor of St. Petersburg, was the architect of the conspiracy. She was beautiful, merciless, and a stronger fanatic even than Zhelyabov. She drove him almost insane; once she demanded that a member of the group who had shown weakness commit suicide, and he did.

The bomb was timed to go off twenty minutes past 6:00 P.M., the family's regular dining hour. That night, though, they were late. Prince Alexander of Hesse and his son were expected for dinner, and their train had been delayed. The Czar and his family were on their way to the dining room when an explosion shook the palace. The room was a shambles. In the guardroom underneath, eleven men were killed and thirty wounded. The Czar first thought of Catherine. He had installed her in the Winter Palace, in an apartment above his own, with an elevator connecting them. She was unharmed; so was his wife, who was asleep, having been given a sedative.

The people were shocked. If the terrorists could get to the Czar's dining room, anything might happen. "[More] explosions were promised in various parts of the capital," the French ambassador, Eugène Melchior de Vogüé, reported. "The names of the threatened streets were given. Families changed their homes and some left the town. The police, convinced of their importance, lost their head. The public prayed for a deliverer."

The deliverer was Count M. T. Loris-Melikov, the minister of the interior. The terrorists promised to kill him, but an assassination attempt failed. By using the stick and the carrot, Loris-Melikov relaxed tension. He called his regime "the dictatorship of the heart." He even abolished the Third Section. Strict security measures were established at the Winter Palace, with special passes for visitors, sentries guarding each floor, and servants forbidden to move between floors. He made the Czar fire some reactionary ministers, limited censorship, introduced press conferences. He became quite popular with the public, rare for an interior minister.

In 1880 Empress Maria was dying; she had such trouble breathing that her rooms had to be filled with oxygen from gas cylinders. Her husband visited her regularly, though he spent a great deal of time with Catherine in Tsarskoye Selo. His children were shocked and resentful. Within a month after his wife died, he married Princess Dolgorukaya, making her his morganatic wife and titling her Princess Yurievskaya. His family was not consulted or warned. The young Grand Duke Alexander, a nephew of the Czar, later wrote about the dinner at which Catherine was formally presented to the family:

> Princess Yurievskaya gracefully acknowledged the formal bows of the Grand Duchesses and sat down in the chair of Empress Maria Alexandrovna. I never took my eyes off her. I liked the sad expression of her beautiful face and the radiance of her rich blond hair. Her nervousness was obvious. Often she turned to the Emperor and he patted her hand gently. She would have succeeded in conquering the men had they not been watched by the women. I felt sorry for her and could not comprehend why she should be ostracized for loving a kind, handsome and cheerful man who happened to be the Emperor of Russia.

Later the mother of Grand Duke Alexander said to her husband, "I shall never recognize that adventuress. I hate her. Imagine her daring to call the Emperor 'Sasha' in the presence of all the members of the imperial family!" And the wife of Vladimir, the Czar's second son, wrote to Alexander of Hesse, ". . . We are forced to receive her and visit her. The Czar goes on visits with her in a closed carriage. Since she is very uneducated and has neither tact nor intelligence, you can imagine the kind of life she leads us. . . ."

The terrorists were active again. Zhelyabov and Sophia ordered mines placed in various places and prepared bombs. The Czar had to be killed. In January 1881 Dostoyevsky told the editor of the Russian *Times*, "You said that I'd shown clairvoyance in my *Brothers Karamazov*. Wait till you see the sequel. . . . I shall make my pure Aliosha join the terrorists and kill the Czar. . . ." Members of the imperial family were terrified. "In wartime one knows one's friends and enemies," wrote the Grand Duke Alexander. "We never did. The butler serving morning coffee might have been in the employ of the nihilists. A servant coming to clean the fireplace was a potential bearer of an infernal machine."

On February 28 O.S., Loris-Melikov placed on the Czar's desk the manifesto that would initiate parliamentary government in Russia. The Czar signed it. Loris-Melikov asked him not to attend the Sunday parade the next day. Zhelyabov had been arrested, but there was the possibility that Sophia Perovskaya and some of her fellow terrorists would do something. The Czar laughed and shook his head.

He attended the parade and afterward told his coachman to get back fast to the Winter Palace because he had an appointment at 3:00 P.M. The coachman took the route approved by Loris-Melikov and guarded by his plainclothesmen, but then he took a short cut along Canal Quai. Sophia noticed the change and signaled her accomplices. A young man threw a bomb against the Czar's carriage. Two Cossacks and three horses were killed, but the Czar was not hurt; he stepped out to see what had happened. The coachman begged him to get into Colonel Dvorzhitsky's sleigh and go back to the palace. As Alexander moved toward the sleigh, a man threw a second bomb. Twenty people were left lying on the ground; once again, as so often in St. Petersburg, the snow was red with blood. The Czar collapsed, his face splashed with blood. "Get back to the palace to die," he said, and lost consciousness. He was brought to the Winter Palace and placed on a couch in his study. Princess Yurievskaya came running in and fell across his body, crying, "Sasha, Sasha!" A few minutes later he was dead, and she dropped down to the floor, her pink and white negligée covered with blood. Outside, thousands of people stood in front of the Winter Palace; when the Grand Duke Vladimir stepped out on the balcony, many knelt down bareheaded. He announced the Czar's death in the Russian way: "The Emperor wished you a long life." Everybody understood; the word "death" was never used. Even the Czar's critics were horrified. Maurice Paléologue, a young French diplomat who had just arrived in St. Petersburg, wrote:

On the very morning of his death [the Czar] was working on a reform which would have launched Russia irrevocably along the track of the modern world, the granting of a Parliamentary charter. . . . And the nihilists have killed him. . . . Oh! a Liberator's is a dangerous job!"

THE BEGINNING OF THE END

Alexander III started his reign by tearing up the reform manifesto, still on his father's desk. He told his advisors that the six terrorists involved in his father's murder would hang.

Leo Tolstoy, who had foreseen the tragedy, dared write to the Emperor that the executions would not deter the terrorists; they would provoke more violence. He wrote:

> . . . it is presumption and folly on my part to demand that you, the Emperor of Russia and a loving son, should pardon your father's murderers, returning good for evil. It is folly, yet I cannot otherwise than wish it. . . . Why not try, in the name of God, to carry out His law, thinking neither of the State nor the people? . . .

The Emperor read the letter and threw it into the wastebasket. The terrorists were hanged in Semenovsky Parade Ground as several thousand people looked on excitedly. Later, many tried to get a piece of rope from the neck of a hanged man; it was supposed to bring good luck.

Alexander III was often compared in appearance to Peter the Great. He was tall and strong and had a Russian peasant's powerful physique. He lived in Gachina, forty miles from St. Petersburg, where he felt safe.

The influence of sinister, evil men on the czars remains symptomatic. Basically weak and insecure, the Romanovs were often dominated by dangerous demagogues and vicious charlatans. Alexander's former tutor, K. P. Pobedonostsev, the procurator of the Holy Synod—a sort of Grand Inquisitor—proclaimed that Russia's Jews must disappear: one third to die, one third to emigrate, one third to assimilate.

Alexander III listened to Pobedonostsev, whom people called "the black czar," and willingly sanctioned the persecution of the Jews. Like many other half-educated, indoctrinated people, Alexander believed in a gigantic conspiracy that was "organized by international Jewry" with the aim of destroying the monarchy. He would always refer to Jews contemptuously as "Yids." Much was made of the fact that Jessica Hellman, who had been close to one of his father's assassins, was Jewish. The first pogroms started in Kiev and Kirovo. Jews were murdered, and their property was confiscated. A pattern emerged which remained a shameful feature of life in Russia. Anti-Semitism in Russia and in Poland later led directly to anti-Semitism in Germany; the persecution of the Jews in Russia was later surpassed only during the Hitler regime in Germany (where many Russian and Polish Jews had gone because they had hoped to be safe there).

In 1882 the May Laws, which created a precedent later followed by the Nuremberg Race Laws, were announced. Russian Jews were not permitted to own land, become lawyers or civil servants, or marry Christians, nor could they appeal against court sentences. They were forced to become small shopkeepers and artisans, which created more resentment among the Russians and led to further pogroms lasting for more than ten years. A quarter of a million Jews emigrated to Western Europe, mostly to Germany and Austria (where they aroused more resentment). It was a vicious circle leading toward Auschwitz and Treblinka. The enterprising and, as it turned out, lucky ones among them didn't stay in Europe but went all the way to America.

In 1892 the Czar's sadistic brother Grand Duke Sergei ordered the Jewish quarter in Moscow surrounded by mounted Cossacks at night. According to an objective witness, Harold Frederic, the author of *The New Exodus:*

. . . Of these unhappy people thus driven from their beds, and hauled off to prison in the wintry darkness, some were afterwards marched away by *étape*, that is, chained together with criminals and forced along the roads by Cossacks. . . . They were scattered— who knows where?, over the whole face of the earth. . . . There was no charge of criminality or of leading an evil life against any of them. . . .

The persecution of the Jews was followed by the forced Russification of many people in the Finnish and Baltic states. Families with German names who had lived in Russia since the days of Peter the Great were ordered to leave overnight. Alexander forbade the use of the German language at his court. His slogan was "Russia for the Russians."

He hated social life and became famous for his eccentric stinginess. Table linen was not to be changed every day. The Emperor's heir, thirteen-year-old Nicholas, was once so hungry that he opened the gold cross he had worn since his baptism and ate the beeswax inside. (Later he admitted it had tasted "immorally good.") At Gachina, the Emperor lived in rooms that were almost shabby. Lady Randolph Churchill wrote of a visit there that "after dinner the table would be removed and Their Majesties would spend the remainder of the evening [in the dining room], though Gachina had several hundred rooms." The Czar was very angry when his wife spent twelve thousand pounds on a sable coat. What he liked best was to drink beer and play the trombone. Members of the court "orchestra" wore shabby clothes and had to drink beer from half-gallon mugs.

Fortunately for St. Petersburg society, there were the Emperor's brothers Vladimir and Alexis, who became famous for their elegance and largesse in the night spots of Paris, where sightseers of *la belle époque* were taken on *la tournée des grands ducs*. At their hangout in St. Petersburg, the Restaurant Cubat, the nights often ended in wild brawls. Vladimir, who was made president of the Academy of Fine Arts, married a German princess, in the Romanov tradition. Alexis, Grand Admiral of the Russian Fleet ("his knowledge of naval affairs could not have been more limited," a cousin said) lived with the beautiful Duchess of Leuchtenberg and her husband, *à trois*, also in the Romanov tradition. It was rumored that the husband was "locked out of his bedroom" and had to sleep in his study. Yet the only brother whom the Czar did not like was Paul, quiet and intelligent, because he married a divorcée from bourgeois society. He was banished from Russia.

In the late 1880s terrorism increased again. One day in 1887 three students were arrested in Nevsky Prospekt; other conspirators were rounded up. Five of them were found guilty of plotting to kill the Czar and were hanged on May 20, 1887. One of them was Alexander Ulyanov, a brother of Lenin.

Alexander continued his father's policies and started the first "cold war" in Russia's history. Thinking in terms of Constantinople, he wanted Bulgaria, which had been split by the Congress of Berlin, and he also wanted satellite governments in Serbia and Greece. Russian agents were sent to the Balkans, where they set up subversive cells. Embassy officials financed "sympathizers" to start riots. Russian army officers in Bulgaria began drilling young people in guerrilla tactics, and agents finally succeeded in starting a mutiny among Bulgarian army officers. Prince Alexander of Battenberg, the Czar's cousin who ruled half of Bulgaria, was kidnaped and forced to abdicate. Queen Victoria was furious. Eventually the Prince was turned over to the Austrians, but he didn't go back to Bulgaria. Alexander III was pleased until he was told that the new regime in Bulgaria under Stambulov was also anti-Russian. Russian agents were dispatched to Bulgaria and managed to kill Stambulov a few years later.

In 1887 Bismarck convinced the Czar that it would be to the advantage of both countries to sign a secret pact, each pledging neutrality in case the other started a war. It was a clever gambit. Austria could not expect German help in a war with Russia, and France could not count on Russia if Germany attacked her. Three years later Kaiser Wilhelm II dismissed Bismarck and did not renew the pact. In 1894 Alexander III concluded a military treaty with France that was directed against Austria and Germany, thus preparing the European stage for the First World War.

Alexander's son Nicholas, the heir to the throne, had fallen in love with the German Princess Alix of Hesse and wanted to marry her. His parents did not approve, since Alix was a granddaughter of Queen Victoria. Nicholas was sent on a boring tour around the world. In 1893 he visited London, where "Uncle Bertie," the Prince of Wales, "sent me at once to a tailor, a bootmaker, and a hatter," he wrote to the Czarina. (The Princess of Wales, Alexandra, was the Czarina's sister. Their father was the king of Denmark.) At the House of Commons, some people thought he resembled the Duke of York, and some thought he looked depressing, "shy, uncertain, indecisive." He was quite decisive about Princess Alix, however, and told his parents he would "marry Alix or not at all."

Alix would, of course, have to give up her Protestant faith and become Orthodox. Nicholas met her in Coburg, where Alix's brother, the Grand Duke of Hesse, had married Princess Victoria, the daughter of the Duke of Edinburgh. Alix refused. "She cried the whole time and only whispered now and then, 'No, I cannot do it,'" Nicholas wrote to his mother. He got unexpected help from the Kaiser. Wilhelm II had become worried by the Franco-Russian treaty and knew that Bismarck had been right. Russia must be neutralized, and Nicholas would do it if he married Wilhelm's cousin Alix. One evening the Kaiser himself took Alix to the house where the Czarevitch was staying. Later Nicholas wrote to his mother:

> We were left alone, and with her first words she consented! The Almighty only knows what happened to me then. I cried like a child, and she did too. . . . The whole world is changed for me, nature, mankind, everything. . . .

They were not yet married in November 1894, when Alexander III died in the Crimean palace of Livadia. Nicholas and Alix (she took on the Russian name Alexandra) were married ten days after the Czar's funeral, in St. Petersburg. The Prince of Wales represented Britain. People called Alexandra "the funeral bride." They didn't know how right they were. The beginning of the end was approaching.

Alexandra was not popular in St. Petersburg. Members of the Czar's family called her cold and humorless. She spoke bad Russian and had bad taste. "Shy, silent, and awkward, she didn't seem to have the talent of drawing people to her," wrote Princess Catherine Radziwill. Alexandra made no secret of her feelings toward the nobility. "I feel that those who surround my husband are insincere. No one is doing his duty for Russia. They are all serving him for their personal advantage." She was shocked by the manners of society in St. Petersburg. "The heads of the young ladies are filled with nothing but thoughts of young officers." She didn't like the balls at the Winter Palace; she didn't like to live in the capital. The Czar and his family—four daughters and Alexis, the heir to the throne—lived quietly in Tsarskoye Selo, seeing few people.

Alexandra was deeply shocked when the doctors told her that little Alexis was suffering from incurable hemophilia. Alexis had inherited the terrible disease through Alexandra's mother, Princess Alice, Queen Victoria's daughter. (Queen Victoria was a carrier of hemophilia.) The Czarina censured the "ignorance" of the doctors and sought escape in religion. Only God could help her child. Her attitude was later cleverly and brutally exploited by Rasputin. Unfortunately her influence on "Nicky" was strong. The Czar was soon known to be irresolute, "a ruler who cannot be trusted," wrote Count Sergius Witte, the brilliant minister of finance. P. N. Durnovo, the minister of the interior, said, "Mark my words, he will be a modern Paul I." Trotsky called him "a charmer, without will, without aim, without imagination, more awful than all the tyrants of ancient and modern history." Trotsky was not exactly objective in his judgment. But even the Czar's second cousin Wilhelm II called Nicholas "not treacherous but weak, and weakness fulfills all the functions of treachery."

Nicholas had grandiose, unrealistic ambitions. He wanted to capture Manchuria and to annex Korea. He talked about conquering Persia and seizing the Bosporus and the Dardanelles. He was bewitched by the old Romanov dream of Constantinople. The Czar's ministers of war and the navy were in favor of a fast commando operation against the Turks—thirty thousand troops would be taken from Odessa to the upper Bosporus before the British could react—but fortunately Count Witte convinced Nicholas that Britain and Austria would immediately come to the aid of Turkey. Three years later the Czar proposed a conference at The Hague to discuss an international limitation of arms, after he'd heard that Austria-Hungary was building up her artillery. Twenty nations accepted the invitation. The Prince of Wales called the idea "the greatest nonsense I ever heard of."

After the Boxer Rebellion in China, Nicholas gave orders to occupy Manchuria, against the advice of almost all his ministers. In 1903 he ordered Russian troops into northern Korea, though he was warned this might mean war with Japan. Nicholas and many people in Europe were convinced that after a short war, Russia would win a triumphant victory. But by the end of 1904 the Russian troops had suffered several defeats, Port Arthur was taken by the Japanese, and after the Russian fleet was almost annihilated at Tsushima, the Czar summoned Witte (who had resigned after the invasion of Korea) and asked him to negotiate for peace with Japan.

These suicidal political activities took place against a background of mounting terrorism inside Russia. In 1902 D. V. Sipyagin, the minister of the interior, had been assassinated. His successsor, V. K. Plehve, who had organized a number of pogroms against the Jews, was killed by members of a terrorist society, Battle Organization. Its leader was Yevno Asev, one of the great double agents of all time. The revolutionary movement spread all over the country. There were two main groups. The Social Democrats (S.D.), who believed in Marxism, were active among the factory workers in the suburbs of St. Petersburg and elsewhere. In 1903 the Social Democrat leader, G. V. Plekhanov, broke with one of his lieutenants, Lenin. The Social Democrats split into the Mensheviks and the Bolsheviks. There was also the party of the Social Revolutionaries (S.R.), who refused the idea of a revolution carried out by the industrial workers and instead worked for a revolt among the peasants. The two parties often exchanged members and information. Lenin, the leader of the Bolsheviks, was active in propaganda. The S.R. preached terrorism; its core was the Battle Organization, which took responsibility for most political murders after 1900.

"In a sense, nobody could live in St. Petersburg without a consciousness of volcanic anger about to erupt; nobody quite knew when or how it would happen," wrote E. M. Almedingen, who remembered her anger as a child when she read at the gates to the Summer Garden, "Dogs, Beggars, and All Lower Ranks of the Army and Navy Not Allowed Inside." The yard porter told the servants in her house that "the policemen will be strung up on lampposts and the workers will come into their own," and she saw "marches of university students and factory workers, red flags waving above their heads . . . the visible pattern of tumult." Such was the social climate in St. Petersburg in the early years of the century, while Russia was losing the war against Japan. The stage was set for the explosion, but when it came, its leader was not a revolutionary or a terrorist but a priest, Father G. A. Gapon, who led a peaceful demonstration of factory workers to the Winter Palace on Sunday morning, January 9 O.S., 1905. A strike had begun at the Putilov Engineering Works and spread to other factories. The demonstrators hoped to present a petition, signed by 135,000 workers, to the Czar, asking for an eight-hour day, freedom of speech and religion, and amnesty for political prisoners. Nicholas II, informed of the demonstration, deliberately left St. Petersburg and stayed in Tsarskoye Selo. He didn't bother to go to the Winter Palace. Instead he had the police alerted and troops called out.

At the entrance to Palace Square, the demonstrators, chanting hymns, carrying icons and portraits of the Czar, were stopped by the soldiers. Some demonstrators were still chanting and praying but others began throwing stones and pieces of ice. The cavalry charged with drawn swords. The people didn't budge. The commanding officer warned that the troops would fire. There were angry shouts: "Go ahead, fire!" They did, leaving piles of bodies in the snow. No one knows exactly how many people were killed; estimates range from several hundred to four thousand. Nearly all historians agree that "Bloody Sunday" was the beginning of the events leading to the October Revolution in 1917. The monarchy was finished in Russia, though Nicholas ruled for twelve more years.

After the tragedy, Father Gapon joined the revolutionaries. "Take bombs and dynamite; I absolve you!" He toured the capitals of Western Europe, was received as a hero, but after his return to Russia came under the influence of the police chief Rachkovsky and betrayed all he knew abut the Battle Organization and its chief, Asev. Gapon asked the police chief for 100,000 rubles. Members of the Battle Organization found out about Gapon's betrayal and killed him in a deserted house near the Finnish frontier.

A few weeks after the massacre in Palace Square, the Czar's uncle, Grand Duke Sergei, was assassinated by the Battle Organization. In October, the lights went out in St. Petersburg, food deliveries were stopped, and there were wild riots. Outside the city, estates were raided by the peasants. In the Black Sea, the crew of the battleship *Potemkin* mutinied; the revolt soon spread to other ships; barricades were set up in Odessa and Kharkov. Leon Trotsky, a member of the Menshevik branch of the Marxist Social Democrats, announced the formation of *soviets* (councils), each member of the council representing a thousand workers. The Czar sent troops to the factories. News of the lost war against Japan led to new waves of terrorism. Civil war was imminent. Witte asked the Czar to make certain constitutional concessions to rally the liberals, who might otherwise join the extremists.

Nicholas gave in. The Imperial Manifesto of October 1905 created a sort of semiconstitutional monarchy. Freedom of conscience, speech, assembly, and association was promised. An elected parliament would be set up—the Duma ("thought," meaning "a place of collective thought"). The manifesto infuriated the leftist extremists, who increased their activities, and the rightist extremists, who said the Jews were to blame and started new pogroms. The Czar asked for Witte's resignation and appointed I. L. Goremykin, seventy-four, "an old fur coat taken out of camphor." The Duma was never effective. Instead of doing some serious, constructive thinking, the members expressed cautious wishes. There was much empty oratory. The promised reforms were literally talked to death. The Czar did accomplish something, though, when he appointed P. A. Stolypin as prime minister. The British ambassador called him "the most notable figure in Europe." The Czar wrote to his mother, "I cannot tell you how much I have come to like and respect this man." Even Stolypin could not sell the nation the parliamentary system. The Russians were not ready for a democracy that remained merely a slogan. The democratic principles had never been tried and tested. The landlords still owned the land; the peasants still had to rent it.

Stolypin was unafraid even of Gregory Rasputin. Rasputin, an illiterate monk, claimed to be a faith-healer able to help the Czarevitch. He had been brought to Alexandra by the wives of two grand dukes, Montenegrin princesses who believed in Rasputin's "superhuman" powers and in spiritualism. It was said that several times Rasputin had stopped the Czarevitch's hemorrhages. Afterwards Rasputin had almost hypnotic influence upon the Empress, who called him the *starets*, or holy man. The truth was that the "holy man" was a brutal and dissolute drunk who loved wild orgies. St. Petersburg ladies who went to consult him because they had "problems" often ended up in bed with him. Stolypin, a decent man, ordered the starets investigated and sent a detailed report of Rasputin's orgies to the Czar. Nicholas refused to do anything about the report after Alexandra said, "He is a saint. They all hate him because they know we love him." Stolypin ordered the "saint" out of St. Petersburg and earned the deep hatred of the Empress. She was quite pleased when Stolypin was assassinated a few months later, during an opera performance in Kiev. His friend and successor, Count V. N. Kokovtsov, wrote in his memoirs that the Czar did not bother to visit Stolypin, who lived for three days after he'd been shot, and showed no sympathy. Their Majesties wanted to express their condolences to Stolypin's widow but she refused to receive them. Later, the Empress told Kokovtsov, in a tactless moment, "I am certain that Stolypin died to make room for you, and this is all for the good of Russia." Kokovtsov was deeply shocked.

During the Romanovs' tercentenary celebrations in 1913 in St. Petersburg, the Empress was strangely withdrawn and failed to attend the receptions at the Winter Palace. It was rumored she was suffering from heart trouble and nervous hysteria. Almost no one knew the reason: she was sick with worry about her son's hemophilia. The incurable condition of the Czarevitch was the best-kept secret in Russia. Everybody knew he was sick but no one knew that the small boy was an invalid, very close to death.

Perhaps to forget his worries, Nicholas escaped into his obsessive dreams of marching into the Balkans and occupying Constantinople. He didn't prevent the formation of the Balkan League. In the capitals of Western Europe the diplomats were aware of the danger of war. Poincaré called the Balkan League "the germ of war against Turkey and Austria." In 1913 the British ambassador in Vienna, Sir Fairfax Cartwright, wrote with remarkable foresight to London, "Serbia may some day bring a universal conflict on the Continent. . . ." Only the Pan-Slavists in St. Petersburg and the Bolshevik revolutionaries, strange bedfellows, were hoping for war. That same year Lenin wrote to Maxim Gorky, "A war between Austria and Russia would be a very useful thing for the revolution." He, too, proved absolutely right.

THE REVOLUTIONS

Lenin was living abroad at the time but was in touch with the six Bolshevik deputies who were members of the Fourth Duma; eight Menshevik members took orders from Trotsky. Lenin's man in St. Petersburg was Joseph Stalin, who had launched the newspaper *Pravda* in 1912 there, with a circulation of forty thousand. (Two years later, Stalin was exiled to Siberia.)

The situation in St. Petersburg was deteriorating. Lenin's propaganda was paying off. In the early months of 1914 there were more than four thousand strikes in local factories. The only cheerful voice was that of David Lloyd George, who made the incredible statement on January 1, 1914, "Never has the sky been more perfectly blue." Lloyd George's vision was blurred; he paid not enough attention to the reports he received from his ambassadors.

On June 28 in Sarajevo Gavrilo Princip, a member of the Serbian terrorist organization the Black Hand, assassinated Archduke Franz Ferdinand of Hapsburg, heir to the throne of Austria-Hungary, and his wife. The "perfect political murder" that started the First World War has never been completely explained. Most historians agree that it was bound to happen sooner or later, owing to the respective positions in the Balkans of Austria and Russia. "The world will probably never be told all that was behind the murder," Sir Edward Grey, the British Foreign Secretary, wrote in his memoirs. His vision was better than Lloyd George's when he said to a friend, looking out from his window in Whitehall, "The lamps are going out all over Europe. We shall not see them lit again in our lifetime."

Some of the protagonists of the conspiracy that led to the assassination in Sarajevo died soon afterwards. There remains no doubt though that Russia played an important part in the plot. Colonel Dragutin Apis, head of Serbian Intelligence, had been a close friend of the Russian assistant military attaché in Belgrade, A. I. Verkhovsky. In June 1917 Apis was executed by the Serbian government on a charge of conspiring with the Austrians. At that time Verkhovsky was minister of war in the Kerensky government in Petrograd (as St. Petersburg was then called). It was a small terrorist world.

Another key figure in the mystery was Vladimir Gachinovich, a Bosnian terrorist. He was the son of an Orthodox priest, had studied the writings of the great nihilists Bakunin and Nechayev, and had become a member of the Black Hand. He lived in exile in Switzerland and was found murdered a few months after the death of Colonel Apis because he knew too much. It never became known who killed him—the Serbian government, his fellow terrorist members of the Black Hand, or the Austrian agents.

After the assassination of Archduke Franz Ferdinand and his wife, the tragedy evolved with the inevitability of Greek drama. Austria's ultimatum to Serbia on July 23 could not conceal Vienna's intention to absorb Serbia as it had annexed Bosnia and Herzegovina in 1908. Three days later Vienna rejected Serbia's reply, declared war on Serbia on July 28, and began shelling Belgrade the following day. On July 30 Austria and Russia ordered general mobilizations. The next day Germany issued a twenty-four-hour ultimatum to Russia to demobilize. The Russians didn't even bother to reply, and Germany declared war. Some historians take a more charitable view. "Austria, in acting against Serbia, was taking the only step by which she believed she could preserve her very existence as a state," wrote Sidney Fay, the American historian. "Russia . . . did not have any such vital interest at stake; her existence as a state was not in jeopardy; her interest was more to preserve and increase her prestige." In the light of subsequent events this interpretation is

doubtful. When France joined Russia and England joined France
after Germany's invasion of Belgium, there were people in St.
Petersburg who feared the war might finish off the monarchy.
Rasputin telegraphed the Czar, ". . . with war will come the end
of Russia and yourselves and you will lose to the last man." A
prophetic statement, but it was too late.

There was mad enthusiasm in Russia for the war against Austria and Germany. Once again—as when Napoleon had burned
Moscow—the Russian nation was united, rulers and ruled, peasants and aristocrats. When Nicholas II and his wife stepped out
on the balcony overlooking Palace Square (where so many Russians had been killed in January 1905 under his regime) many
people fell on their knees. "At that moment, the Czar was really
the military, political and religious leader of his people," wrote
Maurice Paléologue.

Rasputin had been right, for once. By the end of 1914 the Russians were defeated in East Prussia; late in 1915 Russia had lost
Poland, Lithuania, Courland, and much of Galicia. Within the
first twelve months, the Russian armies lost almost four million
men—dead, wounded, and prisoners. By December 1916 the casualties were almost eight million. There was confusion and corruption, and a complete lack of leadership.

Nicholas had come under the influence of Alexandra. The Empress in turn was dominated by Rasputin. He was the most powerful man in Russia. There were rumors that the Empress was his
mistress, that the "holy man" was a German agent. Nicholas lived
at army headquarters, near his cousin, Grand Duke Nicholas
Nikolayevich. The Empress stayed in Petrograd. In her letters to
Nicholas—letters full of passion and fear—she called Rasputin
"our friend." Everybody in Petrograd was scandalized. The
Council of State was in despair, the ministers demanded Rasputin's removal and threatened to resign. The Empress had the
ministers dismissed. Rasputin practically ruled Russia; during the
next eighteen months, the country had four different prime
ministers, all appointed by him. The Empress wrote strange letters to her husband. Once she admonished him to comb his hair
with Rasputin's comb before seeing his advisors. Nicholas's advisors and relations asked him to grant Russia a constitutional

government but Alexandra refused. "Show everyone that you are master . . . !" Demoralization continued in Petrograd; prices were rising, and it was said there were not enough hospitals for the wounded.

At last, many people could stand it no longer. Some demanded that the Empress be removed from the capital. In the Duma, Vladimir Purishkevich denounced the "dark forces" that destroyed the monarchy, and asked the ministers to tell Nicholas that this could not go on. "Revolution threatens and an obscure muzhik [peasant] shall govern Russia no longer."

The following day, a Russian aristocrat, Prince Felix Yusupov, went to see Purishkevich. They agreed that the Czar would not listen to criticism of Rasputin and would never dismiss the starets. Rasputin would have to be killed before all was lost. Other members of the conspiracy were Grand Duke Dmitri, a cousin of the Czar, an army officer named Sukhotin, and a physician, Dr. Lazovert.

Rasputin's death was as improbable as his life had been. Yusupov invited him to his beautiful palais overlooking the Moika, one of Giacomo Quarenghi's masterpieces. In his old-Russian-style cellar boudoir, Yusupov offered Rasputin cream- and chocolate-filled pastry that had been treated with cyanide, and poisoned wines—Marsala, Madeira, sherry, port. The sweet wines would conceal the taste of the cyanide. Yusupov and Rasputin were alone in the boudoir, while the other members of the conspiracy remained upstairs. A gramophone was playing "Yankee Doodle." After half an hour Yusupov went upstairs, white faced. He told them that Rasputin had eaten all the pastry, had drunk two glasses of sweet wine—and was singing happily. According to the diary notes made the following day by Purishkevich, it was now decided that Rasputin must be shot. Yusupov went for his Browning, joined the holy man, who was staring at an icon, and shot him in the back. Rasputin collapsed on the polar bear skin in front of the sofa.

Yusupov went upstairs again to call his friends. Suddenly he heard a roaring shout and turned around. Rasputin got up and turned against him. The Prince started trembling; he was now convinced of the starets's supernatural powers. Rasputin was foaming at the mouth. The conspirators stared dumbfounded as

he opened the door and walked out into the snow-covered courtyard.

"Felix!" he shouted. "I'm going to tell everything to the Empress." It was 4:00 A.M., December 17 O.S., 1916.

Now Purishkevich ran down after Rasputin with his pistol and
fired four shots. The last hit him in the head. Near the gate,
Rasputin collapsed. Purishkevich wrote, "I stepped close and
kicked him in the sleeve as hard as I could." Rasputin was dead,
but the conspirators took no chances. They bound him with
heavy chains and dropped the body from Petrovsky Bridge
through a hole in the ice covering the Little Neva. The body was
found three days later and buried in the imperial park at Tsarskoye Selo. The Empress placed a letter on the breast of the holy
man, asking "my dear martyr . . . to give me thy blessing."

Today the Yusupov Palace is the Cultural House of the
Leningrad Teachers. A large bust of Lenin stands near the stairway. The former boudoir is a storeroom.

The first riots began in Petrograd on February 23 O.S. (March
8 N.S.), 1917, when women couldn't get bread at the bakeries.
The riots soon turned into rebellion, and rebellion became revolution. People marched through the streets, carrying banners
demanding, "Give Us Bread." The Czar stayed at faraway army
headquarters and ordered the Petrograd garrison to restore order.
Nicholas had lost touch with his people. The peasants no longer
called the Czar their "Little Father." Instead, they said, "We shall
win after the generals hang from the gallows." It was said that
shells had been rationed and that wounded soldiers were dying
because they could not be taken to the overcrowded hospitals.

The Petrograd garrison did not restore order; the soldiers
began fraternizing with the rioters. Nicholas dissolved the Duma
by telegram. For the first time, the Duma refused to obey. Instead, a Provisional Government was formed in Petrograd. Alexander Kerensky, a member of the Social Revolutionary Party and
vice-chairman of the Soviet (council) of Workers' Deputies, became minister of justice. Nicholas didn't seem to understand
what was happening. "The fat-bellied Rodzianko wrote me a lot
of nonsense," he said. "I won't even bother to answer." Mikhail
Rodzianko was the President of the Duma, and he had not writ-

ten nonsense. The Czar abdicated several days later, on March 2 (March 15 N.S.), in favor of his son, Alexis. But then he changed his mind: ". . . Not wishing to separate from our beloved son, we leave our heritage to our brother."

The brother and designated czar, Grand Duke Mikhail, went from Gachina to Petrograd and paid a visit to Kerensky, who told him frankly that he could not guarantee his personal safety. That was sufficient for Mikhail, who sat down and signed a statement announcing *his* abdication. The Romanovs were finished—three hundred and four years after Michael Feodorovich, the reluctant founder of the dynasty, a boy of sixteen, had ascended the throne in 1613. Occasionally they had shown good will and a certain ability; more often their record was blemished by madness and murder.

For a while, the imperial family was permitted to remain under house arrest in Tsarskoye Selo. Their condition worsened after Lenin and Trotsky returned to Russia. In July 1917, after widespread Bolshevik riots, Kerensky had the family moved to Tobolsk in Siberia. There they still had a few servants and were permitted to write letters which reveal that in misery and exile Nicholas II and Alexandra showed dignity, nobility, and strength, qualities they had not conspicuously demonstrated before. In March 1918 Alexandra wrote to her friend, Anna Virubova, "How I love my country with all its faults! . . . Believe in the people, dear. The nation is strong and young. Just now darkness and anarchy reign. But the King of Glory will come and save, giving wisdom to the people who are now deceived." But after they were insulted by their guards, young revolutionaries, Alexandra admitted, "The strange thing about the Russian character is that it can so suddenly change to cruelty, evil and unreason. . . ."

In May 1918 the family was moved again, this time to Ipatiev House in Ekaterinburg (now Sverdlovsk) in the Urals. On July 16 O.S., 1918, after midnight, Nicholas and Alexandra, their son and four daughters, their doctor, and three servants were taken by guards to a small room in the basement. A squad of the Cheka —the political police later known as the GPU—appeared with revolvers. The prisoners were shot. Whether Lenin had personally ordered the executions has not been proved though some historians claim it. The truth will never be known.

Lenin had arrived in the late evening of April 3 (April 16, N.S.), 1917, at Petrograd's pink and gray Finland Station with a group of thirty-two men, women, and children. His wife, Nadezhda Krupskaya, was with him. They had left Switzerland and crossed Germany and Finland in a sealed coach (the train's locomotive is now enshrined at the Finland Station in a glass pavilion), with the connivance of the Imperial German High Command. The Germans hoped by disorganizing Russia to win the war quickly. Lenin got out and was handed a bunch of red roses while a band played the "Marseillaise." He wore a topcoat and bowler and seeemed nervous but soon calmed down as he mounted an armored car in front of the station, illuminated by searchlights. He made a short, harsh speech which became history. Lenin called upon the workers and soldiers of the Revolution to reject the Provisional Government and to seize all power. He was taken to the villa that had belonged to the prima ballerina Kschessinska (the Czar's former mistress) and stepped out on the balcony. "Dear comrades, soldiers, sailors, workmen! The Russian Revolution made by you has begun. It has opened a new epoch. Hail to the world Socialist Revolution!"

Lenin, the complete realist, did not express vague hopes but stated radical demands. The split between his Bolsheviks and the moderate Mensheviks was irrevocable. Lenin outlined his exact program though the power was still with Kerensky's Provisional Government. Time and the course of events were on Lenin's side. Living conditions got worse. Another strike broke out at the Putilov Works; again a large crowd marched down Nevsky Prospekt. Near Gostiny Dvor the procession was stopped by soldiers shooting and killing many people. The crowd went on to the Taurida Palace (Catherine's gift to Potemkin), the seat of the Provisional Government. Kerensky failed to issue decisive orders. Lenin left the city and went into hiding close to the Finnish border. He was waiting for his time to come.

It is paradoxical that it was the people of Petrograd—unemotional, slow-spoken, sober, reserved—who started Russia's revolutions, not the politically minded citizens of Moscow nor the fast-moving, fast-talking people in the south.

"The Leningraders," one of them told me, "are very patient up to a certain point. We are not impulsive; it's the climate, I suppose. But we like to think things through. And when we cannot stand it any longer, we lose our patience and erupt. It has happened in this city—not once, not twice, but many times. And when we Leningraders start something, we like to finish it off, right to the glory or to the bitter end."

Alexander Nikolayevich Yemelyanov, who spent his childhood in the place where Lenin hid, several years ago spoke to a German journalist, Ulrich Schiller.

My father arrived at three in the morning, on the last train from Petrograd, with the revolutionaries. I was in the hayloft and looked down. Lenin shook hands with my mother and said she must not say a word to anyone. My mother, a proud woman, was irritated. "I know the rules of the conspiracy," she said. Later she cut the hair of Lenin and Gregory Zinovyev. That was easy in Lenin's case but Zinovyev's hair was thick and strong.

Lenin was taken to a haystack well hidden in a birch wood. It is a small memorial site today, and the haystack is always renewed. Every morning young Alexander rowed for half an hour and walked another ten minutes to bring Lenin food and writing paper.

When I got there, Lenin would often be writing. He was working on *State and Revolution*. He complained about the humidity. All night the fog rose from the water. He said it was bad for his health. We had to get him away. . . . Once I heard Lenin talk to my father. Lenin asked, "Nikolai Alexandrovich, do you think we should seize the power?" "Absolutely, Vladimir Ilyich." "And why? Is the mood of the people propitious?" My father said, "Kerensky's Provisional Government has not solved the workers' problems. The peasants have no land. We have no peace." Then Vladimir Ilyich said, "If Milyukov, Guchkov [members of the Provisional Government], and so on would solve these problems, we would hand them over our membership books. . . . But they haven't solved them. That means we have to take over." My father was silent. But with Lenin one could hide nothing. He asked my father why he didn't answer. Father said, "You may lose touch with the comrades with whom you made the Revolution." Lenin said, "You are right. Nikolai Alexandrovich. . . . Power corrupts people. If someone in the Party should ever suffer from the cult of personality, he will be sent into the factories to be cured."

After the Revolution Alexander Nikolayevich Yemelyanov became a locksmith. During the Second World War he was interned. "I had criticized Stalin for violating Lenin's principles of party life. I spent nearly twenty years in Vokuta and other labor camps."

Early in 1917 the Petrograd Soviet moved to the Smolny Institute; in October the Revolutionary War Committee set up headquarters there. The Bolshevik group of the Soviet was in room No. 18. In September 1918 the Bolsheviks gained control of the Petrograd Soviet. Lenin planned his coup for October 25 (November 7 N.S.)—the "October Revolution"—on the eve of the Second All-Russian Congress of Soviets. On October 24 he left his hideout and made his way to the Smolny.

It was an unlikely place to start a world revolution, one of the oldest structures in town. At the order of Empress Elizabeth, Rastrelli had built the beautiful baroque Smolny Cathedral with its five cupolas, interiors in white and gold, and gray marble floor. (It was bombed in the last war and is not yet restored.) Behind the cathedral was a convent where the Empress hoped to spend her old age. "Smola" means "tar"; her father, Peter the Great, had kept his tar stores for shipbuilding there. Later, Quarenghi built the severe-classicist boarding school for girls established by Catherine II. E. M. Almedingen, who studied at the Smolny, remembers:

Pupils stayed seven years. Even the holidays were spent there, the park behind the house offering enough exercise. The curriculum, designed after the pattern of French convent schools, could not be said to shine educationally. The idea was to turn out socially accomplished young ladies, not scholars. A pupil, having left the establishment, might not be certain whether Naples was in Italy or Spain, and believed the French to be wicked because they ate frogs. But she spoke perfectly, could dance and play the harp and clavichord, and [knew] how to behave in the presence of royalty. . . .

Until Lenin decided the move to Moscow, the Soviet Government resided at the former institute for well-bred young ladies.

There was confusion when Lenin arrived at the Smolny. Committee meetings were held in former classrooms, soldiers stood around aimlessly or queued up for cabbage soup and a piece of bread. "On the steps of the Smolny, in the chill dark, we first saw the Red Guard—a huddled group of boys in workmen's clothes, carrying guns with bayonets, talking nervously together," John Reed wrote in *Ten Days That Shook the World*. Reports said that the garrison of the Peter and Paul Fortress had gone over to the Military Revolution Committee, and it was soon joined by soldiers all over Petrograd. The moment for action had come. Lenin, just arrived, made the decision.

Lenin's apartment, No. 67, is now a shrine. In the front room there is an exhibition of posters, maps, pictures, photostats of Lenin's letters, some handwritten orders, and a photograph showing two sentries in front of the room, with bayonets fixed on their rifles. A colored map on the wall traces Lenin's journey from the hiding place near the Finnish border all the way to Petrograd and the Smolny. His workroom overlooks the inner courtyard, probably for security reasons. It is small and modest, with two armchairs and a sofa covered with calico, and a table. There is a side table with Lenin's pens and other little things, and the field telephone from which he issued his orders. The wires, fixed primitively along the wall, have been left as they were. The member of the Leningrad Party organization who took me there (guided tours are no longer permitted) said that nothing had been changed. Behind a wooden partition in the rear one sees two simple beds, two chairs, a white-tiled stove. Krupskaya's small hand mirrror, with the inscription "Niagara Falls, Canada," was given to her by a soldier. All very simple, but Lenin liked it there. "The transition from illegality and being hounded is too sudden, one gets dizzy," he said to Trotsky.

By noon on October 25, the soldiers of the Petrograd garrison had occupied two bridges across the Neva. Lenin ordered Palace Square cordoned off. Inside the Winter Palace, Kerensky and his ministers were deliberating in the Malachite Hall, which only a few months earlier had been reserved for members of the Czar's family. The Provisional Government was guarded by several cadet officers from Peterhof and Oranienbaum, by a women's battalion, and by an artillery detachment with six guns. The cadets were shooting at people trying to cross the square, but after a while they said they would leave unless they were reinforced. Confusion was mounting. The Bolsheviks occupied the General Staff Building across from the Winter Palace. Soldiers on trucks distributed leaflets all over town. People coming out of theaters and cinemas were heard arguing amicably with the soldiers. At the Maryinsky Theater, Karsavina had danced at the ballet. Chaliapin had sung in Verdi's *Don Carlo*.

At the Winter Palace, some invaders got in through the windows and some defenders got out through the side entrances. What exactly happened at this point, is still a matter of argument. The official version is that Lenin and Trotsky ordered Peter and Paul Fortress to open fire at the Winter Palace. But the guns were rusty, so the cruiser *Aurora* received orders to shell the Winter Palace. On October 27, *Pravda* published a letter written by Belyshev, chairman of the committee aboard the *Aurora*, stating that they had not fired real ammunition from the cruiser's heavy guns; that might have destroyed the Winter Palace and the Hermitage. But postage stamps and picture books show the *Aurora* with her guns blasting away, and there are patriotic stories and poems. It doesn't matter. The *Aurora*, permanently anchored in the Neva, is now a much-visited shrine, getting a new coat of paint once in a while.

At ten minutes past two on the morning of October 26 the Bolshevik commander entered the white Malachite Hall, where the cabinet was still in session, and said, "I announce to you, members of the Provisional Government, that you are under arrest." They were taken to the fortress. It was one of the least violent and most far-reaching revolutions in history. Some soldiers began pocketing small "souvenirs" from the palace, but they were told to file out and empty their pockets. Lenin had said that everything now belonged to the people. Nothing must be touched. He saved the city from destruction.

It is becoming difficult to find people who remember the October Revolution and are willing to talk. One old man I met gave a somewhat different description. He'd been in Palace Square that night with many others. They were told to wait for the signal that would come from the *Aurora*. "'We needed the signal; we had no watches." It came shortly after 9:00 P.M.—one blank shot from a cannon of the cruiser, followed by two blank shots from the fortress. The attackers in Palace Square had four artillery guns. Some machine-gun and rifle fire came from the Winter Palace. The men in the square asked the artillery commander to start shelling the palace but he wouldn't do it. He said Lenin had given strict orders not to damage the palace of the Czars.

"By three o'clock it was all over, and my comrades and I had become the new palace guards."

A Leningrad historian whom I met compared Lenin's October Revolution to the earlier "revolution" set in motion by Peter the Great. (He admitted that "evolution" might be more exact.) "In 1917 Russia was economically backward, comparable to the underdeveloped regions of Spain, Portugal, southern Italy. Lenin knew that something drastic had to be done to lead the tired, apathetic people toward progress. In 1717 Russia was culturally backward, centuries behind Western Europe. Peter the Great knew that only a supreme, even brutal effort would lead the country out of its isolation. The social forces were different but the aims were similar."

There has been speculation as to what might have happened if the transfer of the government from the Smolny Institute to the Kremlin had really been temporary, as Lenin intended. "History might have convinced him after the October Revolution that our city must remain the permanent capital of the Soviet Union. Today, the very idea frightens our citizens. As Russia's capital, Leningrad might have lost its identity. Look at Moscow—big, faceless, ugly. We are better off being 'the second city' politically and economically, and still the first culturally and artistically. Though I admit that in literature the action is in Moscow. The

Muscovites say that Leningrad is not a city but a museum, that we have become 'provincial.' They've forgotten that the forces of past and recent history were here, or that Leningrad's scientists continue the heritage of the Academy of Sciences which Peter set up in 1724, after consulting with Christian von Wolff and Gottfried von Leibniz."

Traditionally, the sailors of the Russian Navy were among their country's most violent revolutionaries. One of the Bestuzhev-Ryumin brothers, an officer from the naval fortress of Kronstadt, was among the leaders of the Decembrist rebellion in 1825. A Kronstadt sailor, Sukhanov, in charge of the Narodnaya Volya's military section, was shot in 1882 by order of Czar Alexander III. Sailors played an important part during the mutiny in Odessa, climaxed by the affair of the battleship *Potemkin* in 1905, and during the following year. The Soviet of Kronstadt opposed Kerensky's Provisional Government from its beginning and, with the help of the Bolshevik sailors of the Baltic fleet, proclaimed itself the independent "republic of Kronstadt."

Kronstadt on Kotlin Island was the creation of Peter the Great: the King's Fortress. Nicholas I continued Peter's design and modernized the fortifications. At the time of the October Revolution, Kronstadt was the "impregnable" base in the Baltic. The 1914 edition of Baedeker's *Russia* recommmends a steamer excursion from St. Petersburg: "four times daily, in one and a half hours, fare 65 kopeks. . . . Permission to visit the harbor, the docks and a man-of-war may be obtained on weekdays from the Chief of Staff."

Not any more. Today Kronstadt is off limits to all foreigners, including diplomats. One cannot go to look at Liberty Park with Baron Klodt's statue of Peter the Great, the beautiful Italian Palace built for Prince Menshikov, St. Andrew's Cathedral, designed by Zakharov for Catherine II. Kronstadt remained impregnable during World War II when Hitler ordered the Baltic fleet destroyed and Kronstadt razed. In September 1941 German planes dropped leaflets: "Leningrad to the ground! Kronstadt to the sea!" Hitler issued Order No. 35: "In co-operation with the Finns, mine barriers and artillery fire must be employed to blockade Kronstadt and prevent the Russian fleet from entering the Baltic

Sea." On September 23 the Germans used 180 planes to attack the fortress and the ships. Kronstadt had only five fighter planes to defend itself. The Germans knocked out the water system, cut the electricity, hit the hospital, and badly damaged the historic center of the town. But the big naval guns were still firing and Russia's Baltic fleet remained in action. Kronstadt was not razed to the sea.

Today no one in Leningrad wants to talk about Kronstadt, the first town to declare itself for the Bolsheviks in 1917. During the October Revolution the sailors of Kronstadt were right behind Lenin. In the summer of 1919 Kronstadt was temporarily occupied by the White Russians, but the Bolshevik sailors recaptured the naval fortress. In the autumn they joined the battle following the second attack of the White Russians under General N. N. Yudenich. Still, Kronstadt remains unmentioned today because in March 1921 "the pride and glory of the Russian Revolution" (as Lenin called them) rose in revolt against the Bolshevik Government.

Under the slogan "Free Soviet for Kronstadt!" the sailors established a revolutionary commune. They said that "the Bolsheviks in the Kremlin have betrayed the revolution." They captured the fortress, most of the town, and two battleships. The sailors' regime lasted sixteen days. The men in the Kremlin were badly shaken. Lenin hesitated to take action against the most faithful of the faithful, but after much soul-searching he decided to send a small army across the frozen Gulf of Finland. The soldiers attacked the fortress during the night of March 16 N.S. There were heavy losses on both sides until the sailors were subdued. Lenin bitterly called Kronstadt "the flash that lit up the reality better than anything else."

There have been other "Kronstadts" since, the most recent ones in Budapest, in November 1956, and in Prague, in August 1969.

THE SIEGE: THE DEAD
AND THE LIVING

On August 30, 1941, over nine weeks after Hitler's invasion of the Soviet Union, German tanks occupied the little railroad station of Mga on the Leningrad-Moscow line. The fall of Mga cut off Leningrad from the mainland and started the siege that lasted 880 days, until 8:00 P.M., January 27, 1944. That day there was no dancing in the streets: the Germans were still very close, and the war was going on. But Leningrad was saved.

Today, in Leningrad, the survivors rarely talk about the siege. After thirty years, the memories are still too painful, though they do come up in unexpected moments. A taxi driver pointed to St. Isaac's Square in front of the Astoria Hotel and said to me, as if reminding himself, that he'd helped to plant cabbage and potatoes in this square during the siege. A woman said they'd sacrificed some fine furniture, cut up and used as firewood for their small stove, so they would have a few hours of heat. "But," she said with quiet pride, "not a single tree was cut down in the parks of Leningrad. The trees must be kept. They were a symbol."

I said that few trees were left at the end of the war in Berlin's once beautiful Tiergarten.

"I know. The trees were considered no symbols in Berlin, where it is never as cold in wintertime as in Leningrad. The Germans had different symbols, maybe the wrong symbols." She looked into space. "The bookstores were open here after most other shops had closed. The bookstores were always crowded.

The Neva, with Peter and Paul Fortress in the distance

The Winter Palace: the façade along the Neva

Prince Felix Yusupov, who organized Rasputin's assassination

The Empress Alexandra in the uniform of The Empress Alexandra
Feodorovna's Regiment of Lancers

The equestrian statue of Czar Nicholas in St. Isaac's Square

Peter III and Catherine II (the Great) with their son Paul, in 1756. Painted by R. M. Lisiewska

Some theaters were playing a long time though they couldn't heat them. It was always hard to get tickets."

A man called D., a writer friend in Leningrad, calls the siege "a terrible trauma and invaluable experience." Hardship, hunger, and sickness stripped people completely, "revealing the innermost values and innermost vices." D. was born in 1908, a fact he considers important. Mature people had a better chance of survival than younger ones when the daily bread ration was gradually cut from 250 to 125 grams, about the equivalent of two sandwich slices. The "bread" consisted of fifty per cent defective rye, fifteen per cent cellulose, ten per cent cotton seed, ten per cent salt, and fifteen per cent soya flour, sawdust, and things no one wanted to know about. The winter of 1941–42 was the coldest in the memory of the old people. On some days the temperature was down to thirty and forty degrees below zero Celsius. The small supplies of coal were requisitioned for hospitals. To get some water, people had to cut a hole in the thick ice of the Neva and carry home a couple of buckets—hard work for healthy, well-fed people, and often impossible for sick, starved ones. Yet in the end many died not of cold and hunger but because they lacked faith.

"They perished spiritually rather than biologically," D. says. "A neighbor of mine, same age, had the same small rations, the same big hardships. He wasn't sick, but he condemned himself when he lost faith. He didn't work and began listening to rumors. He'd heard the Germans were already at the Kirov tractor plant, six kilometers away. They might be in our street next week, maybe tomorrow—and you know what that would mean. A Polish refugee had told him what the Germans had done to the people of Warsaw. In Leningrad it would be much worse. He wouldn't listen to reason. He gave up spiritually and emotionally and fell into apathy. He just faded away."

D. kept working as a journalist. Only *Leningradskaya Pravda* was still printed daily, one single sheet. The other papers had closed down after the local supply of newsprint was exhausted. But there was still the radio station; fortunately the seven-story Radio House was not hit. The staff lived in a large fourth-floor room filled with tables, cots, chairs, books. They had two tiny stoves. When people were too weak to get up to the studio, they would broadcast from the large room. They knew they must keep the radio going. People with no food, no water, no heat, no hope would stay in bed listening to the radio. (It was severely forbidden to listen to foreign broadcasts.) Some people read to keep themselves from thinking. D. found out that many soldiers read *War and Peace,* while the sailors seemed to prefer *Crime and Punishment.*

"Radio House became the center of Leningrad's literary life, or what was left of it. No patriotic pep talk; our people wouldn't listen to rhetoric. News and reports and poetry readings. As long as the streetcars were running, I would take the No. 9 up to the front, or visit the factories turning out weapons and shells. I talked to workers and soldiers. My impressions were read over the radio. No strategy comment because we knew nothing about strategy. Strictly matter-of-fact reports.

"I had no doubt personally that everything would come out all right. That may sound strange to you; it does to me too, nowadays. There was no reason for optimism, but everybody seemed to agree with me. We never talked about the Germans though we knew that they were watching Radio House through their field glasses. People may have been afraid of the Germans but they didn't talk about it."

D. had a moment of panic when he read what the German dive bombers had done to Rotterdam and to Amsterdam, the dream city of Peter the Great when he designed St. Petersburg. D. tried to tell himself that Leningrad was no Rotterdam. Owing to Leningrad's antiaircraft defense system, the Luftwaffe didn't manage to annihilate whole city blocks, as in Rotterdam, but destroyed only isolated targets. Shellfire did more damage than the bombs. Most houses in Leningrad were hit by a shell during the siege. Artillery movements and bombing attacks were announced on the radio. Some people sought shelter, but many remained in their apartments. The children got used to these announcements. Once D. came home and was told by his three-year-old daughter, "Daddy, we are under shellfire," and she slipped under the blanket.

"We would draw sketches together. Once I drew the sky with the stars, and asked her what they were. 'Planes,' she said. The children didn't watch the stars. They were looking for the planes."

Everybody said that Leningrad was "too important to be lost." It must not be desecrated; it must remain Russian.

"We didn't think of the palaces, the churches, the museums. But this city is a spiritual treasure, our national heritage. We are trustees of something transcending the history, architecture, beauty. We couldn't let down Peter, who had founded the city, and Lenin, who had preserved it. It was neither local nor Soviet patriotism that made us almost stupidly stubborn. It was something I cannot even describe, something of personal, almost intimate significance to everybody, a state of mind for which I have no rational explanation. It wasn't just hope. I believe many of us felt that History was on our side. We were talking a lot about Napoleon but rarely about Hitler. Why hadn't Napoleon ever tried to seize St. Petersburg?"

There were moments of terror and hell—and of greatness and dignity. As hardship and danger increased, people became physically weaker and spiritually stronger. At the Institute of Agriculture, the scientists were growing potatoes—samples had been sent up from various parts of the country—trying to find out whether some varieties could be grown in northern latitudes. No one working there ever thought of taking any potatoes home. The scientists and assistants were as hungry as everyone else. They knew the potatoes might get spoiled during the experiments. But there was no question of eating one. D. remembers a friend, a professor of botany in charge of the hothouses of tropical plants at the Botanical Gardens. A small reserve of coal had been allotted to the hothouses. The professor's home was unheated, as cold as anybody's. It never even occurred to him to take home a few pieces of coal to heat one room for one hour. (One night the professor was killed by a shell as he walked home.)

A Leningrad woman who moved to Moscow after the war told me her heart is still in Leningrad. "During the siege, we had to move three times. Our old house was shelled; then we stayed with friends, whose apartment burned down; and the third place was bombed out. Years later, my sister found letters from our parents in the ruins of the bombed house. Such things happened to many people in Leningrad. Most people know the siege only from books and some pictures. But Leningraders who have been through it feel like members of a large but exclusive club. We share so many things; we know so much. Even now elderly peo-

ple in Leningrad say 'take' and 'give' instead of 'buy' and 'sell.'
During the blockade, money had no value. We lived only on government rations. When we talk about these things among ourselves, there comes a moment when no one says anything any
more. There is no need for words."

Failing to break the physical resistance of the defenders, the
Germans tried to destroy the people's morale with low-altitude
bombing, hitting the hospitals filled with soldiers wounded at the
front. Other targets were the ammunition factories, where the
workers went on with stoicism bordering upon heroism. Then the
Germans smuggled in agents who went around telling people it
was hopeless, why not give up? Many agents were caught, but
many were not.

"The worst thing was to be alone," D. remembers. "You sat in
your dark, cold room and heard the planes coming in, and you
felt angry and helpless. Many people would go out into the
street, where they were not alone. The authorities were right
when they gave us a little vodka as part of the ration. Oddly, one
rarely saw someone drunk that first winter. Maybe it was the
cold."

Even during the worst days of the siege, when the Germans
were very close and doing terrible things, D. did not hate them.
He was often bothered by the thought; he sensed it would be his
patriotic duty to hate, but he could not. Neither was he able to
analyze his lack of hatred. Most of the people he knew shared his
attitude. They might be angry for a while, after something terrible had happened, but there was no basic feeling against the German nation. Often there was pity for the German soldiers, who
had walked off to war almost intoxicated. It was widely believed
in Leningrad that sooner or later the German soldiers would perish, though at the moment the situation certainly seemed to
favor them.

"I suppose it was part of our unrealistic behavior," D. says.
"They were a streetcar ride away; they had all the food they
needed; and yet we were convinced, most of us anyway, that the
Germans would be finished *somehow*. It made no sense to me
then, and it doesn't now."

Shortly after the end of the war, D. was in Berlin as a journalist. He saw at once that the destruction in Berlin was much worse

than in Leningrad, but this gave him no satisfaction at all. He watched in astonishment how the population, mostly women, began clearing away the mountains of rubble. They didn't talk much and probably didn't like it, but there was a strong sense of discipline. Orders had beeen issued by somebody, and they were doing it. The sense of discipline, of bowing to authority, was apparent wherever he went. The Germans didn't seem to do these things so much for themselves, convinced they had to be done, but rather because they had been given orders, and orders are orders.

Once D. noticed that a big crowd formed near the ruins of what had been Knobelsdorff's magnificent State Opera House on Unter den Linden. D. joined the people and was told that something was going on: *"Da ist was los."* People in the rear, stretching their necks, reported that *hoher Besuch,* some high-ranking visitor, was inspecting the ruins.

"Everybody seemed to stiffen, as though standing at attention, even the people in the rear. They *enjoyed* standing at attention in front of an unseen authority. It was very strange. There was speculation in the rear, where they couldn't see, on who the *hoher Besuch* might be. Someone said, 'Looks like an American general,' and some people really pressed their palms to the seams of their pants as though the general was going to inspect them. Eventually the man in uniform turned out to be a French captain, which I considered a letdown but the Germans didn't. They stood stiffly, craning their necks until the visitor had gone. The absurd experience explained a good many things to me. We Russians have also our idiosyncrasies—I suppose every nation has—but we didn't rebuild Leningrad after the war because we had orders. Of course we had orders but that was beside the point. We rebuilt the city because we loved it. It was our national heritage, a national symbol."

After the German invasion of the Soviet Union, the military leaders in Leningrad had no doubt that their city would soon be attacked, but they were not prepared for the all-out attack. The Leningrad Command covered an immense area stretching from the Baltic Sea to the Arctic shore of the Kola Peninsula. The Baltic Fleet had for some time been on number-2 alert, almost but not *quite* ready for action. Leningrad's top man, Party Secretary

Andrei A. Zhdanov, was on vacation in Sochi, the Black Sea resort. His deputy, Alexei A. Kuznetsov, called an emergency meeting of the local Party leaders and generals at the Smolny Institute after he'd received a telephone call from Moscow. German planes were already bombing Kiev, Minsk, Murmansk, and other cities.

Kuznetsov issued his first orders around five o'clock in the morning. At the Leningrad General Staff Building—the beautiful palace which Carlo Rossi had built across from the Winter Palace —the mobilization orders were put into effect. At noon, the people of Leningrad listened to Vyacheslav M. Molotov's voice on the radio: "We have been attacked. . . . The enemy will be crushed. Victory will be ours."

Lines formed at once in front of the State Savings Banks and in the food stores. The Russians have a long history of hoarding. The people of the city were like burned children. Even vodka was being hoarded. But there was no panic. The evening performance of Johann Strauss's *The Gypsy Baron* at the Maly Theater was sold out.

The attack might come any moment. The city was an important industrial center, with almost 800,000 workers in Leningrad's five hundred factories. Eighty-two per cent of Russia's turbine generators were made there. The Kirov (formerly Putilov) Works was the Soviet Union's largest machinery plant. The entire Soviet Fleet was supplied by the Baltic shipyards. Stalin was more concerned about Leningrad's industrial potential than about the "second" city he had always hated. The secret struggle between Leningrad and Stalin began soon after Lenin's death in 1924. Three years later, Grigori Zinovyev, a close associate of Lenin and Leningrad's Party leader, was purged. He was succeeded by Sergei Kirov, said to be a Stalin man, able and ambitious. He became popular, *too* popular, during the Party Congress in January 1934, when he got more votes than Stalin in the elections to the Central Committee.

On December 1 Kirov was shot by Leonid V. Nikolayev at his office in the Smolny Institute. Kirov's death was the beginning of Stalin's secret police terror and mass murder. Many years later it became known that Kirov's assassination had been "arranged" by the secret police with the connivance of Stalin. Just in case some "arrangers" might talk, Stalin purged several police officers involved in the Kirov affair. He next broke up the powerful Leningrad Party organization and firmly established the hegemony of Moscow. The methods were always the same. First, the intellectuals, writers, artists, and young sympathizers of Kirov were arrested and disappeared. Then Party members and industrial managers were purged. A new man from Nizhni Novgorod (now Gorky) would streamline the Leningrad Party organization. Andrei A. Zhdanov was ruthless and ambitious. He became one of the most powerful men around Stalin, whose daugher Svetlana married Zhdanov's son Yuri.

On July 1, 1941, ten days after the German invasion, Zhdanov set up the Leningrad Defense Committee. Factories were speedily converted to war production, making tanks, armored cars, shells, explosives. A ring of fortifications was built around the large city. Every able-bodied Leningrader was drafted for eight hours of work, digging trenches, helping to build shelters. Even factory workers had to pitch in after their ten-hour shift. The personnel of the Hermitage Museum was put into emergency service. The theaters, which usually closed late in June, were told to remain open; many gave two performances a day.

A number of women and children were evacuated, but more wanted to stay to help defend Leningrad. Even old people refused to leave their beloved city. Painted camouflage nets sewn by the personnel of the theaters were strung all over the Smolny Institute to make it look like the Summer Garden. The newspapers reported that Galina Ulanova, the beloved prima ballerina, was among the seamstresses.

Early in August, Field Marshal Wilhelm Ritter von Leeb started the German attack against Leningrad. Colonel General Franz Halder, Chief of Staff, wrote in his diary, "Army Group North obviously should not meet with irresistible difficulties." Halder, a first-rate tactician, knew of Hitler's Leningrad fixation. The Führer had a mystical belief about "Petersburg." Ever since the Teutonic Knights and the Hanseatic League had dominated the region, the Germans have considered the Baltic their *mare nostrum*. (Even today some German historians refer to Catherine II as "the German Czarina.") Hitler considered Leningrad "the cradle of Communism" and "the soul of Bolshevism." If he could physically destroy the cradle, he might spiritually annihilate Bolshevism. It was a naïve and dangerous notion.

The Germans exerted considerable psychological pressure on Leningrad. They designated military police units to maintain order "after the city's capture" and prepared special license plates for army vehicles (now displayed at the Red Army's Central Museum). They distributed guidebooks and city maps among their soldiers; even the route of Hitler's triumphal procession was laid out exactly. And all the time, German planes dropped leaflets on Leningrad warning the population that their city would be "leveled to the ground." On August 20 Zhdanov told a Party meeting at the Smolny, "The enemy is at the gates, it is a question of life or death."

The next day, Hitler issued a directive: "Not until we have tightly encircled Leningrad, linking up with the Finns, and destroyed the Russian Fifth [Leningrad] Army, shall we . . . destroy the Center Army Group" (which defended Moscow). Unlike Napoleon, the Führer, a military genius of a very special sort, considered the northern capital his greatest prize.

The Leningrad Command was getting ready for the worst. Internal security was tightened and guards were placed at all sensitive spots where the Germans might drop parachute units. Factories and naval yards were protected by pillboxes, sandbags, antiaircraft batteries. Air-raid trenches were dug in the public parks. Yet Stalin was said to be dissatisfied with the defenders, calling Zhdanov and Marshal Kliment Voroshilov "specialists in retreat," probably in order to remind them that they were living on borrowed time. In Tallinn, the Baltic Fleet suffered a worse disaster than the British at Dunkirk. Of twenty-nine transports evacuating Tallinn all but four were lost.

In Leningrad, evacuation continued according to plan. The important treasures of the Hermitage and the Russian Museum were removed to Gorky, Perm, and Sverdlovsk. The Leningrad Public Library shipped 400,000 important items out of 9,000,000. The Pushkin archives and the libraries of Diderot and Voltaire were evacuated. Important books were placed in the library's deep cellars, in the catacombs of the Alexander Nevsky Monastery, and in the subterranean labyrinths of Peter and Paul Fortress. From the palaces in Pushkin, Pavlovsk, and Petrodvorets (Peterhof) many treasures were removed just before the Germans arrived.

The members of the Leningrad Philharmonic and the Pushkin

Theater—"living art treasures"—were sent to Novosibirsk, the Maryinsky to Perm, the Maly Opera to Orenburg, the Conservatory to Tashkent, and almost one hundred scientific institutes to various places in the east. Late in July, even the animals of the Zoological Gardens had been evacuated. Only the people of Leningrad remained—too many of them.

Zhdanov made the mistake of not reporting to Moscow the capture of Mga, but Stalin was not fooled about the serious situation of Leningrad and sent a delegation to the besieged city. It included Vyacheslav Molotov; Georgi Malenkov, who competed with Zhdanov for the number-two position at the Kremlin; and Alexei Kosygin, then a relatively unknown expert. At a meeting at the Smolny Institute, Zhdanov wanted to defend Leningrad "under all circumstances and at all costs." (Soviet historians assume that he didn't really know how Stalin felt about the city.) Both Molotov and Malenkov wanted to abandon the doomed city. They returned to Moscow, where it was said that Zhdanov was a traitor trying to conceal the inevitability of defeat. Only President Mikhail I. Kalinin, a native of Leningrad, wrote in *Izvestiya* he was confident that Leningrad would defeat the Germans.

Stalin sent his top tactician, General Georgi Zhukov, to Leningrad "to try the impossible." They didn't know that the Germans had already occupied the Neva fortress of Shlisselburg. Again the Leningrad Command had failed to report the bad news to Moscow. On September 4 Stalin cabled to Churchill, "We have lost more than half the Ukraine and the enemy is at the gates of Leningrad," urging Churchill to open the second front. In Leningrad, pictures of Stalin vanished and pictures of Zhdanov began to appear everywhere.

Leningrad was now completely surrounded. Early in September, Dmitri Shostakovich told the people of his native city, over the radio, that he had finished the second movement of his Seventh Symphony (later known as the *Leningrad* Symphony). "Life in the city must go on as usual," Shostakovich said. He had been asked to leave his home in the Petrograd district and refused. In October he and his family were evacuated, "almost forcibly," to Moscow and then to Kuybyshev. The *Leningrad* Symphony was first performed in Moscow on May 29, 1942.

On September 4, German long-range guns began shelling the city as the Germans watched the bombardment through their field glasses. They could see the *Aurora*'s red flag flying from the tower of the Admiralty. The tower and the gilded spire of Peter and Paul Fortress had been camouflaged by amateur mountaineers, who climbed up and covered the shining surface with gray paint. (After the war, they scaled the tower and spire again and removed the paint with solvents.) The German guns were within range of the Winter Palace. The *Bronze Horseman* statue was protected by a large sandbox all around it, after the possibility of lowering the monument to the bottom of the Neva had been discussed and the idea discarded. Observation posts were set up on the roof of the New Hermitage and above the Hall of Arms in the Winter Palace, and more antiaircraft guns were installed.

On September 6 the Germans dropped high-explosive and incendiary bombs all over the city. They hit the large Badayev warehouse, which extended over an area of four acres, destroying large supplies of grain, meat, butter, and sugar. The Leningraders were shocked; this, they knew, meant starvation. Until then they'd had the same food rations as people all over Russia. There was still white bread, workers got eight hundred grams of bread a day; there was butter and meat, and people with money could buy caviar, crab meat, and Crimean champagne.

After the Badayev fire, the authorities estimated they had reserves for only three weeks. All foodstuffs were distributed to various locations; there must be no repetition of the disaster. Dmitri V. Pavlov, a noted distribution expert from Moscow, arrived to take charge of food supplies and got ready to feed three and a half million people, including half a million troops around the city. Until then the German bombers had concentrated on hitting mainly hospitals; they bombed a large hospital on Suvorov Prospekt, killing and maiming an unknown number of people. Now they began bombing warehouses and stores. A bomb hit Gostiny Dvor on Nevsky Prospekt, Leningrad's largest department store, killing ninety-eight people. The authorities bitterly regretted that they hadn't more strictly forced people to leave while there had been time. Hundreds of thousands had gone, but large numbers of refugees had arrived from the Baltic states that had been overrun by the Germans. There was a widespread belief in Leningrad that to leave was to show cowardice. But most people stayed because they loved their city, even under siege.

By the middle of September, Field Marshal von Leeb had set up his headquarters at Gachina. He could see the camouflaged spires and gilded church domes of the beautiful city that he hoped would soon be his. He had twenty divisions, and his troops were in top condition. There was not much time left before the beginning of the Arctic winter, which comes early in Leningrad. And the Führer was getting impatient.

On September 16 the German advance units were two miles from the Elektrosila plant, a short streetcar ride from the center of Leningrad. Even the optimists were no longer certain the city could be held. Women and even children were commandeered to work on trenches and fortifications. Internal security was tightened. There was a strict curfew from 10:00 P.M. to 6:00 A.M. Anyone who was stopped in the street by a patrol might be shot on the spot unless he had a good excuse. Rumors said that German intelligence had recruited thousands of agents among anti-Soviet nationalistic groups—Poles, Ukrainians, Finns, Lithuanians, Estonians—who spoke perfect Russian. The Leningrad Command ordered all dockyards, bridges, and factories to be mined immediately. Should the Germans succeed in breaking through into the city, Leningrad would blow itself up. Trusted "troikas," troop patrols accompanied by "dedicated Communists," were selected for the suicidal task. All plants around the city were evacuated so that the Germans would not be able to use them for the production of weapons or ammunition. *Leningradskaya Pravda's* headline said, "LENINGRAD—TO BE OR NOT TO BE." It was no secret that Stalin wouldn't mind if Leningrad were lost. But it was not known that Hitler had instructed Field Marshal von Leeb that "Petersburg must be leveled to the ground." The two dictators had at last agreed on *something*.

Many historians believe that had the Germans made an all-out attack in those days they might have taken Leningrad, though it would have been defended block by block and house by house, as Stalingrad was later on. The Leningraders were digging in. There were machine-gun nests on the roofs, tank traps in the streets, and embrasures and hastily built pillboxes. The Germans were then nine miles from the Winter Palace. Machine guns were

posted on the roof; the crews were ready for German para-
troopers. Zhdanov loved Leningrad and partly disregarded Stalin's orders: the Winter Palace, and a few other palaces—among
them Petrodvorets, Pushkin, and Tsarskoye Selo—were *not* mined.

Around September 20 the German frontal attacks grew
weaker. Soviet intelligence reported that Hitler had ordered von
Leeb to release several Panzer divisions from Leningrad to be
sent to the Moscow front. More German troops were pulled out.
The great military leader had decided that success would come
anyway in Leningrad, that winter and hunger would do what
his troops hadn't so far been able to achieve. By early October the attack lost momentum and then came to a halt. The Germans were digging in for the winter.

Stalin recalled General Zhukov for the impending battle of
Moscow. The Germans brought some of their biggest guns
(Krupp, Schneider, Skoda) to Leningrad. The city had flour
reserves for thirty-five days and meat for thirty-three. There was
fat for forty-five days and sugar for sixty. But the Public Library
remained open. A small reading room in the basement was always filled with people reading by the light of small oil lamps. It
was very cold there, and the librarians received many queries on
how to make matches and candles.

On November 7, the anniversary of the Bolshevik Revolution—
the biggest holiday in the Soviet Union—children got an extra ration of half a cup of sour cream and a hundred grams of potato
flour. There was no parade (though there was one in Moscow).
Some speeches were read over the radio, followed by music.
Leningradskaya Pravda wrote, "We will be cold but we shall survive. We will be hungry but we shall tighten our belts. We shall
hold out until we win." Brave words but the members of the
Leningrad Command knew that the supplies left were small and
getting smaller. President Mikhail I. Kalinin, a former Putilov
worker, wrote to Stalin, "We must establish reliable routes for
supplying Leningrad in winter conditions." To everybody's surprise, Stalin gave orders to organize a small airlift, two hundred
tons of high-calorie food a day; a drop in the bucket but every
drop helped. The people of Leningrad never lost hope. Until late
November they were saying the blockade might end any day
now.

The authorities were less hopeful. They were gambling on the weather, waiting for the ice to firm on Lake Ladoga, Europe's largest lake, seven thousand square miles. Plans to use the frozen surface had been made around the middle of October. Workers began expanding the primitive port facilities at Kokkorevo and Osinovets near Leningrad, and across the lake at Kobona, Lavrovo, Novaya Ladoga, and Voibokalo. No one knew whether the ice would hold the weight of heavy trucks. The scientists said that one foot of ice would be created in eight days at a temperature of minus five degrees Celsius. A truck carrying a one-ton load would need eight inches of ice.

Ice roads were not new in Russia; even railroad tracks had been laid on ice. But the Ladoga route was something that had never been tried before. It would be thirty miles long, and the Germans would certainly try to bomb it. On November 8 the Germans had occupied Tikhvin, a small town in the east, closing the ring around Leningrad—except for Lake Ladoga. Five million people might have to depend on the ice route for survival.

Soviet air reconnaissance reported that ice was forming early that year. The people at the Leningrad Command became more hopeful. On November 15 two reconnaissance patrols took off from both ends of the the lake, testing the ice. The soldiers had axes and wore white camouflage clothes. One man broke through the ice but was rescued. Both groups agreed that the road might soon be opened. On November 19 the first horse-drawn sledge crossed the ice and returned from the mainland with some food supplies. It was the eighty-third day of the siege. The daily bread ration in Leningrad was down to 125 grams. There were flour supplies left for two days.

On November 22 the first column of sixty trucks brought thirty-three tons of flour to Leningrad. One truck broke through the ice and the driver died in the cold water. During the following week forty trucks were lost. Some broke through the ice and others were shelled by German guns or strafed by Messerschmitts. As the ice thickened, more trails were staked out across the lake. Eventually, there were sixty different trails, with a total length of almost a thousand miles.

The poet Vsevolod Vishnevsky had written in his diary, on November 19:

Last night we were thinking of the recent past . . . Strela . . .
theaters . . . restaurants, . . . favorite dishes (it makes one's
mouth water) . . . shashlik, in Kars style, Georgian soup, greens,
greens . . . almonds, borsht, Kievsky cutlets, pies, champagne. . . .
And in reality . . . today soup and cereal. Tomorrow soup and
cereal. How boring.

Snow fell, and the streetcars stopped running. Some stood in
the streets, immobilized, white fortresses in snow piles. Children's sleds became the only means of transportation. People
used them to take the sick to the hospital or the dead to the
cemeteries, or to a nearby place where the bodies were piled up.
At night it was very quiet in the dying city. People died quietly.
"Someone would pull a small sled with a dead person on it, and
suddenly he would fall down in the snow beside the sled and was
dead too," a chronicler wrote. Snow continued to fall, mercifully
covering the corpses lying everywhere in the streets. Once in a
while soldiers would pick up the dead, dynamite a few trenches
in the hard, frozen ground at the cemetery and throw the bodies
into the improvised mass grave. No one bothered to record the
names. Other people brought their dead to the reception room of
the nearest hospital. Some came there just to die. When the big
German guns shelled the city, the streets were empty. Then the
guns fell silent, and there were the cold, apathetic people pulling
their sleds. By the middle of December some snow drifts reached
up to the second floor of the houses. Around Radio House it was
said that five or six thousand people died every day in the city.

People even began to eat their dogs. They loved them, but
they were unable to feed them. Some became afraid of their
dogs. People also ate the ground meat of cats and mice. Many
children suffered from dysentery. A child's breakfast ration was
twenty-five grams of bread with a little hot salted water. For
lunch they got a soup made of frozen beets and a little slice of
bread. Many people died of dystrophy and diarrhea caused by
the inedible components of the "bread." Some were so hungry
that they scraped off the wallpaper, trying to boil the paste that
was said to contain a little potato flour. Some chewed paper, for
hours. Doctors reported that teen-agers between fourteen and
eighteen died in larger numbers than older people, that men died

faster than women, though all got the same rations. Some boiled old leather briefcases into a sticky mass and made something called "meat jelly." And there were a number who just lay down on their beds in the cold rooms and didn't get up again.

Hunger and sex are the most powerful human drives but the survivors say that there was almost no sex in the city of Leningrad during the terrible winter of 1941–42. Women didn't even attempt to look attractive. In December somebody had heard from someone else that one could eat lipstick, a little at a time. "People did go to bed together—but only to feel the warmth of their bodies because it was so terribly cold," a man remembers.

Zhdanov ordered several "convalescent centers" set up, where scientists, writers, artists, and generally "people of importance to the state" would get somewhat more generous rations and limited medical attention for two or three weeks until they felt stronger. One center was set up at the Hotel Astoria for authors, painters, musicians. Boris V. Asafyev, the composer, spent several weeks at home in his bed, "conserving strength," while he composed in his mind the music of his new opera *The Bronze Horseman,* after Pushkin's poem. Once in a while, during the few hours of daylight, he would get out of bed and write down the music he had memorized. Zhdanov and his top aides received the ration of front-line soldiers. No one in Leningrad got much more than those worst off.

The search for food went on continuously. Supplies of cottonseed cake were found, not believed to be edible since it contained some poison. But the scientists treated the cottonseed at high temperatures, removing the toxic ingredients. During the worst weeks a ten per cent measure of cottonseed cake was added to the bread mixture. All warehouses, grain elevators, and freight cars were carefully swept; several tons of flour were reclaimed. At the Razin brewery a cellar filled with grain was found, and grain was also discovered in several warehouses in Kronstadt.

In the middle of the winter, when people were silently dying all over the city, the Municipal Council set up a commission of architects to plan the restoration of Leningrad after the end of the war. They met in the cold cellars of the Hermitage, wearing thick mittens, working by the light of a few candles. Their food rations were the same as everybody's, but their imagination remained unrationed, and their plans for Greater Leningrad were later put into operation.

That winter a person's ration card became his most important document, the difference between near-starvation and death. If somebody lost his card—during an air raid, a fire, the shelling of a house—he was almost certainly doomed. In the earlier weeks, substitute cards had been issued after some formalities. Some people would invent disasters, bringing along "witnesses," and later they would share the extra ration with the "witness." By late January 1942 it was said that to get a new card you would have to have permission from Zhdanov himself. The cards were renewed at the end of each month; every citizen had to appear in person. People were envied when a member of the family died early in the month and they could use the dead person's card until the end of the month. Some tried to forge ration cards; others stole them. Apartment-house owners or janitors broke into rooms where someone had died and took away the card. At the beginning of the month, after the cards had been renewed, the crime rate went up. The police couldn't cope with the thieves. Patrols of front-line soldiers stopped suspicious persons in the streets and made spot checks. A person caught with a ration card that didn't belong to him might be shot at once.

The Germans printed counterfeit ration cards, which were dropped by planes or circulated by their agents. There were rumors of people stealing food in distribution centers, of black marketeers. The Leningraders were exceptional as a group but they were only human. There were cowards and thieves among them—and worse. As the cold, hungry winter wore on, murders for food were reported. People were killed for their ration cards or for a loaf of bread. Crimes were committed by desperate, normally law-abiding citizens who couldn't bear to see their wives, parents, children suffer and die. Some murderers were German agents, trying to break down public morale. It was rumored that Nazi agents were trying to stir up a "hunger revolt." There was no mail delivery but letters arrived at Party headquarters, signed illegibly, asking that Leningrad be declared an open city. "Let the Germans come in, they will give us plenty of food." The German High Command remembered that the revolution in Petrograd in March 1917 had been started by cold, hungry women standing in line in front of the bakeries.

History did not repeat itself, however. There were no riots in front of food stores. People began to discover the hard way what dieticians have preached for a long time, that the human body needs much less food than is generally assumed, that many people in many countries overeat constantly. A Leningrad scientist who studied the problem of starvation told me, "We know today that the human body can stand complete fasting for as long as some thirty days. All one needs is a little water every day, provided you rest most of the time, and burn up little energy. But you may die of 'hunger,' by eating a little bread and nothing else every day, which is a totally wrong diet."

During the siege, some doctors in Leningrad who still had time and the needed peace of mind to make observations noticed that certain diseases due to overeating—stomach problems, gall bladder and kidney infections, diabetes, and so on—disappeared during the siege. There were very few heart attacks, relatively speaking, perhaps because most people lost weight. Very few suffered from the common cold. Unfortunately these advantages were outweighed by starvation diseases such as dystrophy and fatal diarrhea.

At midnight on December 31 the guns of the Soviet ships in the Neva celebrated by booming a salvo against the Germans. The sound of the "Internationale" was heard over the radio, followed by the chimes of the Spassky Cathedral in Moscow. There were no extra New Year's rations, as had been rumored in Leningrad. A kilogram of black bread was selling for six hundred rubles on the black market. Vodka, jars of cabbage, and cigarettes were also for sale but at exorbitant prices that put the black market out of reach for most people. But there were two hours of electric light. Everybody said it was wonderful.

Early in January 1942 Zhdanov authorized the destruction of many wooden structures. People began burning a little wood in their *burzhuiki*, small makeshift stoves that were not safe at all. Within a few weeks, over three hundred fires were caused by *burzhuiki*. When a building began burning, it usually was left to

burn down. There was no water, and the fire brigade had ceased
to operate. D. once passed a burning house and was shocked by
the strange sight.

"People from the neighborhood came carrying their buckets as
the heat of the flames melted the snow and ice around the house.
They stood in line, quietly and in order, and when their turn
came, they filled their buckets and went home. No one thought
of using the water to put out the fire."

Dmitri V. Pavlov, the food rationing boss, later estimated that
there wasn't enough food in January and February for two hundred thousand people "just to keep them from dying." Yet the
terrible toll would have been much higher without the Lake
Ladoga life line. On December 9, 1941, the Soviets had recaptured Tikhvin. The small railroad to Volkhov was reopened. Fast
Zis-5 three-ton trucks were used on Lake Ladoga, making the trip
across the ice in one hour. Repair shops and first-aid stations
were set up on the frozen surface. Special patrols would put
wooden crossings over sudden crevasses. The drivers received pre-
miums for exceeding the delivery norms. Over twenty thousand
people were on duty on the frozen lake, but it was literally killing
duty, at forty degrees below zero, with murderous northerly
winds. Zhdanov told the men, "The supply of Leningrad hangs
on a slim thread. . . . It depends on you men of the ice road."
They were talking about "the road of life" when they talked of
Ladoga. The speech was classified secret. The people of Leningrad didn't know about it.

The men on the ice road did all they could but it wasn't
enough. In December 1941 more people died in Leningrad than
during the whole preceding year. After the recapture of Tikhvin,
a conference was held at the Kremlin under Stalin. Plans were
made to break the blockade of Leningrad with three army groups
—the Leningrad, the Volkhov, and the Northwest. Zhdanov attended the conference. After his return to Leningrad he took a
calculated risk by increasing the bread ration by seventy-five
grams—a thin slice—each day though he knew there were only
five days of flour supplies. Suddenly a wave of optimism spread
through the cold, hungry city. The railroad station of Mga would
soon be recaptured; the railroad line to Moscow would be
reopened; "enormous supplies" were said to be stored at various

distribution points around Tikhvin. In a short time Leningrad would be liberated.

By mid-January, the optimism was gone as suddenly as it had come. It was public knowledge that the Soviet soldiers were underfed, weak, and sick. Replacements did not match the losses. Front-line rations were five hundred grams of bread, three times the civilian ration, but sixty thousand soldiers suffered from dystrophy and thousands from scurvy. They were in no condition to fight the well-fed Germans. Deaths from starvation diseases along the northern front that winter surpassed deaths from enemy action. It was said that the rats had come from Leningrad to the front, where they found more food. Soviet soldiers said that smart rats would go right on to the German lines.

The German bombers continued their attacks against the road of life. Zhdanov placed the Lake Ladoga ice route under the command of General A. M. Shilov, feared for his toughness. Fighter planes of the Soviet Baltic Fleet were ordered to attack strafing German aircraft. Hundreds of Young Communists were ordered out on the ice. It was said in Leningrad that if one truck failed to arrive, five thousand people in the city would die of starvation. Many trucks got stuck in enormous snowdrifts that could not be cleared away. The small Irinovsky railroad station on the line to Leningrad was no longer operating. Too many people were sick or dying.

The first ugly rumors began to spread in the middle of the winter. Many people refused to believe them unless they'd met someone who had seen somebody who. . . . Cannibals in Leningrad! It *couldn't* be true. Even today no one will talk about it. The survivors deny it vehemently, perhaps a little *too* vehemently. Actually there is no proof, only guarded references. But once in a while one meets somebody who admits, in strictest confidence, that he was at least conscious of the possibility.

"You couldn't help thinking of it. All of us, civilians and soldiers, old and young people, were pale and weak and undernourished. And all of a sudden you would meet a strange-looking man, well-fed and greedy, with a brutal, cunning look in his eyes. You wouldn't say anything, you were too embarrassed even to think of it, but you would react instinctively. Maybe the man was working in a food store and managed to steal some food, and hadn't been found out yet and shot. Maybe he was the manager of an apartment house and stole ration cards. Or—maybe he was one of the thugs at Haymarket. . . ."

Haymarket (Sennaya, now officially known as Peace Square) had been a dangerous slum since the early days of St. Petersburg, populated by "Dostoyevsky" characters. Dostoyevsky had lived in the district and wrote about its people. After the October Revolution the area had been cleaned up. The Dostoyevsky characters disappeared at the time of the officially enforced oblivion of Dostoyevsky during the dark days of Stalinism. Dostoyevsky, the expert on the seamy side of life, was not exactly popular with Party ideologists extolling the strengths and virtues of the new Soviet citizen.

During the siege, Haymarket made a comeback and became the center of Leningrad's black market, the meeting place of criminal types. After the Badayev fire, one could buy glass jars filled with "Badayev earth." After the big warehouse burned down, molten sugar had seeped down into the cellars and the earth underneath. Some of the sugar was later recovered by groups of workers under official supervision. But at night people would come with axes and picks and take home some of the frozen soil. At one time, a jar with soil taken from the upper layers would bring as much as a hundred rubles at Haymarket. The buyer would take the jar home, melt and boil the earth mixture, and strain it through a fine sieve and a linen cloth. There wasn't much sugar in it, but there wasn't much potato flour in wallpaper paste either.

According to official records, there were five police dogs kept by the Leningrad police in February, possibly the last dogs in the city. Small children were growing up without ever seeing a dog, a horse, or a cat. Their parents showed them in books what these animals were like. It was said that even the birds wouldn't come back in spring. All kinds of weird stories were told, and no one was much surprised when the first rumors about "meat patties" drifted through the hungry city. Two patties sold for four hundred rubles in Haymarket. Some people shrugged off the rumors. Horsemeat maybe, or the meat of dogs. But the rumors persisted that the patties were made of human flesh. By that time, even the skeptics would say nothing. Anyway, who could afford four hundred rubles for a couple of meat patties? If someone bought them, he was welcome to his meal.

But there were people who wouldn't let their children go out alone in the street when it was dark; and darkness came very early. At Radio House they told the story of a front-line soldier who had come to Leningrad on a brief visit to his family and had disappeared. The authorities investigated the case and stated that he was not a deserter; most probably he had been murdered. His body couldn't be found though. He was last seen in the Haymarket district before he disappeared. There were other stories, perhaps mere gossip, whispered among people while they stood in line, hungry and shivering, waiting for the bakeries to open. Somebody had heard about army sappers dynamiting the frozen earth to make mass graves at the Piskarevsky and Serafimov cemeteries. The sappers had seen bodies with shoulders and thighs missing. Other people remember the strange, rotten, sweetish taste of the Neva water that winter. They would boil the water before drinking it, but the taste didn't go away. Naturally, since sometimes bodies were dropped through a hole in the frozen surface of the Neva and the canals. The poet Daniel Leonidovich Andreyev wrote:

> We have known everything . . .
> That in Russian speech there is
> No word for that mad war winter . . .
> When the Hermitage shivered under bombs . . .
> Houses turned to frost and pipes burst with ice . . .
> The ration—100 grams . . . On the Nevsky corpses.
> And we learned, too, about cannibalism.
> We have known everything. . . .

Late in March 1942 a new wave of optimism swept the city. Suddenly there was hope again among the survivors. Nothing had happened to justify the hope; the military situation was still desperate. But hope is rarely based on reason. At any rate, the Lake Ladoga ice road was still operating. Members of the Communist youth brigades were sent to the post offices to sort out mountains of mail. Some telegrams were found and delivered by boys and girls. The telegrams might be two or three months old.

When the young people came to an apartment, they might knock at the door, and when no one opened, would call the neighbors and force open the door and find somebody lying dead inside. Someone would say, "A good thing that the rooms are so cold." And somebody else might give a shrug: "Too bad we didn't know about it, could have used an extra ration card."

"People became hard and cynical," says D. "People would change in these cold, hungry months, and some changed for worse."

Early in April some streets were cleared and a few streetcar lines were put into operation, among them the lines No. 3 and No. 9, going right up to the front. Not many people rode there, but psychologically the reappearance of the streetcars was very important. They were greeted like old friends one missed badly. People riding in the streetcars were shouting, and those in the streets were waving and laughing. Some ran home to tell their families they'd seen the cars running again. No doubt, Leningrad would soon be liberated; certainly Comrade Zhdanov had a secret plan. More power stations began operating. Party Secretary Kuznetsov had told a meeting of factory managers that their plants must begin at once to produce shells and small ammunition. Just wait a few weeks, and you'll see what happens. . . .

Karl I. Eliasberg, director of the Radio Committee orchestra, was ordered to conduct a concert. There had been no concert in Leningrad for the past four months. Eliasberg began to look for the members of the orchestra. Twenty-seven of them had died. Others were still alive but so weak that they were simply unable to play. Only eight members of the orchestra were ready to perform. They were joined by thirty musicians who reported for the first rehearsal after several appeals for musicians were read over the radio. Eliasberg himself was hardly able to conduct. He and his wife had spent two weeks at the convalescent center of the Hotel Astoria, suffering from severe dystrophy. The concert took place on April 5, at the Pushkin Theater because Philharmonic Hall had been damaged by shellfire.

It was a short concert. The musicians were too weak to perform a long program and the listeners were too weak to listen to one. After Glazunov's "Triumphal Overture," the orchestra played excerpts from Tchaikovsky's *Swan Lake,* and ended with the overture of Glinka's *Ruslan and Ludmila*. The theater was ice cold; when the musicians exhaled, people saw a white fog coming out of their mouths. Eliasberg had almost fainted on his way to the theater but he felt fine the moment he stood in front of the orchestra. The musicians, too, forgot about being cold and hungry and weak. The concert was a great success.

The Lake Ladoga road had to be given up on April 24, the 257th day of the siege, as the ice began melting. It had really been "the road of life." According to a report by Alexei Kosygin, over half a million people had been evacuated by way of Ladoga from Leningrad to the mainland. In the opposite direction, 270,000 tons of food had been brought into the city, saving the lives of most remaining Leningraders. The last shipment consisted of fresh onions. Leningrad was still alive. Its population had shrunk, owing to deaths and evacuation. In April 1942 the authorities issued 800,000 fewer ration cards than at the beginning of the siege. More than ten times as many people died of starvation in Leningrad as were killed in Hiroshima; many more died during the evacuation. The death toll became a political question; the Soviet authorities tried to report it low, on orders from the Kremlin. Stalin didn't want Leningrad to acquire the halo of a tortured city. In his book *Leningrad v Blokade* (Leningrad in the Blockade), Dmitri V. Pavlov wrote, "The life of the Leningraders was so grim that there is no need for historians or writers dealing with these events to strengthen the colors or deepen the shadows." Russian historians and writers were well advised to follow the official line.

Spring came at last, and the hope of new life. There had been no epidemics during the winter, thanks to the extreme cold. Now the danger was acute. The people of Leningrad—still weak and sick—were urged to clean up. The bodies still lying in the streets were taken away and buried. Three hundred thousand women registered for clean-up operations. There were no May Day celebrations, only a few speeches and music on the radio. The Germans contributed the accompaniment, donating free shells. Some exploded in St. Isaac's Square in front of the Astoria Hotel just as the new commander, Lieutenant General L. A. Govorov, was attending a reception.

Govorov had started his military career in 1916 in the Czarist army, became a brilliant artillery expert, and with many others was arrested by Beria's secret police in 1941 during a major purge. It was said that he was saved from the execution squad by President Kalinin and Marshal Timoshenko (who earlier had been saved by the intervention of Nikita Khrushchev). Govorov became a hero during the Battle of Moscow, where he practiced his principle of the offensive use of artillery fire, "accurate counterbattery blows against the German artillery." Govorov didn't wait for the Germans to start a barrage. He ordered his men to find the German artillery positions and destroy them. He was a tough man of few words; soldiers said that "no one had ever seen him smile." Stalin sent him to Leningrad because he was convinced that only an artillery genius could break the siege. He was right.

Another new commander in Leningrad was Lieutenant General Andrei A. Vlasov, also a hero of Moscow, a scholarly military man. Later, in June 1942, after a terrible defeat that cost the lives of more than ten thousand Russian soldiers, Vlasov disappeared. In Moscow it was assumed, and hoped, that the general had shot himself. But Vlasov had surrendered to the Germans on July 12 and became head of the Vlasovite anti-Soviet movement. He became the Soviet Union's most prominent traitor in World War II. Today he is an unperson there, but Vlasov was a complex figure. He certainly couldn't be compared to the White Guard General Yudenich, who promised in 1919 "to hang a Bolshevik on every lamppost in Petrograd." Vlasov was a military scientist, who once told Marie Curie, "My blood belongs to my fatherland." He was also a weak man, a protégé of Malenkov, and later of Goebbels's propaganda machine. It is hard to believe that he didn't know about the atrocities committed by his soldiers at the end of World War II, especially in Czechoslovakia, where the Vlasov soldiers were more feared even than the dreadful German SS. After the end of the war it was reported in the West that Vlasov "fell into the hands of the Russians." He had been a marked man since the day he surrendered to the Nazis, and he knew it. His execution

Alexander II

Alexander II and his family, about 1871. Seated left to right: Czar
Alexander, his daughter-in-law Maria Feodorovna holding the fu-
ture Czar Nicholas II, and Czarina Maria Alexandrovna. Standing
left to right: Grand Duke Paul, Grand Duke Sergei, Grand Duchess
Maria (later Duchess of Edinburgh and mother of Marie of
Rumania), Grand Duke Alexis, the Czarevitch Alexander (later
Alexander III), and Grand Duke Vladimir.

Father Gapon, leader of the 1905 demonstration in St. Petersburg

Peter the Great. A contemporary portrait

Kronstadt. From a nineteenth-century engraving

Nicholas I. A contemporary engraving

Gregory Potemkin. A mezzotint after the
original portrait

was announced on August 2, 1946—a little over two years before his antagonist, Zhdanov, was executed.

After the defection of Vlasov and the loss of Russia's Second Shock Army, Leningrad's chances for survival looked worse than ever. The Leningrad Command ordered that Leningrad must become a military city, with as few civilians as possible, just those needed to secure essential services. On July 6 Zhdanov announced, after a meeting with Stalin, that only 800,000 people would be permitted to remain in Leningrad. All others would be evacuated. The tragedy of the preceding winter must not be repeated. Over 300,000 people would shortly be evacuated by the shipping service on Lake Ladoga that had been set up in May, replacing the former ice road. A new pipeline had been laid on the bottom of the lake between the mainland and Leningrad that could supply the besieged city with fuel.

The Leningrad Command knew that a new German offensive was planned for September 1942. Field Marshal Georg von Küchler, the new commander of the German Army Group North, was to follow Hitler's directive No. 45. The Führer wanted Leningrad taken by September, "at all costs."

Fortunately, the people of Leningrad didn't know it. In the city the mood was relaxed, almost cheerful, although the Germans were bombing and shelling. The sun was shining, the streetcars were running, there were no dead bodies lying in the streets. Along the Moika and the Fontanka fishermen were seen, dedicated to their peculiar pursuit of happiness. Everybody tried not to think of last winter. Black market prices went down, a certain indication that things were improving. The bookstores were crowded. One could get even theater tickets, if one tried hard enough. Everybody knew, of course, that the Germans were on the offensive all over Russia, that they would soon start their all-out attack against Leningrad, that they had brought up the heavy guns they had used to conquer Sevastopol. But no one talked about it.

"Everybody was trying to avoid reality," D. remembers. "On August 9 I attended the first concert at the repaired, reopened Philharmonic Hall. The Seventh, *Leningrad* Symphony by Shostakovich. The composer had sent the score and the parts from

Moscow by plane. The concert was broadcast and the Germans listened in. I suppose the Nazi music lovers didn't like the music, because during the second movement they tried to ruin the concert firing their heavy guns until General Govorov's artillery found and silenced them. Govorov sat in front of me, and he seemed to enjoy the concert."

During the fall the Soviets tried several times, and always failed, to relieve the German pressure on Leningrad. Everybody was thinking about the approach of another terrible winter but the mood in the city was not noticeably depressed. On the evening of November 8, 1942, a reception was held at the brightly illuminated large hall of the Smolny Institute, where Lenin, twenty-five years earlier, had stepped out on the platform and said, "We will now proceed to construct the Socialist order." An underwater cable had been laid on the bottom of Lake Ladoga connecting Leningrad with the Volkhov power station on the eastern shore. The entire Party and military hierarchy was present, including General Govorov, who was called away to a telephone. It was the voice of Stalin, ordering Govorov to proceed with "War Game No. 5," the code name for the offensive that was to break the Leningrad blockade.

Govorov went straight to his office on the upper floor of the Smolny and looked over the top-secret plans that he'd kept in his safe. During the next weeks, he worked out his plans for the attack in great detail. He realized clearly that this was his, and Leningrad's, last chance. This time nothing must be left to improvisation. Govorov knew that his opponent, Colonel General Georg Lindemann, had twenty-five top divisions at his command.

On December 8 Stalin ordered Govorov to start Operation "Iskra" ("Spark"), which would break the blockade. Lindemann had no illusions about the future when, in an order to his troops, he called Leningrad "the source of the Bolshevik Revolution. . . . For the Soviets, the liberation of Leningrad would be as important as the defense of Moscow or the battle for Stalingrad."

On New Year's Day 1943 there were only 640,000 people left in the city; a year before, there had been four times as many. Operation Iskra began on January 12, in the early morning, with a

two-hour barrage of almost five thousand Russian guns. Govorov's gunners did a fine, precise job; three days later, he was
promoted by Stalin to the rank of colonel general. On January 17
Govorov ordered his troops to close the gap between the forces
along the Leningrad and the Volkhov sectors of the front. On
January 18 the Russian troops in both sectors joined forces. The
Germans had to give up the fortress of Shlisselburg; during the
past months they had executed many of the Russian inhabitants
of the fortress and sent many as slave laborers to Germany.

At 11:00 P.M. Radio Moscow announced that "troops of the
Leningrad and Volkhov fronts have joined together . . . and have
broken the blockade of Leningrad." Suddenly the streets of Leningrad were filled with happy people. There was dancing and
music; speeches were read, and poems were recited on the radio.

"It seemed as though each of the people left in the city was
celebrating," D. remembers. "There were red flags everywhere. It
was the 506th day of the blockade. Some people said the siege
was almost over. They were wrong, of course. The Germans were
still a streetcar ride from the Winter Palace. But our troops held
Shlisselburg. We were still surrounded, but not *completely* surrounded."

On February 7 the first train left the Finland Station for the
mainland by way of the Shlisselburg bridge across the Neva.
There was music again, but the people on the train knew it
would be a dangerous journey. The gap the Soviet troops had
forced at Shlisselburg was less than five hundred yards wide. On
both sides were powerful German guns. During the next months,
the gap was cut "perhaps twelve hundred times" by German
shells, and always repaired. People called it "the corridor of
death." Sometimes the corridor could not be used in daytime, and
the trains ran at night, without signal lights. Special Engine Column 48, an elite rail unit, took over the operation in midsummer.
During the last months of the year, the trains delivered 4,500,000
tons of freight to Leningrad.

Zhdanov and General Govorov, however, had few illusions
about the situation. Stalingrad had turned the tide, and the first
supplies from the United States were beginning to reach the Soviet Union. But the German troops were still all around Leningrad, and heavy German guns on the Sinyavino Heights were

shelling the railroad tracks in the corridor of death, day and night. From the Pulkovo Heights the German officers were still watching Peter and Paul Fortress and the cupolas of the Smolny Cathedral through their glasses.

The people of Leningrad were suffering from delayed shock. After the brief exultation in January, people began to realize that their joy had been premature; many became deeply depressed. In February the bread rations were increased; employees got five hundred grams of bread a day and dependents four hundred, but there were warnings that the increases were temporary and might be rescinded. Everybody realized that the narrow gap at Shlisselburg might be locked any day. In his May Day speech, General Govorov warned the citizens that a German attack might be "imminent." Zhdanov reminded the people that Leningrad was still a military city. The Germans punctuated these speeches by heavy barrages. They hit the Public Library and a streetcar on Nevsky Prospekt, killing most passengers, but later Govorov's counterbattery salvos silenced them. People in Leningrad followed the exchange of artillery fire as though it were a chess game; many had become experts and could tell what kind of guns had fired the shells, and where the next ones might land.

The Bolshoi Theater came from Moscow for guest performances. At the stadium, the Dynamo Club won the soccer championship. Little attention was paid to the second anniversary of the war, on June 22. The scientists in Leningrad began writing a book about the achievements of science in the city during the blockade (the manuscript was never published). No one was starving but no one looked well. American powdered eggs and powdered milk, butter and sugar were for sale, and after a while the Leningraders said that American butter wasn't bad but Russian butter tasted better.

(I told D. about the emaciated survivors in German concentration camps in Austria and Bohemia who had been liberated by American troops and were taken to military hospitals or special recovery centers. They were happy and grateful—for a while. After two weeks some began to complain because American coffee wasn't "strong enough" and the fried eggs weren't exactly as they liked them. He was not surprised. "Human nature is the same everywhere," he said, with a shrug.)

The German shelling became worse during July and August. Many people who had spent a lot of time in the streets during the first winter because they didn't want to stay alone in their homes now were afraid to venture out. Many couldn't stand the whining noise of the shells. The square in front of the Finland Station was hit so often that people called it "the valley of death." Several theaters and cinemas were closed, streetcar stops were removed, and white and blue signs appeared on Nevsky Prospekt and in other streets reading, "In case of shelling this side of the street is the most dangerous." During the month of September almost twelve thousand German shells fell on the city, but the people still walked in the public gardens amid cabbage and turnip fields. The women wore their best summer clothes. No one talked about the approaching winter but everyone was worried.

General Govorov began making plans for the liberation of Leningrad in September 1943. Again he proceeded with almost scientific precision. The three-pronged offensive—from Oranienbaum, the Pulkovo Heights, and toward Novgorod—would start in the middle of winter, when the Russian troops were aided by ice, snow, and bitter cold, natural allies that had always defeated previous invaders. Govorov complained that he had not enough guns, and Zhdanov had to plead with Stalin until more guns, antiaircraft batteries, Katyusha rocket launchers, tanks, planes, and other weapons were sent to Leningrad. At the end of the year, General Govorov commanded more than 1,240,000 troops and had an enormous concentration of fire power. His opponent, Field Marshal von Küchler, had less than 800,000 troops and 10,000 guns.

In the early days of January 1944 Govorov talked to his field commanders and artillerymen. Once more he impressed on them the need for concerted action and a fast initial attack that would throw the Germans off balance. Gachina must be quickly recaptured. Long-range guns must methodically destroy all German strongpoints. In the field, each commander knew the German position he had to turn against. The operation began in Oranienbaum on January 14, the 867th day of the siege. The fog was so thick that the reconnaissance planes and bombers remained grounded. The Soviet forces jumped off after a concentrated ar-

tillery barrage by the heavy Russian guns, the batteries at Kronstadt, and the guns of the Baltic fleet. The Second Shock Army
advanced two miles. The commanders cursed the fog; only the
sappers were delighted as they cleared the mine fields without
being seen by the Germans. Govorov, who had been in Oranienbaum for the jump-off, flew back to Leningrad in such a thick fog
that his plane circled for almost forty minutes before the pilot
was able to locate the airfield.

At 9:30 on the morning of January 15 the Russian guns began
the biggest barrage, one hundred minutes of concentrated fire.
Everybody in Leningrad knew that this was it. "The earth was
shaking in the city and the sky seemed to be filled with crashing
sounds," says D. "I believe many people who never go to church
were silently praying. Later we heard at Radio House that over
200,000 shells had been fired against the German positions. In
Leningrad there was hope and there was also fear. We knew that
if this attack didn't come off, it would be the end of the city we
loved. The German counterattack would be terrifying and there
would be little left of the beauty of Leningrad. There were
doubts and rumors. It was said that after the blockade every citizen would be sent to a rest home. I don't know what we did during the following days. Mostly we were waiting. Some people
were so tense that they bought a pint of vodka for three hundred
rubles. The days were long, and the nights were longer."

By January 22 there was no doubt that the Germans were in
disorderly retreat. They were falling back on all fronts so fast
that the Russians could hardly keep up with them. But there
were more rumors and many more hours of tension until the citizens of Leningrad saw rockets—red and white and blue—in the
dark skies above the city. Instinctively, with a reporter's
awareness of them, D. looked at his wristwatch. It was eight
o'clock in the evening on January 27, the 880th day of the siege.
The blockade of Leningrad was over, but the ordeal of the
defenders was not. Not quite.

AFTERMATH AND HORROR

One of the first things they did, D. remembers, was to remove the sandbag camouflage around the monument to Peter the Great. "Everybody went to Decembrists' Square to pay a visit to Peter." In his poem *The Bronze Horseman* Pushkin had asked, "Where are you flying, proud horse / And where will your hooves fall?" For a short, glorious time following the end of the siege, everybody was talking euphorically about "the renaissance."

"Our task," said Zhdanov, "is not just reconstruction but the restoration of our city—not only to restore as it was but to create a city even more comfortable than it was."

Leningrad's leading architects had drawn the plans of the renaissance during the siege, incorporating various features of Paris, Washington, and other Western capitals. The historical center around the Winter Palace was too small for the city of the future. There would be a second center in front of and around the Smolny Institute. The area around the Finland Station would become a large memorial in honor of Lenin. The architects had planned a city that would eventually have seven million people, extending toward the south and southeast, providing direct access to the Baltic across the Gulf of Finland.

The architects had shown an admirable sense of optimism. The Germans had destroyed fifteen million square feet of housing in Leningrad, 840 factories, 41 bridges, 526 schools, 101 museums. They had ruined 187 of the more than three hundred eighteenth- and nineteenth-century buildings classified as historical monuments. Thirty-two shells and two bombs had hit the Hermitage. Over 300,000 square feet of rooms and 60,000 square feet of glass and windows had been broken at the Winter Palace. Many people in Leningrad argued that some ruins should be kept as a permanent reminder of German barbarity and Russian heroism, but the authorities decided to restore everything. After a visit to the town of Pushkin, Olga Berggolts wrote:

> Again from the black dust, from the place
> Of death and ashes, will arise the gardens as before.
> So it will be. I firmly believe in miracles,
> You gave me that belief, my Leningrad.

On April 30, 1944, a memorial exhibition opened in Solyany Park. It was not improvised but had been planned with meticulous care since December 1943, in the middle of the siege. The Leningrad Military Council issued the orders, apparently convinced that the blockade would be broken. Outside, on Market Street, heavy German guns and German tanks were exhibited. Inside, there were fourteen rooms filled with over sixty thousand exhibits, including dioramas made by Leningrad artists. People came to the exhibition to relive once more "the heroic defense of the city," but many had a sense of letdown as they walked past the exhibits.

"The facts were all there," D. remembers. "Even the bomb was there, a thousand-kilo monster, that had fallen near to the Erisman Hospital, fortunately without exploding, during the early weeks of the siege, in September 1941. The names of the two heroes who had defused it were there. Yes, all the facts one could assemble. But there were the intangibles that could not be recreated and exhibited. How can you exhibit the suffering, the horrors, the terrible routine of daily life in the dying city?"

Many Leningraders said it was a fine exhibition for people who had *not* been in Leningrad during the siege. But for the survivors of the ordeal it failed to re-create the atmosphere, the tragedy, the moments of pain, and the worse moments when pain was not felt any more because one had become drugged by too much pain. The moments between waking and sleep when one was only half-conscious of being alive. Perhaps somebody would one day

write about it—somebody of the stature of Tolstoy. Perhaps somebody had already written about it. It was known that all writers
who had lived through the siege of Leningrad were working on
something.

A vast literature exists on the siege, mostly in Russian, but no
work of Tolstoyan dimension. It may have been written but it
was never published. The best English-language book on the
siege, Harrison E. Salisbury's *The 900 Days*, has fourteen small-
print pages of bibliography listing books and periodicals dealing
with every aspect of the blockade and the battle of Leningrad.

Salisbury's accurate, thorough study is not popular in official
Soviet circles. Several people in Leningrad whom I met had read
it (some were reluctant at first to admit it) and agreed that it
was good and "true." Salisbury wrote the deeper truth, that
above all it was the people of Leningrad who saved their city,
though he gives full credit to the Party and to the military men
and the soldiers. And he wrote the truth about what he calls "the
Leningrad Affair"—the sinister conspiracy of Stalin, Malenkov,
and Beria following the siege, which aimed at eradicating its very
memory. They didn't succeed; the story of Leningrad could not
be suppressed. But the men in the Kremlin who came after Stalin
did not permit the truth of the aftermath to be known. Most people in Russia know nothing about it today.

Zhdanov was ordered back to the Kremlin after the plenary
meeting of the Leningrad Party in April 1944. The people of
Leningrad regretted his departure; he had become popular during the siege. He had been tough but just; he had enjoyed no special privileges; and he had kept a cool head during the worst moments of the long crisis and had not broken down under the
enormous strain when he had known, with very few others, the
truth about the terribly slim margin between the city's life and
death.

He had not been equally popular inside the Kremlin, where
the intrigues and power struggles never stopped during the days
of the siege. Between August and October 1941, when the fate of
Leningrad was in the balance, Zhdanov never knew whether the
next hour might bring a summons to Moscow, and the death sentence. Marshal Nikolai Bulganin once told Nikita Khrushchev,

"When a man is called to the Kremlin he doesn't know whether he will emerge alive or not."

During the war Zhdanov had never been a member of the small, powerful group of men who had complete access to Stalin, the truly powerful ones: Molotov, Beria, Malenkov. After his return to Moscow, Zhdanov's star was in ascendancy. Two years later, in 1946, he was the number-two man at the Kremlin, with immense power. His former deputy in Leningrad, Alexei A. Kuznetsov, was with him in Moscow supervising State Security, which meant spying on Beria on behalf of Zhdanov. Malenkov was temporarily out of power, perhaps because he had once been too close to General Vlasov, the traitor. Zhdanov ingratiated himself with Stalin but he paid a terrible price for his ambition—the infamous campaign known as *Zhdanovshchina* culminating in the persecution of some of the finest writers and artists in Leningrad.

In August 1946 Anna Akhmatova, the great Leningrad poet, and Mikhail Zoshchenko, the great Leningrad satirist, were expelled by the Leningrad Union of Writers on brutal, ridiculous charges that no one believed. Akhmatova, who had been awarded the Medal for the Defense of Leningrad, was said to be a whore. Zoshchenko was accused of being a pimp. No one tried to defend them, and they were not permitted to defend themselves. The secret orders to the Writers' Union had come from Moscow, directly from Zhdanov. Stalin wanted the Russian people to forget Leningrad's heroic role during the war. The first scapegoats were to be writers and artists. It has always been that way in Russia, from Dostoyevsky to Solzhenitsyn. The names change, the method remains the same.

Vera Ketlinskaya had started writing her novel *The Blockade* in her cold flat during the siege, while her mother's frozen body was lying in the next room. She had to wait three years to see her book published, in a ruthlessly censored version which she hardly recognized. The terrible truths, the shocking things everybody knew who had lived through the siege, the moments of fear—all that was taken out, and the rest was watered down. Her manuscript had been too "negative." Olga Berggolts had written a play, *Born in Leningrad*, full of bitter things, truthful and painful. Much too negative, it was said. The play was never produced. Other Leningrad writers who had written what they felt during the blockade—among them Sergei Khmelnitsky, Leonid Rakhmanov, Yevgeny Ryss—were unable to publish their manuscripts. And thus one will never know whether someone in Leningrad wrote another *War and Peace* about the siege.

Zhdanov's desperate gamble did not save him. His archenemy Malenkov came back into power. He had once told Stalin that Zhdanov, an architect of the Ribbentrop pact, had fatefully miscalculated Hitler's demoniacal vision. Now he convinced Stalin that Zhdanov was responsible for Marshal Tito's successful rebellion against the Kremlin, the first crack in the Soviet power bloc, for which Tito has not been forgiven to this day. What happened at the Kremlin in July and August 1948 can only be guessed. The death of Andrei A. Zhdanov was announced on August 31, 1948. He was said to have died "of medical malpractice." He may have been poisoned. Alexander Poskrebyshev, Stalin's powerful cabinet head, admitted before his death that poison had been used in various cases during the purges in the 1940s.

After Zhdanov's death, many men were purged who had been with him in Leningrad during the siege: his former deputy Kuznetsov; Mayor Peter Popkov; Nikolai A. Voznesensky, chief of the state planning commission, and his brother, the rector of Leningrad University; the Party secretaries and the managers of the big Leningrad plants; and others who had been associated at some time with Zhdanov. Marshal Georgi Zhukov was demoted to an unimportant command in Odessa. Alexei Kosygin, in charge of the successful evacuation of hundreds of thousands of Leningraders, was not certain for months whether he would get that summons to the Kremlin.

One day in 1949 the Museum of the Defense of Leningrad was closed and its director, Major Rakov, disappeared. Many exhibits and documents concerning the siege were taken to the archives of the Secret Police and the Ministry of Defense. (Major Rakov turned up after the death of Stalin; he had spent several years in a concentration camp.) A new museum was opened in 1957, but it was much smaller.

Only after the death of Zhdanov did the pattern of "the Leningrad Affair" emerge more clearly. The aim of the thorough campaign was to eradicate the memory of the epic of Leningrad.

Beria and Malenkov went to absurd lengths. All records, statistics, documents concerning the siege disappeared. No volume of Zhdanov's wartime speeches exists. The wartime files of *Leningradskaya Pravda* are "not publicly accessible." Works dealing with the achievements of Leningrad's scientists during the siege were not published. Every effort was made, no matter how unimportant, to make people forget the siege of Leningrad. The official documents of the Council of the Defense of Leningrad were removed to the archives of the Ministry of Defense in Moscow. There they remain hidden, not available to historians. Leningrad was to become a noncity populated by unpersons.

Bizarre charges were made. The Council for the Defense of Leningrad was accused of a plot "to deliver the city to the Germans." The Leningrad leaders had planned "high treason." The "conspirators" had tried "to set up a new regime with the help of foreign agents." The accusations revived the Florentine aspects of the court of St. Petersburg, where everything imaginable had happened since the days of Peter the Great. Hundreds, and perhaps thousands, of people disappeared who had been prominent during the siege. "Nothing in the chamber of Stalin's horrors equaled the Leningrad blockade and its epilogue, the Leningrad Affair," Harrison Salisbury concludes.

But the truth remains alive at Leningrad's Piskarevsky Memorial Cemetery, located in the Vyborg district, an enormous, wide green lawn with some trees and many small marble plates in the ground. Symbolic gravestones, each a reminder of many thousands of dead. On one side are stones for the civilian population; on the other, stones adorned with small hammer-and-sickle emblems for the soldiers who died defending the city. No one can tell how many people are buried in this vast mass grave. No death notices were made and no archives kept during the first winter of the siege. No one in Leningrad believes the "official" number of dead—632,253—published by the Stalin regime at the end of the war. An overall total of deaths, civilian and military, on the order of 1,300,000 to 1,500,000 seems reasonable. More people died in Leningrad than in any other city in modern times during a war.

At the far end of the lawn a stone platform was raised for the eternal flame, with the words of Olga Berggolts etched on the marble wall, next to the flame:

Here lie the people of Leningrad,
Here are the citizens—men, women, and children—
And beside them the soldiers of the Red Army
Who gave their lives
Defending you, Leningrad,
Cradle of Revolution.
We cannot number the noble
Ones who lie beneath the eternal granite.
But of those honored by this stone
Let no one forget, let nothing be forgotten.

In the small memorial hall to the right of the entrance into Piskarevsky Cemetery, a few pages from a child's diary are exhibited. (They are copies; the original is in the Leningrad Museum of History.) There is a short entry on each page, written by an eleven-year-old schoolgirl. Tanya Savicheva lived with her family in No. 13, Second Line, Vasilevsky Island. Some entries:

Zhenya died 28 December, 12:30 in the morning, 1941.

Babushka died 25 January, 3 o'clock, 1942.

Leka died 17 March, 5 o'clock in the morning, 1942.

Dedya Vasya died 13 April, 2 o'clock at night, 1942.

Dedya Lesha died 10 May, 4 in the afternoon, 1942.

Mama, 13 May, 7:30 in the morning, 1942.

Savichevs died. All died. Only Tanya remains.

Tanya Savicheva was younger than Anne Frank, and not much of a stylist, but the analogy is obvious. A photograph shows Tanya, looking much older than her age, with big, sad eyes. Almost every day schoolchildren from all over the country are taken through the memorial hall, looking at Tanya's picture, reading her diary pages. I noticed a small boy, perhaps Tanya's age, meticulously copying her lines into his small notebook.

It was assumed that Tanya had died herself sometime after making her last entry. Later it became known that after her mother's death, in the spring of 1942, she had been evacuated to a children's home in Shakhty, a village in the Gorky area. But it was too late to save her. She was suffering from chronic dysentery and died after much pain in the summer of 1943. She was twelve years old. An older sister who returned to the apartment after the siege found Tanya's diary in a box with her mother's wedding dress.

The walls of the memorial hall are covered with enlarged photographs. Following them clockwise one gets a short chronological pictorial review of the siege. First, the early attacks by German dive bombers. Evacuees at a railroad station. Bodies of air-raid victims in a snow-covered street. A German shell hitting a building. Fires, incendiary bombs, destruction. A streetcar immobilized in a high snowdrift, like an icebreaker stuck in the Arctic Seas. An old woman, her face half covered behind a woolen headkerchief, desolately pulling a child's sled with a corpse on it. Another woman pulling a sled with a man sitting on it who is too weak to walk. Dead bodies piled up outside Okhta Cemetery. A corpse leaning in a sitting position against the fence of the Summer Garden, where Pushkin loved to walk. The man sat down there and never got up. The ice road across Lake Ladoga, the first ray of hope. Soviet soldiers in front of a conquered gun emplacement. The Soviets at the entrance of liberated, destroyed Petrodvorets (Peterhof) Palace, which Peter the Great had wanted to make his Versailles. The last photograph shows groups of German prisoners of war on Nevsky Prospekt, escorted by two Russian soldiers.

On January 27, 1944, Vera Inber, writer and diarist, wrote, "The greatest event in the life of Leningrad: liberation from the blockade. And I, a professional writer, have no words for it. I simply say: Leningrad is free. That is all."

THE GLORY OF THE
HERMITAGE

The Winter Palace—the present version is the fifth and probably the last—was designed in 1754 by Francesco Rastrelli. It had nothing in common with the original Winter Palace, small, almost primitive, made of wood, which Peter the Great had ordered built in 1711. The original palace was replaced after five years by Georg Matternovy's larger version, which was later renovated by Domenico Trezzini. Subsequent rulers kept changing and adding. When Rastrelli got his orders, and unlimited funds, from the extravagant Empress Elizabeth, he had the whole thing torn down and started all over again in his exuberant, eccentric style.

The temptation was terrific and Rastrelli decided to make the most of it. A Florentine, educated in Paris at the time of Louis XIV, he had traveled all over Europe. In St. Petersburg he began with minor projects, the interiors of the Shafirov and Cantemir palaces. His penchant for baroque extravagance soon became obvious. Trying to be more Russian than the Russians, he created the St. Petersburg baroque style, using French rococo elements and Italian ornaments, and giving his façades a specifically Russian look by installing rounded domes, giant caryatides, and a profusion of statues along the roof line. But the baroque is dangerous in the hands of an undisciplined artist. In Vienna, Fischer von Erlach and Lucas von Hildebrandt showed both magnificent imagination and impeccable taste in their masterpieces, Erlach's Charles Church and Hildebrandt's Upper Belvedere for Prince

Eugene of Savoy. In St. Petersburg, Rastrelli happily sacrificed taste and proportion for pomp and magnificence. He is mostly remembered for the Winter Palace and for the Great Palace (Ekaterininsky) in Tsarskoye Selo, when he went all out for colossal effect, but he created *beautiful* buildings when he didn't have too much money. He was not too successful when he finished the half-built Anichkov Palace at the corner of Nevsky Prospekt and Fontanka, which Elizabeth gave to Alexis Rasumovsky. But he created two fine buildings on the Nevsky, the Vorontsov Palace in the Anichkov Garden, and the beautiful Stroganov Palace, with a green and white façade along the Moika. Perhaps his finest work is the lovely five-domed Smolny Cathedral, a symphony in china-blue and white, crowned by silvery cupolas. It was his baroque version of the old Russian churches in Moscow. He had planned a high bell tower above the main entrance but it was not constructed; the model is preserved at the Academy of Arts. Rastrelli had a great sense of color; much of the light blue, light green, pink, and red shades of the St. Petersburg palaces was created by him.

But he lost all self-control when he decided to build an enormous Italianate palace along the Neva, under the cool, northern sky of St. Petersburg. It took eight years to finish the Winter Palace with its two façades—toward the river and toward Palace Square—and the eastern wing facing the Admiralty. There is a profusion of high reliefs in white and charcoal, and along the roof line are ornamental vases and more than 150 statues. The façades are painted apple-green and white. Everything about the Winter Palace is extraordinary. It is over a 150 yards long and covers an area of two million square feet. It has 1,050 rooms and 117 staircases, 1,786 doors and 1,945 windows. Inside there are huge galleries and large pillars of malachite. Occasionally there is also great beauty—the staircase of Carrara marble leading to the czar's apartments, or Rastrelli's Jordan doorway, used by the czars at the Epiphany. The exuberance surpasses everything built in the Western world.

In 1765, three years after Catherine II came to power, she ordered the French architect Vallin de La Mothe to build a two-story pavilion next to the immense palace. Her admirers claim that she felt lost and lonely in Rastrelli's extravagant interiors and wanted a more intimate residence. Her detractors state that she considered the palace too small for her sumptuous festivities. Both are right. Catherine called the new building the Small Hermitage, taking the name from Jean-Jacques Rousseau's predilection for hermitages. The Empress admired the Swiss philosopher who preached the simple life. At the Small Hermitage she hung her fast-growing collection of great paintings.

In 1775 she commissioned the Russian architect Y. Feldten, director of the Imperial Academy, to enlarge the pavilion by adding two more wings, later known as the Old and the New Hermitage. And in 1784 Giacomo Quarenghi of Bergamo was ordered to add the Loggia, to shelter the copies of the decorations that Bramante had created for the *Loggie* of the Vatican and which Raphael had later re-created for Pope Leo X. Catherine's agent in Rome, Reiffenstein, who was director of the Russian Academy, had had copies made of the fifty-two frescoes made by Raphael and his pupils. It took eight years to do the copies on canvas; they were finished in 1785. Three years later Quarenghi's gallery was finished and today students of Raphael's murals go to Leningrad rather than Italy to see the well preserved *Loggie.* Quarenghi also built a small, elegant theater in pink and white for intimate court entertainment. It had an auditorium for five hundred people and was connected by a covered bridge to the main building.

In 1837 Rastrelli's Winter Palace was completely burned out. Nothing remained but the walls and Rastrelli's beautiful Ambassadors' Staircase. But his spirit lives on. Within one year after the catastrophe, everything had been redone exactly as it was—the marble pillars, the malachite walls, the painted ceilings, the inlaid wooden floors. The Marquis de Custine, attending the ball in 1839 that was given for the reopening of the palace, wrote:

It was magical. The admiration and astonishment which struck the whole court at the renewal of the palace within a single year lent a dramatic interest to the chilly solemnities of ordinary formality. . . . What a stroke of will, I thought. The style of the ornaments recalled, although made yesterday. What I saw seemed already antique. . . . Everything was colossal, innumerable. A thousand people were seated at table in one room.

The following year Czar Nicholas I ordered a complete enlargement, done by Leo von Klenze, the German architect who designed the Pinakothek and the Glyptothek in Munich, and the Russian court architect A. I. Stakenschneider. The neoclassical façade of the Hermitage—a portico supported by eight pillars, against which rest ten atlantes of dark-gray Finnish granite—was finished in 1852.

Until 1922 the art works were shown in the fifty-six halls of the Hermitage pavilions. Only after the end of the Second World War did the Leningrad City Council decide to put the entire Winter Palace at the disposal of the Hermitage authorities. Now over two and a half million objects are shown on more than fifty thousand square meters of walls in 374 halls. There are over fourteen miles of halls and galleries. Some visitors collapse; two doctors are always on duty, giving first aid.

But the glory of the Hermitage is not due to its size or scope, from the prehistoric to this day, nor to the high percentage of great masterpieces, the comprehensive collections—Spanish, seventeenth-century Dutch, Flemish, the various French schools. The great charm is the display of beautiful art as an organic part of the Winter Palace's interiors. It is not so much a museum as an extravagant palace with wonderful chandeliers, mirrors, painted ceilings, malachite, and Carrara marble, and great paintings, sculptures, gold, and china. The Neva, viewed through the high windows, becomes part of the ensemble. Rastrelli's brilliant idea was faithfully preserved. The visitor feels like a guest in a truly imperial home.

Most of the three million visitors every year are Russians who experience a strong sense of continuity with history. The most popular exhibits are not the Leonardos or Rembrandts but the rooms displaying "the heroic past of the Russian people." There one sees old peasants and elderly women wearing headkerchiefs who grew up in Czarist Russia and can hardly believe that they are walking through the palace of the Czars, the vast gold and bronze throne room with the twenty-seven-square-meter map of Russia made of semiprecious stones, the cities and rivers indicated by rubies and emeralds. They barely dare walk through the more intimate, velvet-hung throne room of Peter the Great.

The Czar is very much present at the Hermitage, spiritually and in effigy—his figure, dressed in silk; his books and carpentry tools; standards of his regiments; military paintings of his victories.

Peter's interest in the arts was limited to certain artists. Memling (he tried to get the *Last Judgment* from Danzig's Marienkirche), Rembrandt (he ordered the purchase of *David's Farewell to Jonathan*), Rubens, Van Dyck, Pieter Brueghel. He liked seascapes because he loved ships. What he enjoyed best though were idealized portraits of himself and pictorial glorifications of his achievements—not the most promising attitude for building a great collection. But after gold objects were found in Siberian tombs, he ordered that they be preserved. He sensed the importance of antiquities going back to the Scythians in the sixth century B.C., and they now belong to the glories of the Hermitage.

Catherine II found her way to the arts through her interest in reading. "The Empress is never without the works of Voltaire, the *De l'Esprit* of Helvetius, the writings of the Encyclopedists and of Jean-Jacques Rousseau," wrote the Chevalier d'Éon. She made her first important purchase, 225 paintings from the Berlin art dealer Johann Gotskowski, because she'd heard that Frederick the Great wanted them. Now she had some fine Rembrandts, *Potiphar's Wife* and *The Incredulity of St. Thomas*, Frans Hals's beautiful *Man with a Glove*, and other Dutch and Flemish masterpieces. Not bad for a start, especially since the Empress had no idea what she was buying. She made all her purchases sight unseen, relying on her advisors' judgment. Her ambassadors in Western Europe kept her informed of important sales. Word circulated in Paris that Denis Diderot, the formidable editor of the *Encyclopédie*, the most important literary document of the era, was looking for someone to buy his manuscripts and his library. Diderot needed money to finish his work, which took twenty-five years to complete, and he liked women, food, and good wines. Catherine appointed Diderot "librarian of his own books" and at once paid him his salary for the next fifty years—truly an imperial advance payment, though perhaps not strictly ethical. The Empress was now accepted as a "serious" art patron by Diderot and his friends, the Paris *philosophes*. They became her most valuable sources of information.

In 1766, Catherine II was thirty-seven. She had been Empress for four years and she had tasted the sweet uses of power. She consciously fashioned her regime after that of Peter the Great, who remained her ideal. Peter never had much use for ministers and bureaucrats and relied on his intimates, Lefort and especially Menshikov. Catherine too had her favorites who worked hard, in her bedroom and elsewhere. She read every line Peter had written. The former German princess believed she could learn the secret from the great Romanov of how to rule the Russian empire in Russian style. She hoped that to posterity she would measure up to Peter. No one among her intimates was surprised when she decided to order a statue of Peter the Great. She asked Prince Dmitri A. Galitzin, her ambassador to France, to find a good sculptor and said she would spend 300,000 livres on the project. Galitzin suggested a few candidates but all wanted more money. Augustin Pajou asked twice as much as Catherine was willing to pay. Then Diderot wrote that Étienne Falconet might accept the commission if his conditions were met. Falconet stated them explicitly in a letter to General Betzky, the director of public buildings. The Senate would be responsible for supplying all materials. Falconet demanded "total and indispensable freedom which I need to work; no impediment or constraint other than taste and propriety . . . an annual salary of twenty-five thousand livres for eight years. This sum, together with what I have been able to make in France, will be enough to guarantee me a decent and peaceful old age. . . ."

Catherine was pleased; the statue would cost much less than she'd expected. Actually it cost more because Falconet needed twelve years to do it. He began by ordering an enormous block of Finnish marble from Karelia, three hundred miles away from St. Petersburg. The block was brought there by the basically simple though somewhat laborious method of putting wooden logs underneath. Log was placed after log, every few inches another one. It took four long years to transport the block. The statue in Decembrists' Square shows Peter astride a wild horse trampling a snake, with the granite block underneath forming a wave. The Czar wears a long Russian coat, which his boyars, ironically, were not permitted to wear; and he doesn't face exactly toward the west, as one might expect. Peter's head was finished by Marie

Collot, Falconet's niece and pupil. The great sculptor was not present when the statue was installed in 1782. He had left St. Petersburg after a fight with the Czarina. The inscription, in Latin and Russian, says, "To Peter the First, Catherine the Second." The Empress was a success in her own way but she still liked to be compared to Peter.

In Paris, Prince Galitzin managed to buy a very great Rembrandt, *The Return of the Prodigal Son,* from a collector who remained anonymous. (Some eighteenth-century collectors, not unlike some today, didn't mind making a quick profit provided they remained unknown.) When Galitzin was transferred to The Hague, Diderot carried on in Paris. In 1768 he informed the Empress of the collection of the late Gaignat who had been secretary to Louis XV. With customary arrogance Diderot reported that Gaignat "had collected some fine works of literature almost without knowing how to read, and some great works of art without being able to see more in them than a blind man." Unfortunately another collector, the Duc de Choiseul, had the inside track. Diderot managed to get only four pictures, but one of them was a fine Murillo.

The transaction worried Diderot a great deal because it often took a long time to get the money from St. Petersburg to Paris. It was also difficult to get letters through to Catherine. There were spies who read his letters and probably reported the content to other royal collectors. Diderot began writing his letters to Falconet, who passed them on to the Czarina, often adding his own advice. "After all," he wrote once, "I know something about painting. It is practically my profession." Catherine, on the other hand, admitted to Falconet that she "didn't understand enough" about the pictures. Not many rich collectors will make such an admission. But Diderot and the *philosophes* appreciated her frankness. She was an empress and incredibly rich but she was no snob. That understood, they got on well with her: *they* understood a lot about art but they were not rich. It was the old story of the wealthy art patron and the impecunious artist. Catherine could afford to be humble because she was so powerful. She had her own museum, her own theater, her opera and ballet companies, her own chamber orchestra.

The year 1769 was a vintage year for Catherine. The war

against the Turks was going well, and she was becoming deeply interested in Gregory Potemkin, though Gregory Orlov was still the official favorite. Potemkin was serving as an aide to General Rumyantsev, the Russian commander, but at the end of the war Catherine said that Potemkin "has done more than anyone else to end the Turkish war." On the battlefield of collecting she won a major victory in Dresden, where she managed to get the magnificent collection created by the late Count von Brühl, minister of foreign affairs to Augustus II, King of Poland and Elector of Saxony. Brühl had helped his sovereign to create the great collection that was the nucleus of the world-famous Dresden Gallery at the Zwinger; at the same time he created a nice little collection for himself—four Rembrandts, among them the wonderful study of the *Old Man in Red,* and *Portrait of a Learned Man;* four beautiful Ruisdael landscapes; five Rubenses, including two of the master's greatest works, *Landscape with a Rainbow,* which has been called "a universe rather than a landscape," and the exciting *Perseus and Andromeda,* a masterpiece for which the lucky Brühl had paid exactly sixty-three florins.

The lucky Catherine also got one of the greatest paintings by Guido Reni, *Building of Noah's Ark,* and Nicolas Poussin's inspired masterpiece *The Deposition.* There were five Ostades and several paintings by Bellotto and Watteau. Brühl had been catholic in his tastes and so was Catherine. She had no special favorites; she had an instinct for beauty, in paintings and in men, though it wasn't always external beauty.

She would have liked to collect living painters as well as their paintings. Bellotto had been court painter in Dresden and Vienna; she made him a generous offer to come to St. Petersburg, where he might find as much inspiration as in Venice. Bellotto turned her down and went to paint Warsaw, as court painter to Stanislas II. Catherine regretted his decision. She knew that Bellotto would have seen and immortalized much of the deeper beauty of St. Petersburg that remains hidden to ordinary mortals.

She had some happy moments when the Brühl collection arrived at the Hermitage. The crates were opened and the Czarina looked at the beautiful paintings which were hers and which she had never seen before. "Only the mice and I admire all this," she said, in a furtive moment of self-reproach. Only her intimates, among them Falconet, were permitted to see the paintings. She received them in the Hermitage on Thursday evening; there was no etiquette on such occasions. A few tables were set up, the guests were told to "sit down where you choose and when you please," and there were no servants present. That was the smart thing to do because the members of her nobility had so many servants they couldn't tell the exact number. (Catherine had hundreds of servants at the Winter Palace, but it thrilled her to fill a plate with delicacies for her lover of the moment. Again she followed in the footsteps of the admired Peter the Great, who amused himself playing the part of "servant" to his friend Lefort.)

Prince Galitzin, now the Russian ambassador at The Hague, helped the French *philosophes* to have their works printed there, and thus kept in touch with the goings-on in the art market. He was always trying to find something special for his empress, and like the late Count Brühl, he collected also for himself. In 1768 he attended the sale of the Coblentz collection in Brussels. Count Coblentz had been the Austrian minister there. Galitzin bought forty-six paintings for Catherine, including five Rubenses and Gerard Dou's fine *La Dévideuse*. He also bought almost six thousand drawings, some by Rembrandt and Rubens. These, with the many drawings in the Brühl collection, gave Catherine one of the finest collections anywhere.

In 1770 Diderot, now almost a full-time art dealer, decided that Catherine must get the great Crozat collection. Pierre Crozat, called "Crozat the poor," had been treasurer of France and assembled a magnificent collection of paintings, prints, drawings, sculpture. (His brother, the "rich" Crozat, had made an even larger fortune from the Louisiana monopoly.) The Crozat collection was said to be terrific: two Raphaels, a Tintoretto, a Guido Reni, four Veroneses, more than a dozen Rubenses, seven Van Dycks, and eight Rembrandts, including the very great *Danaë*, the beautiful nude—a rarity in Rembrandt's paintings—that had caused a scandal among the Puritans of Amsterdam. Another Rembrandt masterpiece was *The Holy Family*. The collection also included several paintings by Watteau, Claude Lorrain, Sébastien Bourdon.

The collection would be expensive and Catherine had some second thoughts. She sent Falconet to Paris. He reported that the Guido Reni (*Virgin*) looked dubious to him, and he was doubtful about some other paintings, admitting that he was not certain but acting "in all good faith." Catherine didn't mind. She had learned that an absentee collector cannot always be right; a certain percentage of failures had to be accepted. She wrote to Falconet, "In order to deal properly with the fine arts one must have fewer interruptions than We have had here in the last weeks." She was referring to the war in Turkey and to the negotiations with Prussia and Austria which in 1772 led to the partition of Poland, and increased Catherine's empire by thirty-six thousand square miles.

Early in 1772 Diderot concluded the big deal: over four hundred pictures for 460,000 livres. (A few months later, the smaller, much less important collection of the Duc de Choiseul was sold for almost the same amount.) Many people in Paris were upset about a sale that would deprive France of such great art treasures. Diderot admitted that "the collectors, the artists, and the rich are all up in arms" but declared that he was "taking absolutely no notice." Always believing that attack was the best defense, he said, "It is just too bad for France if we must sell pictures in time of peace while Catherine buys them in the middle of a war."

The crates were shipped by sea. The voyage took almost half a year and Catherine was getting worried; even an empress cannot lose half a million livres too often, and she hadn't forgotten that two years before a boat with a smaller collection had been lost. The worst part of it was that she wasn't even sure what to expect: Diderot had not bothered to send her a list of the paintings. Absentee collecting was a noble and fascinating game, especially when played against the kings of Poland, Sweden, and Prussia.

At last the ship arrived at the docks of St. Petersburg, very close to the Hermitage, and Catherine and her mice had a wonderful time admiring Diderot's acquisitions. They included Raphael's *Virgin and Child with St. Joseph*, the *Pietà* by Paolo Veronese, Tintoretto's *Birth of St. John the Baptist*, Cima da Conegliano's *Annunciation* and Pellergrino Tibaldi's *Holy Family with St. Elizabeth*. There was *Judith*, believed to be a Raphael, later recognized as a Giorgione. Among the Rembrandts there were the beautiful *Portrait of an Old Man* and *The Parable of the Laborers in the Vineyard*. And a few months later, at the sale of the Duc de Choiseul collection, Diderot managed to get Murillo's *Boy with a Dog*, Gerard Dou's *Doctor*, Rubens's *Portrait of Suzanne Fourment*, Jan Steen's *Sick Old Man*, and other fine works of the Flemish and Spanish schools. Diderot paid only 108,000 livres for the paintings.

Catherine, not always given to gratitude, decided to invite her honorary art dealer to St. Petersburg. She also ordered a catalogue of her paintings drawn up in manuscript, for her gratification only. She wrote to Diderot that it was time he saw how the paintings he'd bought for her were hung. (They were close to each other on the high walls of the Hermitage, from floor to ceiling.) Diderot arrived in October 1773 and stayed almost half a year at the Myatlev Palace. Falconet, afraid of Diderot, a difficult house guest, said he had no place to put him up although the sculptor owed his job and his house to Diderot. The *philosophe* had many private talks with Catherine; they were truly encyclopedic and far-ranging, on the arts, literature, music, government, education. Gradually the relationship changed, from a formal one between the very rich art patron and the philosopher making a little money as her dealer and agent, to mutual respect, perhaps almost to friendship. The Empress asked Diderot to help her set up a university in St. Petersburg, and there was talk about putting out a Russian edition of the Encyclopedia, but Diderot was tired and getting homesick for Paris. He left early in March 1774, after Catherine had asked him not to say good-bye. "Saying good-bye is always too sad."

Diderot's success as a part-time art dealer had long irritated the professionals in London, Rome, and The Hague. Catherine was informed in advance of all important sales, and received many offers. She had established herself as a serious buyer, and her credit rating was excellent. She had at last attained her aim— to bring the great collections from Western Europe to St. Petersburg. With the genuine collector's instinct she now began to concentrate on the Netherlands. In 1778 she tried to get the collection of Govert van Slingelandt, described to her as very important, but she lost out against a Dutchman, Stadholder

William V, who guaranteed to the heirs that the collection would remain in Holland. Opposition was growing in Europe against the sale of "the national heritage" to a foreign sovereign. It was conveniently overlooked that many collections had been formed by removing considerable national heritage from Italy and Spain.

Having failed to get the admired Voltaire to St. Petersburg while he was alive, the amazing Catherine after his death in 1778 tried to have his remains shipped there, promising the heirs to build a grandiose mausoleum for the great man. When this didn't work out either, she tried to get his library, seven thousand books. Her new agent was Baron Friedrich Melchior von Grimm, a Frenchified German, editor of the excellent *Correspondance littéraire*. Grimm persuaded Mme. Denis, Voltaire's heir, to sell her uncle's literary estate for the sum of 135,398 livres, 4 sous, and 6 deniers. Grimm had instructions to make sure that the sale included all letters that the Czarina had written to "the great man." In return, Catherine added her portrait in a diamond-decorated gold box, and a personal note. "To Madame Denis, niece of a great man who loved me." The transaction was considered a national disgrace in France, and Mme. Denis was bitterly condemned. The French ambassador in St. Petersburg was asked to prevent the sale "in a discreet manner." Catherine was very pleased and ignored all protest. Voltaire's books are still in Leningrad, and Voltaire students must go there for research.

Catherine was becoming interested only in difficult coups. Easy deals meant nothing to her any more. She could be tough, even stingy, with professional art dealers who had made the mistake of bringing their paintings to St. Petersburg. She loved to buy pictures blindfolded, so to speak; it was more exciting and more feminine. Once she wasn't ashamed to haggle with Pierre-Étienne Falconet, the son of the sculptor, who had been commissioned to paint her, her son the Grand Duke Paul, and his wife Natalia, because the price of the paintings seemed "exorbitant."

After the near-crisis in France, Catherine caused a national crisis in England when her ambassador, Count Mussin-Pushkin, succeeded in buying the extraordinary collection that Sir Robert Walpole, the prime minister under George I and George II, had put together. Sir Robert had had taste and money, the prime requisites of the great collector. London was shocked; Dr. Johnson led a public uproar. Catherine was delighted with the scandal and informed Grimm that she had her claws on the Walpole paintings, and would "no more let them go than a cat would a mouse." The Walpole collection went to Russia—198 paintings. Several Rubenses, including *Landscape with a Broken-down Cart*, Rembrandt's fantastic *Abraham's Sacrifice of Isaac*," the *Family Group* by Jacob Jordaens, and fifteen Van Dycks, including the portraits of Lord Philip Wharton and Sir Thomas Wharton. French paintings—Bourdon, Claude Lorrain, Gaspard Dughet, Poussin—and from Italy a Guido Reni, an Albani, two Luca Giordanos, four Salvator Rosas, a Bonifazio di Pitati.

Next came the collection of the Comte de Baudouin, which Grimm called one of the best in Paris—119 paintings. It included eight Rembrandts—among them *Girl Trying On an Earring, Portrait of Jeremias Decker*, and *Portrait of an Old Man,*—which alone are worth a special journey to Leningrad. Also ten Van Dycks, five Ostades, and works by Rubens, Ruisdael, Jordaens, Teniers, Dou, Brouwer, Heyden. Grimm had been right but Catherine hesitated because Baudouin had left it to Her Majesty to decide conditions. Catherine waited four years and then she wrote that Baudouin "is not going to be happy unless he sells his collection. It seems that I am destined to make him happy." She and fifty thousand rubles, which was truly a bargain.

By that time Catherine was becoming difficult and choosing more carefully. She was also thinking of money. Toward the end of her regime, after the long, expensive wars against Turkey, the annual budget of Russia was eighty million rubles while revenue from taxes was only twenty million. Yet when she really wanted something, money meant nothing to the Czarina. She spent over half a million a year on her favorites. She financed the deficit by having more paper rubles printed and by announcing public loans which amounted to over 300 million rubles. It all sounds familiar; and since no one dared lose confidence in her, the Russian obligations were bought up in Russia and elsewhere. With the Czarina on the throne, the investment seemed secure. Thus she was able to build up one of the greatest collections ever assembled, and all this achieved in less than thirty years.

Toward the end of her regime Catherine became more liberal about allowing other people to see her treasures, though it was still necessary to get permission from General Betzky. Permission was often given to distinguished foreign visitors, who had to be accompanied by a curator, and to students of the Academy of Fine Arts. They would visit both the Little Hermitage and the Old Hermitage and also Quarenghi's gallery with the copies of Raphael's *Loggie*. A catalogue done after Catherine's death in 1796 by Labensky, the curator of paintings, showed a grand total of 3,926 paintings, enough to make other monarchs green with envy.

Catherine inspired generations of wealthy Russian collectors. Some members of the Russian nobility were immensely rich and had enormous incomes. Sheremetiev was said to have forty thousand serfs; Bezborodko had thirty thousand. Catherine rewarded her nobles and especially her personal favorites and official lovers with enormous gifts of land, money, and serfs. She is believed to have given over 800,000 peasants, men and women, to private owners. There were half a million nobles in Russia (the total population was below thirty million) and they were entitled to own both the land and the serfs living on the land. According to the Table of Ranks set up by Peter the Great, any man could join the army, the civil administration, or service at the court and might eventually attain nobility, own land and people, and be exempted from capitation taxes. Noblemen were not born, as in Western Europe, but made. Many served in St. Petersburg and Moscow and stayed away from their estates for years, a practice which often alienated their serfs and later became a serious social problem.

The Russian noblemen employed at least six times as many personal servants as the aristocrats in Western Europe, and paid them no wages. Servants were fed, but the sort of food they got was not expensive. "The number of servants is dreadful," wrote Martha Wilmot. "Think of two, three, or four hundred servants to attend a small family; a Russian lady scorns her two feet to go upstairs; two powdered footmen support her lily-white elbows and nearly lift her from the ground." Prince Yusupov had a private theater at his palace, and his own theater and ballet companies; all members were servants (and serfs). Prince Kropotkin had a private symphony orchestra of a hundred serfs. His second butler doubled as a flutist, and a footman was one of the trombone players.

A nobleman's wealth depended upon the number of serfs he owned. In 1772 thirty-two per cent of them owned fewer than ten serfs each and lived in near poverty. But the Galitzins, Stroganovs, Shuvalovs, Demidovs, Bieloselskys were rich and gradually turned their houses into private museums. In St. Petersburg, as earlier in London and Paris, members of the nobility were the most prominent collectors (later they were joined by the wealthy bourgeois). The aristocrats followed the example of the Czarina, filling their St. Petersburg palaces and Paris residences with art treasures; their descendants continued the tradition. Prices were going up continuously, and the great collections became formidable investments. But many collectors truly loved and understood art. Under Catherine's guidance, Potemkin became something of an art expert. Alexander Lanskoy, one of her young lovers (who was, incidentally, selected by Potemkin when he went off to another war against the Turks) did so well as an art collector that Catherine said "he had improved himself."

Catherine's son and successor, Czar Paul I, contributed nothing to the Hermitage, his mother's creation. He turned the Winter Palace into army barracks and had some beautiful paintings taken from the Hermitage to his own palaces in Pavlovsk and Gachina. Alexander I wisely left Curator Labensky in charge. His tutor, La Harpe, who had been educated in Paris, taught young Alexander much about the arts there. (Later the Czar would send gifted Russian students to the École des Beaux Arts in Paris.)

In Rome Labensky acquired Caravaggio's *Lute Player* from the Giustiniani collection, and Spada's *Crucifixion of the Apostle Peter*. Vivant Denan, a diplomat and art connoisseur, worked with Labensky to find art treasures for the Hermitage, among them Pieter de Hooch's delightful *Woman with Her Servant* and Murillo's *Jacob's Ladder* and *Isaac Blessing Jacob*. In 1815 the Hermitage acquired from Malmaison several paintings which Napoleon had given to Josephine. Among them were four of Claude Lorrain's most beautiful landscapes, fine paintings by Paulus Potter, Jan van der Heyden, and David Teniers, and a Rembrandt.

These had been looted by Napoleon's envoys from the collection of the Landgrave of Hesse-Cassel. Czar Alexander knew the paintings had been stolen but that didn't bother him. This form of art collecting has remained popular with powerful men from Napoleon to Hitler. Alexander also made some legitimate purchases from the Dutch banker Coesvelt, fifteen works of the Spanish school, among them Velasquez's *Portrait of Count Olivares,* three Murillos, and Francisco de Zurbarán's wonderfully moving *Virgin Mary as a Child.* He was lucky again when his court physician, Craighton, discovered the masterpiece *Virgin and Child,* now attributed to Giorgione.

The next Romanov, Czar Nicholas I, remains, after Catherine II, the most important imperial patron of the Hermitage, though he didn't have the Empress's taste; he had, for instance, a weakness for paintings of battle scenes (as, much later, did Kaiser Wilhelm II of Germany). Nicholas thought the Hermitage had too many works of the Dutch and Flemish schools and not enough of the Italian and Spanish schools. He refused, however, to buy several Goyas from the collection of Manuel de Godoy, minister of Charles IV of Spain; he didn't like Goya. He approved the purchase of five Titians, among them the tragically beautiful *Mary Magdalene* and *Virgin and Child,* and a fine *Madonna* by Palma Vecchio. In 1845 the Hermitage had another stroke of luck when the Russian ambassador in Vienna, Tatichev, bequeathed his small, exquisite collection to the Czar. It contained a *Madonna by the Fireside* by the mysterious fourteenth-century Master of Flemalle, a *Madonna* by Morales, and the van Eyck diptych *The Crucifixion and Last Judgment* (now in the Metropolitan Museum in New York).

After the Winter Palace burned down in 1837 and was quickly rebuilt and restored, Nicholas decided to make the Hermitage a public museum. In 1849 a new catalogue was compiled for the Czar by the curators, who divided the more than 4,500 paintings into several categories: 815 would be exhibited, many remained in the reserves, and some 560 were classified as of minor interest. On February 5, 1852, the Hermitage opened its doors to the public—the magnificent Siberian antiquities on the ground floor, the various schools of painting on the second. The Czar was the last monarch to share his treasures with the people. The Uffizi in

Florence had become public in 1737; Vienna's Belvedere Museum in 1781; the Louvre after the French Revolution in 1793; Amsterdam's Rijksmuseum in 1808.

The curators were worried about lack of space and whether they had really selected the most important works. The following year Nicholas took a step that is now much regretted at the Hermitage because, as it turned out later, it created a dangerous precedent: he decided to sell 1,219 paintings from the 4,552 in the imperial collections. It was explained that there had been "changes in taste." The curators had deliberated long and carefully, but they still made mistakes, selling Lucas van Leyden's triptych *The Healing of the Blind Man of Jericho* and Jean Baptiste Chardin's beautiful *Attributes of the Arts,* which, fortunately, remained in St. Petersburg and was brought back to the Hermitage after the Revolution. The sale remains known as a disaster at the Hermitage, and they don't like to discuss it.

Alexander II left the management of the great museum to the curators. The Hermitage had become a big, important institution with its own management and policies. A new catalogue was published, and the pictures were hung, not to provide pleasure for the visitors but according to the various schools and the importance of the paintings. The curators decided about purchases. One of them, Gheneonov, remains unforgotten in the annals of the museum. In 1866 he bought from the Duke of Litta in Milan, for 100,000 francs, Leonardo da Vinci's beautiful *Madonna Litta,* which is now considered the most important painting at the Hermitage. (People standing in front of the painting are photographed by a camera secretly installed in the wall. The management doesn't want to take any chances; it remembers what happened to da Vinci's *Mona Lisa* at the Louvre.) The formidable Gheneonov also purchased a small Raphael *Madonna,* an early work of the master, full of moving innocence and pure beauty, from Count Conestabile in Perugia. Empress Maria Alexandrovna loved it so much that she kept it for ten years at her private apartment before she reluctantly consented to give it to the Hermitage, where it is called the *Madonna Conestabile.*

Gheneonov's successor, Vasilchnikov, bought a magnificent Fra Angelico, *Virgin and Child with St. Dominic and St. Aquinas,* that had been done for the Convent of San Domenico in Fiesole. Vasilchnikov was an able diplomat who persuaded Czar Alexander III to permit the transfer of several masterpieces in various imperial palaces to the Hermitage. And so visitors could admire Rembrandt's *David's Farewell to Jonathan,* which had been in Monplaisir, and Tiepolo's *Maecenas Presenting the Arts to Augustus,* formerly in Gachina. The Hermitage now had priority in matters of the arts. The czars no longer "borrowed" art treasures for their palaces; on the contrary, everything beautiful was shown first to the curators of the museum. The Hermitage obtained seventy-three paintings from the fine Galitzin collection, and the curators made some important purchases, Guardi's *View of Venice* and Fragonard's lovely *Stolen Kiss,* once owned by King Stanislas Augustus of Poland.

In 1910, under Czar Nicholas II, a new policy emerged. All great Russian collections up for sale had to be offered first to the Hermitage. The Semenov collection was acquired, mostly Dutch paintings, and two years later the Stroganov collection. Baron Alexander Stroganov had once written, "Good Lord, deliver us from cold-blooded investors and uncultivated connoisseurs." After his death, part of the collection went to Rome, but much of it remained in St. Petersburg in the lovely palace on the Nevsky designed by Rastrelli. A very important acquisition was made in 1914 by Curator Benois—Leonardo da Vinci's *Benois Madonna,* a masterpiece often copied.

Between 1910 and 1932 the Hermitage doubled the number of its paintings. There had been 3,333 pictures at the museum after the sale of 1853. Less than a hundred years later, there were over eight thousand paintings (and over forty thousand drawings and half a million engravings). No other great museum ever grew so fast, but none had the benefit of the October Revolution, which was followed by the nationalization of all great private collections in Russia. Long after the death of Catherine II, her educational efforts paid off handsomely.

In September 1917 the important paintings of the Hermitage had been taken to Moscow, where they were not threatened by the Germans or, later, by the Russian revolutionaries. Many people in Moscow hoped that the country's capital would keep the country's most important art treasures. But historically the works belonged to the Hermitage, and they were returned. After all private collections had been declared property of the nation, the curators began taking inventory in Petrograd. They were overwhelmed. The Russian aristocrats had collected more and better than even the optimists at the Hermitage had thought. The curators found fine primitives from Siena and Florence, paintings by Guido Reni and Jacopo del Sellaio, and Dutch and Flemish paintings in the Stroganov collection. From the Kuchelev-Bezborodko collection the curators selected a Pieter Brueghel the Elder (*The Fair*), a Rubens (*Christ*), a Jordaens, a Teniers, paintings by Ostade, Delacroix, Decamps, Diaz, Millet, Courbet, Corot. From the Shuvalov collection came a Rubens (*Raising of the Cross*), a Jordaens (*Christ*), a portrait by Lucas Cranach the Elder. The Nikolai Yusupov collection contained beautiful French nineteenth-century masterpieces (which the czars hadn't permitted the Hermitage to purchase), two Teniers, Lorenzo Lotto's *Portrait,* and some Dutch masters.

At the Durnovo Palace the curators found El Greco's terrifying *St. Peter and St. Paul,* (the only El Greco at the Hermitage); at the Dolgoruky Palace there was Hendrik Terbrugghen's fine *Concert;* at the Naryshkin Palace they found works by Casanova, Delaroche, Millet, and Ingres. The Olive collection contained a fine Canaletto, *View of the Island of San Michele near Murano,* a landscape by Boucher, and a portrait by Laurent Fauchier. The Kochubai collection, the Gagarin, the Maitlev—the curators were snowed under by an *embarras de richesses.*

They also found unexpected treasures at the former imperial residences in Pavlovsk, Petrodvorets, and Gachina. The finest of them, Titian's *Flight into Egypt* and Paolo Veronese's *Conversion of St. Paul,* were hung at the Hermitage. But soon it became quite impossible to exhibit even the more important paintings. There was no space. Many paintings were sent to other museums in Russia. Guidelines were established: things belonging together must not be divided.

Then the Soviet Government decided, quite reluctantly, to sell some pictures. Foreign currency was badly needed. The rulers at the Kremlin could base their decision on the precedent created in 1853 by Czar Nicholas I. There were public sales and secret transactions (with Andrew Mellon and Nubar Gulbenkian, among others). As a result, the Metropolitan in New York now has two van Eycks, the National Gallery in Washington has van Eyck's *Annunciation* and Rembrandt's *Portrait of a Pole,* the Gulbenkian Museum in Lisbon has two Rembrandt's *Pallas* and *Portrait of an Old Man,* and Tiepolo's *Cleopatra's Banquet* went to Melbourne.

No one at the Hermitage likes to remember these sales. Today the Hermitage has no van Eyck, and it lost Raphael's *St. George* and Botticelli's *Adoration of the Magi.* In Berlin in 1928 almost a hundred paintings from the Hermitage were sold—some by Canaletto, Rubens, Tintoretto; two years later several thousand engravings (among them forty by Rembrandt) were sold in Leipzig. But the Hermitage was lucky when it acquired one of the richest collections of modern paintings. Its Impressionist and, generally, École de Paris works arouse the envy of most other museums. They were not collected by emperors or aristocrats but by two dedicated men, Ivan Morosov and Sergei Shukin, who loved modern painting, knew what they wanted, and built their astonishing collections in less than fifteen years. They would commute between Moscow and Paris in the early years of the century, during the heroic epoch of the Fauvists and Cubists, bringing money to some artists in Paris no one else paid attention to, and beauty to their homes in Moscow.

Morosov commissioned decorative panels by Maurice Denis and two paintings of the Mediterranean by Bonnard. He bought eighteen paintings from Cézanne. The Hermitage now has ten Bonnards, eight Gauguins, four Manets, six Matisses, and three Renoirs from his collection. Shukin was even more daring in his taste. Daniel Henry Kahnweiler remembered, "Shukin was then [1912] almost the only important collector of avant-garde art. He liked big pictures. Whenever I had a group of Picassos, I sent him a telegram, and he would set off at once from Moscow."

Shukin bought six Renoirs on his first trip to Paris. In 1908 he commissioned Matisse to do several panels for the eighteenth-century Trubetzkoy Palace, which he owned. Matisse showed *The Dance* at the Salon d'Automne in 1910, where "the nude figures caused some disquiet," and asked Shukin to hang *The Dance* on the second floor. ("The effort of climbing demands a feeling of

release. *The Dance* represents a ring flung over a hilltop.")
Matisse's *Music* was hung on the floor above, "where one is inside
the house, in harmony with the atmosphere and the silence."
Shukin soon recognized the genius of Picasso; thanks to him the
Hermitage now shows the artist's evolution from the end of the
last century to 1914. Eventually he assembled thirty-one Picassos,
from *The Embrace* (1889) and *The Encounter* (1903) to *Portrait
of Ambroise Vollard* (1910) and *Violin and Glass* (1913). He
also had twenty-seven Matisses, twelve Derains, four Monets,
three Cézannes, three Van Goghs, and works by Douanier Rousseau, Renoir, Guillaumin, Marquet, Pissarro, and others. After the
Revolution he went to Paris as a refugee. He was much less rich
than some of his former protégés, but he was philosophical about
his losses and said he was glad that the paintings he'd collected
would now be seen by millions of people at the Hermitage.

When the guards and guides arrived at the Hermitage Museum, shortly before eight o'clock on the morning of Sunday,
June 22, 1941, they were told to walk down the narrow staircase
into a large room in the basement, where they were issued hel-
mets and gas masks. There would be a civil-defense drill. Such
drills had been held once in a while to co-ordinate air-raid protection measures, but this morning the employees were urgently
needed upstairs. A big crowd was expected. *Leningradskaya
Pravda* had published an article, "Tamerlane and the Timurids at
the Hermitage," about a special exhibition of art works from the
Mongol era in two large halls. The paper had printed dispatches
from Samarkand, where a scientific expedition was studying the
Gur Emir mausoleum, Tamerlane's burial place. The scientists
were collecting material for the celebration of the five hundredth
anniversary of Alisher Navoi, the outstanding poet of the Tamerlane era. *Leningradskaya Pravda* had reported that Tamerlane's
coffin had been opened and his skeleton had been studied. One
leg was shorter than the other. The guides said that the stories
would bring lots of people to the Tamerlane rooms. They were
right. When the Hermitage was opened at eleven o'clock, there
were long lines of people waiting along the Neva embankment.

They didn't stay. A few minutes past noon there were radio reports that German bombers had attacked several cities. An hour

later, orders came from Iosif Orbeli, director of the Hermitage: Admit no more visitors; tell people the news; after they've left, close the doors. All curators and senior staff members were told to come to the director's office overlooking Palace Square.

Orbeli, a dignified man with a white beard, whom his friends compared to an Old Testament prophet, was angry. A few weeks before, he had at last established, after years of effort, the Hermitage's new department of Russian culture. In the storage rooms there were packing cases with a quarter of a million exhibits for the department; new expeditions were being prepared. All this had to be postponed now, for a while anyway, to prepare for the evacuation of the art treasures from the museum. Orbeli had been unable to reach the Committee on Arts in Moscow to ask for specific instructions. He told his staff they were going ahead on their own. The most important paintings—the two Leonardo da Vinci Madonnas, the Raphael Madonnas, the Rembrandts, the Murillos, and so on—would be taken off the walls right away and brought to the stone vaults in the cellars of the Winter Palace. Packing would start the next morning.

Several curators who attended that Sunday afternoon meeting are still at the Hermitage. They remember that everybody was silent and gloomy. They were all afraid—not for themselves, but for their children, the art works. Then somebody pointed at the calendar sheet behind Orbeli's desk. June 22. Somebody remembered that Napoleon had also invaded Russia in June, on June 24 to be exact. Everybody smiled and the meeting closed on a more cheerful note.

It is not true that most treasures were removed within a few days as has been claimed, but the Hermitage people did an amazing job. On July 1, nine days after Hitler's attack, a long train moved out of the October Freight Station loaded with half a million art works. The most important paintings, many in their frames, were in an armored car. Four Pullman cars were filled with special treasures—the *Athena Pallada* that Peter the Great had bought, Rastrelli's sculptures, the crown jewels, precious stones, golden artifacts. The Pullman cars were followed by a flatcar with an antiaircraft battery. It may have been the most valuable train in history; its destination was secret.

A second train left Leningrad on July 20—twenty-three cars,

carrying more than 700,000 art works. This time the Hermitage authorities knew the destination, Sverdlovsk; officially it was also a secret. A third train was prevented from leaving when the Germans captured the small railroad station of Mga, cutting the last line that linked Leningrad with the Russian mainland.

During the siege, life went on in the vast subterranean chambers and cellars of the Winter Palace, where several large bomb shelters had been set up. Alexander Nikolsky, the Hermitage's chief architect, who lived with his wife in the No. 3 shelter (just below the Italian Hall), wrote a diary about their life in the cold cellars and made sketches which he later showed to friends. Three invaluable candles were sacrificed so they could look at them. Almost two thousand people in the cellars were working on long tables and sleeping on cots, and many died there.

They never had the slightest doubt that Leningrad would survive. This certainty helped them, and other Leningraders, to go on. Nikolsky made drawings of an arch in memory of the heroes saving Leningrad. His plans were used after the war in the Park of Victory and the Victory Stadium. Yet when he was working on his plans, victory was several years and millions of human lives away.

On December 10, 1941, Iosif Orbeli presided at the celebration of the five-hundredth anniversary of Alisher Navoi, the great poet of the Tamerlane era. It was held at the schoolroom of the Hermitage, with the windows looking out at the frozen Neva. It was terribly cold. The day before, the streetcars had stopped runnning; *Leningradskaya Pravda* was being printed on a single sheet; the daily bread ration was down to 125 grams.

Orbeli spoke more about the suffering in Leningrad than about the poet whose suffering had ended centuries ago. Once a shell fell nearby, but Orbeli asked the guests not to be alarmed. Vsevolod Rozhdestvensky, the poet, who had been on civilian defense duty all night, read a translation of Alisher Navoi. Nikolai Lebedev, the Eastern literature expert, was suffering from acute dystrophy and had to be carried to the meeting. He read a paper on the poet; they could hardly hear him. Lebedev died later on his cot in the cellar.

Orbeli inspected the ghostly Hermitage almost every day though his rheumatism got worse. On December 29 a shell hit the wing near the kitchen courtyard, another damaged the façade on the Admiralty side, and a third ruined the stone canopy above the entrance. Orbeli worried about the treasures somewhere in the Urals, and about the art works still in the vaults and cellars of the palace. Too many things had been left behind. The Hall of Athens, the Hall of Hercules, and the Hall of Jupiter were filled with packing cases.

During the few hours of daylight Orbeli worked in his city office, where one day he was visited by a famous submarine commander, Captain A. V. Tripolsky. Orbeli took his visitor to his "blockade office" near Shelter No. 3, a tiny room where the director of the Hermitage had a few books and a candle. Leaving the Hermitage, Tripolsky went down the embankment and talked to the crew of the *Polar Star*, formerly the private yacht of the czar, now attached to the Baltic fleet and immobilized in the frozen Neva. The crew laid a cable across the ice into the Hermitage. For a while Orbeli had an electric lamp in his office and a small electric heater, until there was no more fuel for the *Polar Star*.

The Hermitage was the only place in the city with a supply of wood, originally brought for packing crates. During the winter, people who died in the cellars were put into coffins. After the death of the carpenter on January 8, 1942—the 130th day of the siege—the dead were carried to the Vladimir corridor and taken away by soldiers with an army truck.

Boris Viktorovich Sapunov, doctor of philosophy and art history, is curator at the department of Russian culture, eleventh to seventeenth century. A rotund, energetic scholar, Sapunov shares with his fellow curators in the great museums everywhere a sense of infectious enthusiasm, a joy of acquisitiveness bordering upon rapacity, and the conviction that his specialty is the most important of all. Once a year he goes alone to Siberia, or the Urals, or the Lower Volga region, hoping to find a treasure of "his" epoch in a monastery, a locked church, possibly in a private home. He doesn't call his journeys "expeditions," though they are. A plane rarely gets him to his destination. He has to switch to a car, a bus, a jeep, a horse-drawn coach, a mule. Last year, in a swamp near Vilna, he rode on an American World War II tank converted into a milk truck, holding on to an old icon.

Such icons are hard to find now, since even the unworldly Russian peasants have heard of high prices paid for the "sacred paintings" that meant much to a devout Russian—beauty and devotion, earthly decoration and divine protection. An icon was the shortest connection with the Good Lord, a blessing and a promise, an altar in one's home, very important since the nearest church was far away. Icons still mean all these things to the Russian peasants, after decades of the government's trying to make them atheists. (I saw two beautiful icons in the apartment of a prominent Russian writer who said he kept them "for their beauty, not for any spiritual meaning.") Old icons have the chaste nobility and pure loveliness of the early primitives in Siena. Icons are the visible soul of Russia; every Russian who loves poetry and music, which means almost every Russian, has an icon in a corner of his heart.

Sapunov explained this to me so I would understand his problem in taking possession of an old icon "when the people don't know what they've got there." Often Sapunov doesn't know either, and can only hope. Sixteenth-century icons may be hidden under several layers of dark soot that conceal the multicolored beauty. In one of "his" halls at the Hermitage Sapunov exhibits a partly cleansed icon. One third is still as he saw it first, thickly covered with soot; you can hardly distinguish the heads of the saints, just a faint outline of their clothes. The larger part has been cleaned, revealing the stunning beauty and brilliant colors, gold and blue and red. The cleansing job is so absorbing that the best experts can do it only during two or three hours a day. Sapunov indicated that the method was secret. "In principle," they use old fashioned cleansing agents such as egg yolk rather than sophisticated chemicals that might cause irreparable damage. The art works are treated "like important patients," chemically cleansed from germs, photographed, X-rayed. Much knowledge and patience are needed since there are often four or five layers of paint under the soot. Women restorers are more patient than men. Creative artists are useless. "They cannot slip unconsciously into the skin of the original artist, and instead tend to create their own painting."

"My problem," Sapunov said, "is to guess what's underneath that soot and hope it will be right eventually. First I've got to get that icon through dealing with people who are no fools. I talk about their health, their domestic animals, their children, *any-thing*. Patience is important. I may have to talk for days, never bringing up the one subject on my mind. I walk around with them. I'm invited for tea. I may at last casually indicate that the icon over there isn't bad. No answer. After a while I bring it up again. Would they be willing to part with it? Silence. I talk about the Hermitage. They've all heard of it. I tell them that millions of people may one day look at their icon and be inspired by its beauty. Often they just shake their heads. I've got to enlist the help of the mayor, of another official. It's even more difficult in the monasteries, where only a few monks are left; often it's hard to get into a church that is locked and dead. One needs psychology, stubbornness, and the power of persuasion." Owing to this combination, Sapunov always brings something back that turns out to be special, maybe a treasure. Once he found an old sword in Estonia; only two others like it are known to exist. He showed me a thirteenth-century book of Psalms of which he is justly proud.

The Hermitage has a staff of 1,200 people, including its administrative personnel and guards. There are 250 experts, and possibly 150 top specialists in nearly every field. Russian universities have no courses yet for future museum experts. "Eventually they'll be necessary. Restoring is getting to be a very important field. We take gifted young people for a trial period. If they work out, they become staff members. The best of them work somewhat like translators, trying to project themselves into the mind of the artist whose work they restore. It takes from three to five years until they learn thinking that way. Women are more adaptable, putting aside their individuality, and they have better nerves than men. Nearly all old art works are sick and need clinical attention."

Climate and space are now the big problems at the Hermitage. Leningrad's humidity is high. Central heating and various devices proved inadequate in the Winter Palace, which was not built as a museum. Most curators would like to move the Hermitage to modern, air-conditioned buildings, but they know this is unrealistic. The Leningraders want their great museum to remain at the palace. Yet the Hermitage exhibits only a little over ten per cent of its art works; almost ninety per cent of the treasures remain in the reserves. "The Hermitage is an iceberg," says

Sapunov. "It shows, for instance, about a hundred out of its fifty thousand engravings, some by Dürer, Goya, Rembrandt. There is always the fear of keeping things in the reserves that ought to be shown."

Financially the Hermitage is better off than many great museums in the Western world. ("Money is not a serious problem here.") The Ministry of Culture provides a generous budget. Extra money is available for special projects and important acquisitions. The Hermitage finances up to forty expeditions a year, with some now working in Central Asia and around the Black Sea, looking for antiquities. In a country with a strongly entrenched bureaucracy, the policies of the Hermitage are surprisingly unbureaucratic. The various departments present their needs based on gaps in the inventory. Every Monday a buying commission made up of the department heads decides on priorities. In an emergency the director goes to Moscow to submit the case to the Ministry. (The director of a certain museum in Leningrad is known for his skill in getting an extra couple of million rubles.)

Important collections reaching the Soviet Union are first offered to the Hermitage; so are private collections belonging to people who have died without legal heirs. There are no rich donors in Russia, but Sapunov's department has obtained beautiful costumes and furniture from private collectors. The curators often turn down bequests of art not quite up to the lofty standards of the Hermitage. Certain purchases are authorized to be made in the West, for hard currency. Commission stores in the Soviet Union must always give first look to the Hermitage. Sapunov indicated some problems well known to museum curators in the affluent Western society that arise in Russia too.

"People here have money now and many want to get old icons, and there is a formidable international demand. I still have the advantage of knowing where to look for them."

The Hermitage naturally competes with the great museums in the West. But Leningrad's Russian Museum is almost unique, being complemented by, rather than in competition with, only Moscow's Tretyakov Gallery. The Russian Museum is always crowded, mostly with Russians. School classes, groups of soldiers, delegations, peasants, intellectuals, workers all feel at home there with their national heritage. One meets a fascinating cross section of races and peoples, the genuine melting pot of the new Soviet society. In Russia, the Russian Museum is more popular than the Hermitage. Its curators lecture all over the Soviet Union, and people study for their visit to it. It is an artistic and human experience (though non-Russians may have a feeling of being left out). A grade-school teacher told me she prefers to take her children to the Russian Museum. "It has no mythology, which we are not supposed to teach. But how can you explain some of the greatest paintings at the Hermitage to children who know nothing about mythology?"

In 1895, under Czar Nicholas II, it was decided to transfer the Russian paintings and sculptures from the Hermitage to the former Mikhailovsky Palace, built by Carlo Rossi between 1819 and 1825 for the Grand Duke Mikhail Pavlovich, the younger brother of Czar Alexander I, in classical Tuscan style. It faces Arts Square, serene and beautiful, enclosed by several Rossi façades. No. 1, the Little Opera House, once was a theater for French plays. No. 2, formerly the House of the Nobles, is now the State Philharmonia, home of the Leningrad Philharmonic, one of the finest Soviet orchestras. No. 3 was the home of the painter V. P. Brodsky. Mikhailovsky Palace was adapted as a museum by V. F. Svinin and opened in 1898. After the October Revolution it was enriched, by order of Lenin, with treasures brought from churches, monasteries, and private homes. It was badly damaged during the last war but was restored by 1953. Many rooms have kept their former character as places of court entertainment. Like the Hermitage, the Russian Museum is a beautiful palace that happens to be filled with icons, paintings, sculptures, folk art, and even posters.

The greatest treasures are in several rooms on the ground floor, magnificent icons from the twelfth to the sixteenth centuries, and fragments from the St. Michael Monastery, Kiev. There are the unforgettable icons by Andrei Rublev, a monk who painted the apostles with a power of expression unique in Russian art. There is a strong mystical magic in these religious paintings. In churches built in the Orthodox tradition, screens were erected between the congregation and the priests celebrating mass. The screen, the iconostasis, was later covered with religious paintings.

Some early icons were twelve feet high, in glowing shades of
gold. Many, unfortunately, were destroyed by the Mongol invaders, and early icons have become very rare.

One cannot help noticing the traumatic abyss that exists between some fifteenth-century icons and the first "modern" Russian paintings at the time of Peter the Great. At the Russian Museum one becomes aware of Peter's "Great Leap Forward," as he
was trying to take his country from the old ages into modern
times. After the wonderful inner life of the icons there is, suddenly, stilted portrait painting and the forced artificiality of able
Russian painters who copied Western artists. Peter sent them to
France, Italy, and Holland. They were eager pupils, but most of
them remain copyists. There is little that is original about their
portraits of Peter, his wife, his daughters. Ivan Nikitin painted
the Czar on his deathbed, the Western-minded statesman. The
visitors love these paintings.

After the founding of the Russian Academy, there was a strong
classicist influence among the artists who had been abroad, but
gradually the great Russian talent overcame the conservative heritage. Alexander Ivanov's *Christ Appearing to the People* is powerful and very Russian. Or K. P. Bryulov's colossal *The Last Day
of Pompeii*. Ilya Repin painted masterpieces of satirical realism.
His *The Zaporogue Cossacks Write a Letter to the Sultan* is a
magnificent study of mirth—from the cunning smile and half-hid-
den snigger to the roaring shriek. Some painters such as Valentin
Serov worked under the influence of the Impressionists and post-
Impressionists, but the development didn't go far. The "new"
group had a philosophy formulated in its magazine *Mir Iskusstva*
(The World of Art). Sergei Diaghilev, impresario and organizer,
was its editor, Alexander Benois its leader. Bakst, Roerich, Golovin, and Bilibin were among the contributors. They were trying
to get away from realism; for a while they had hope, when Marc
Chagall and Vasily Kandinsky briefly held official posts. But they
were driven out by the commissars, who demanded a social-
realistic representation of the material world. There are busts and
portraits of Lenin, posters and propaganda pictures made during
the Revolution. Before leaving the Russian Museum, I went back
once more to look at the old icons. They were timeless and beautiful.

A DIADEM OF PALACES

In 1708—St. Petersburg was five years old, and the Czar was in Moscow, inspecting his government—Catherine, whom he'd married the year before, prepared a surprise for him. She had a stone house built and a beautiful garden with an avenue of linden trees laid out for him, "on a very pleasant site at a distance of about twenty-five versts [fifteen miles] southwest of the fortress town . . . at the end of an immense plain which offered the most beautiful prospects to the eye." On his return, Peter was delighted. He is said to have embraced his wife, congratulating her on the site, which was "delightful without being aquatic."

Ever since, the Romanovs have sought refuge in the region where the climate was milder than in the town along the Neva. They practically never stopped building palaces there that were ostentatious and much too big. Like St. Petersburg, the site of the retreat had several names reflecting the vagaries of history. Originally it was known by its Finnish name, Saari Muis ("Saari Village"), translated into the Russian Sarskoye Selo. After the death of Peter, it became Tsarskoye Selo ("Imperial Village"). After the October Revolution, when the palaces were temporarily converted into children's camps, it was known as Detskoye Selo ("Children's Village"). In 1937 the town and the great palace were rechristened after Pushkin, who had gone to the lycée there, and in 1831 went to live with his bride in a small wooden house at the corner of Vassenko Street, now another Pushkin museum.

"The whole world is a foreign land to us but Tsarskoye Selo is our home."

Catherine's original stone house with several wings and galleries, designed by J. F. Braunstein, no longer exists. Peter's extravagant daughter Elizabeth, who had inherited the estate from Catherine, summoned the younger Trezzini, Domenico's son, in 1743 and began building in the great style. Aided by Andrei Kvasov and Sava Chevakinsky (who created the beautiful baroque St. Nicholas Cathedral in St. Petersburg, today the largest church open for worship), Trezzini added more luxurious buildings to the simple stone house that had delighted Peter. In 1752 Elizabeth changed her mind again. She had everything torn down and told Francesco Rastrelli to build her a *real* palace.

That suited Rastrelli, who designed an enormous rococo extravaganza, a palace almost a thousand feet long, spectacular and fantastic and not in good—nor even moderately good—taste. The Great Palace (later known as Ekaterininsky Palace, Catherine's Palace, after Catherine the Great) was Rastrelli's idea of Russian architecture, a three-story building, colossal and monolithic, featuring huge round-headed French windows decorated with wrought-iron balconies and separated by gigantic atlantes, with baroque stucco ornaments. The palace was painted bright blue and white, the atlantes and moldings gold. The roof line was decorated with a gilded balustrade and statues of gods. Even Catherine thought that Rastrelli had overdone it. The statues were taken away, the balustrade was painted white, and the other gilt was replaced by a bronze wash. Seen now from the beautiful park that surrounds the palace, Ekaterininsky remains a Russian extravaganza in striking colors, pompous and glittering and also harsh. It is reminiscent of the strident chords in the early ballet music of Stravinsky, who was born not far away, in Oranienbaum (now Lomonosov).

Elizabeth loved the place and spent an enormous amount of money on it. "There are accounts in existence going up to one million six hundred thousand rubles to show what it cost but the Empress gave a lot of money besides out of her own pocket," Catherine later wrote. Elizabeth added dancing galleries, concert halls, shooting boxes, fishing pools, picnic grottoes, and a chapel in gold and blue. The interiors were later altered by Catherine II and other monarchs, but a feeling of unreality and make-believe remains, with stagelike perspectives and stairways that might have delighted Cecil B. De Mille. In 1758 at the parish church, later Pushkin's lycée, as Russia took part in the Seven Years' War against Frederick the Great, Elizabeth suffered a stroke from which she never quite recovered.

When Catherine II came to power in 1762, she began changing the interiors. Rastrelli had installed painted ceilings and richly inlaid parquet floors. He used marble, porphyry, lapis lazuli, malachite, amber, and mother-of-pearl, not to mention the gilt mirrors, crystal chandeliers, and "beds of gold." Catherine was mad about building ("it's a disease like alcoholism") and she decided to make a neoclassical palace out of Rastrelli's blue and white elephant. She had joined the eighteenth-century cult of admiration for ancient Hellas and Rome, and she found the right masters in Quarenghi and Brenna. A copy of Palladio's bridge was installed in the park by the Russian architect Neyelov, who had been in England. For the redecoration of her private apartments Catherine hired an unknown Scotsman, Charles Cameron, who had studied in Italy. It was a stroke of genius, like her ideas about the paintings at the Hermitage.

Cameron began working on the interiors of the Great Palace. The beautiful Lyons Room, named for the blue and white silk brocade from Lyons, has a magnificent floor made of wood and mother-of-pearl, and lapis lazuli candelabra, but the effect is intimate and elegant, never pompous. Cameron showed exquisite taste when he installed the Arabesque Room in Pompeian style, the black and gold Chinese Room, the Green Dining Room, and the Amber Room, completely paneled in amber. He also created several intimate chambers in different styles, a cabinet of mirrors, a "snuffbox" with blue and white walls, a silver cabinet, and a small bedroom with columns of colored porcelain. He built classical little "follies" in the park and garden, and a small Chinese village; and then he started on a masterpiece, an annex to the palace that seems incongruous, having no connection in style. But it succeeded, and his additions remain the best things about the palace: the Agate Pavilion and the Cameron Gallery.

The small Agate Pavilion, in Italian classical style, painted in Pompeian colors, yellow and red, has two bathhouses, with an anteroom containing Greek and Pompeian decorations, and a suite of rooms that are formal and beautiful, truly rooms for an empress. They are filled with marble, alabaster, amber, ornaments in ivory, and classical bronze reliefs. Very beautiful, but would anyone want to live there, even an empress? Outside there is a paved garden from which a sloping bridge descends into the park.

Cameron also built the classical long gallery that remains named after him. A double flight of steps leads up from the lake to Cameron's Ionic-columned Greek temple. The gallery, built at a right angle to the palace, was filled with bronze busts of Catherine's old and modern heroes. (It was noticed that the bust of Voltaire was removed after the outbreak of the French Revolution.) From the lake below, the Cameron Gallery looks like classical fata morgana, a Greek fantasy suddenly rising in the Russian countryside, and adds to the sense of unreality.

The palace was crowded when I saw it; my Intourist guide said it was always crowded during visiting hours. There were schoolchildren and students and soldiers and many old people. Everybody had to put on soft overshoes; even so, the fine floors have to be renewed every four or five years. The Ekaterininsky was almost completely destroyed by the Germans in the Second World War. Photographs show the burned-out shell. The postwar restorers worked with exceptional skill and fanatical fidelity, successfully re-creating old paints and the embroidered silks from China. "Only an expert could see that they are not old," a guide said. "Some restorers went to China to study the old methods." In the great dining room, an enormous banquet table is set up, with a profusion of china, crystal, gold. Standing behind a rope, the visitors stare at the incredible luxury. So that's the way their czars and czarinas lived, while most of the people were impoverished serfs. One understands why the Soviet leadership decided to restore the pomp of the past right after the end of the war, when the Soviet Union's standard of living was so low compared to the West. And the visitor from the West cannot help thinking that nowhere else would luxury on such a pronounced scale have been possible. Versailles, Florence, and Schönbrunn are different. Ekaterininsky Palace in Pushkin is saved by the park, beautiful with its terraces, lakes, boat houses, pyramids, statues, the small

Hermitage, and the fine old trees and large lawns. It is a restful place, except for the MIGs that come screaming from a nearby airfield at low altitudes.

In 1792 Quarenghi began work on Alexandrinsky Palace, in classical style, named after Czar Alexander I. Quarenghi designed a double row of Corinthian columns for the façade. The large park contained several buildings—the Arsenal, the Chapel, the Farm. A small town, Fedorovsky Gorodok, was built in 1914 in old Russian style by the architect Krechinsky for the family of the Czar. After the massacre in front of the Winter Palace in 1905, Nicholas II and his family lived here, feeling more secure than in St. Petersburg. The Czar had his own railroad station there, and even his "railroad regiment." It was from this station in July 1917 that he and his family started their fatal journey to Siberia and later to the Urals.

A few miles from Pushkin, on the Baltic coast, there is Peterhof (now Petrodvorets), thirty miles from Leningrad, overlooking the Gulf of Finland. It had been Peter's idea since 1708, when he had built himself a small summer house at Strelna, a place on the coast where he would watch the ships going to his new harbor at Kotlin Island (Kronstadt). Peter's summer house, built of wood, was later enlarged by Michetti, became a palace designed by Rastrelli, and was finally known as the Great Palace of Strelna after Voronikhin finished his rebuilding in 1803.

In Strelna Peter began dreaming of building his own Versailles. He had admired the original on a visit to Paris. He discussed the idea with his best French architect, Leblond, and they decided to do something that would dwarf even Versailles in some respects. Leblond designed a two-story building on a steep slope, three hundred yards from the sea below. Behind and above the castle, Leblond built a formal garden around fountains and statuary. In front of the castle was a wide terrace facing the sea and, far away, the coast of Finland. From the terrace a large waterfall and statues lead down to a basin featuring a statue of Samson and the lion. A sixty-foot-high jet of water spurts from the lion's mouth. A canal links the fountain with the landing stage on the sea; it is bordered on both sides by round shells spouting water. There were also French and Italian fountains. It was a very early vision of Disneyland, and Peter began construction with customary élan. Thousands of workers were set to digging; others laid wooden pipes that carried water from places thirteen miles away. Not satisfied with his aquatic Versailles, Peter built several pavilions and mini-palaces in the gardens, each with a French name: the relatively modest Marly, with oak-paneled rooms, and the elegant Hermitage, with a dining table moved by a special mechanism that would lower the table through the floor to the kitchen below. Rastrelli was so impressed by the gadget that he installed it again in another Hermitage he later built in the park of Tsarskoye Selo.

But the finest of the small buildings was Monplaisir, built for Peter's wife, in Dutch style, with a lovely kitchen that has gaily colored tiles, and ceilings whose birds and flowers betray the feminine touch. Peter loved to spend a few days there with Catherine. The Dutch and Flemish paintings he'd bought and hung there created Russia's first picture gallery, long before Catherine II began collecting for her Hermitage. Peter died just as the large palace was finished, but his daughter Elizabeth continued with great gusto. First there were only minor changes, and then major ones by the exuberant Rastrelli. He extended the palace along the terrace, altered the windows, and added two wings joined to the middle section by galleries. One wing contained a chapel and was crowned by five golden cupolas, while the other wing had one large cupola with an imperial eagle. Rastrelli painted the palace dark pink; now it is yellow and white. He also added more cascades, more gilded statuary, luxurious ornaments, and a great park. Inside the palace he created grandiose staircases and theatrical vistas, but he was persuaded to leave Peter's modest study untouched, as Nicolas Pineau, a French artist, had done it.

While Elizabeth amused herself in Monplaisir with her friends and lovers, young Catherine was unhappily playing cards with a husband she couldn't stand the sight of. Both were bored. In St. Petersburg Peter had amused himself by drilling a hole in the floor of his room in the Winter Palace and watching his aunt the Empress Elizabeth, making love in her room just below. Then he fell in love himself with Elizabeth Vorontsova. His wife, Catherine, had become interested in Stanislas Poniatowski, an attractive young Polish count. He was twenty-one; she was eight years older. One night when she and her husband were staying in Monplaisir—the Empress had remained in St. Petersburg—there was a scene right out of Casanova's Memoirs. In this case Poniatowski played Casanova's role, and he wrote about it later on:

> I danced a minuet with Elizabeth [Vorontsova] and I said to her, "It is in your power to make several people happy." She replied: "That is already almost done. Come one hour after midnight . . . to Monplaisir where Their Highnesses are lodging."

Poniatowski and Elizabeth entered Monplaisir. Poniatowski found Peter "very gay, welcoming me and calling me 'thou,' saying 'How foolish not to have been frank with me. Then none of this mess would have happened.'" Poniatowski "readily agreed to accept the situation":

> I began at once to express my admiration for His Highness's military dispositions. He was flattered . . . and after a quarter of an hour he said, "Now that we are such good friends, I find there is someone missing here." He crossed over to his wife's room, dragged her out of bed, leaving her only time to put on her stockings and no shoes, and to slip into a Batavia dress without an underskirt, and then brought her in, saying, as he pointed to me, "Here he is! I hope I shall have satisfied everybody."

That night Monplaisir became everybody's pleasure.

The dashing Stanislas Poniatowski was the father of one of Catherine's illegitimate children. Little Anne died in infancy. Stanislas later became king of Poland. Monplaisir, and the rest of Peterhof, remained the Versailles of Catherine's successors. The court disappeared in 1917, but Peterhof, now open to the public, remained a famous tourist attraction. During the siege of Leningrad, in 1942, the Germans shelled the Russian Versailles, almost completely destroying it. Among other things, the interiors had contained many precious gifts which Frederick the Great had sent to Catherine II and which were now obliterated by the successors of Frederick's grenadiers. Once again, history had come full circle.

The great showplace was completely restored at the end of the war, and is again very popular with tourists from Russia and everywhere else. It should be approached from the sea. The cascades, the water jets, the cupolas, the golden statues, the noisy music coming from loudspeakers—it is pompous and vulgar, like a movie set for a 1930s musical. But in the evening, after the tourists have left and the loudspeakers are silent and dusk is falling, the stage set becomes a fairy tale. That is the moment to see the strange grandeur of Petrodvorets.

The only truly beautiful among the former imperial country palaces is also the smallest. Pavlovsk, just a short ride, four miles, from Pushkin, was presented by Catherine to her legitimate son and heir, Paul (after whom it is named) and his wife, Maria Feodorovna. The Empress couldn't stand having her son and daughter-in-law living near her, though she had several hundred rooms at the Winter Palace. The young couple reciprocated the sentiment. Charles Cameron was summoned and told to build the Czarevitch a nice little palace. Work began in 1782. Cameron didn't get along with Paul, who should have left the great Scotsman alone. Later, other architects were called in: Brenna, Gonzaga, Quarenghi, Rossi, Voronikhin. All of them had the good sense to leave Cameron's original design. Pavlovsk is a mixture of styles but is saved by a harmonious synthesis and the miracle of artistic simplicity. Cameron was the only great architect in eighteenth-century St. Petersburg who did not become intoxicated with pomp and the possibility of unlimited funds. He kept his cool Scottish head and classical proportions.

Cameron designed a simple square building crowned by a flat, low cupola perhaps inspired by the Pantheon in Rome. On both sides are semicircular arcades. The elegantly curved galleries enclose the courtyard where Paul used to drill his soldiers. The colonnades are filled with antique statues. Inside there are beautiful staircases; Cameron's lovely Italian circular hall with mauve and white artificial marble walls, niches, and friezes; a green hall with marble pillars; Paul's throne room with large white porcelain stoves; and many almost intimate salons and gracefully furnished apartments. The private suite of the Empress still has some details that miraculously survived, for example, her work table and her curtains. Through the rounded windows one sees the garden.

This is the sort of palace one wouldn't mind living in (if there were no servant problem). In the former throne room a banquet table has been laid for a rather intimate affair (by eighteenth-century standards)—say, only a hundred guests—with hand-woven cloth, fine china, silver, candelabra. Elsewhere there is much detail that makes the palace a lovely little museum—the fireplaces and ceilings, chandeliers and vases, furniture and paintings, gobelins and porcelain. The 1914 Baedeker lists paintings by Rembrandt (*Head of Christ*), Ruysdael, Veronese, Guido Reni, and Ribera in the intimate picture gallery, a sixteenth-century New Testament in French, and collections of cameos and Russian coins. Many of the art works are now in the Hermitage.

Cameron also designed the English park, one of the most beautiful anywhere, with small lakes, brooks, little pavilions behind hedges, Greek temples with statues (many by Gonzaga), and Cameron's Temple of Friendship, a rotunda surrounded by Doric columns that was used as a concert hall, with a statue of Catherine II as Ceres. Rossi built the Rose Pavilion, which was often covered with roses, in 1812. Two years later, Alexander I celebrated here his victory over Napoleon. "Did you see that bench in the park, just by those three big trees, that green bench?" Dostoyevsky wrote in 1869 in *The Idiot*. The old trees are still there.

Pavlovsk too was almost completely destroyed during the Second World War, and was restored with incredible devotion to detail. Again, the best Soviet experts made sure that the colors and fabrics were re-created exactly as they had been, often by antiquated methods. Cameron's masterpiece gives joy to numberless visitors. There are larger, more ostentatious palaces all over the world, but hardly one reflecting "simplicity and nobility," Cameron's aim, so well fulfilled.

"The excursion to Krasnoe Selo where the Corps of Guards occupies a summer camp is mainly of interest to military men," advised the 1914 Baedeker. It did not mention the horse races of the officers that Tolstoy described in *Anna Karenina*. Not far away is Gachina, surrounded by pine forests, originally a country house which Gregory Orlov received from Catherine.

Orlov had to give up Gachina when he was "fired" in 1772. It was presented to Catherine's military-minded son, Paul, because no one else wanted it. After he became Czar Paul I and turned

Gachina into a military camp, it was always a gloomy place. Why anyone who had the lovely palace of Pavlovsk would want to spend one day or a week in Gachina seems unfathomable. It always remains associated with military action. In 1917 Kerensky made it his headquarters. Two years later, General N. N. Yudenich began the White Guards offensive from there. During the siege of Leningrad, the Germans used it as a command post. Antonio Rinaldi's simple three-story structure, connected to its wings by colonnades, encloses a large rectangular courtyard. Neither Gachina nor the large park that surrounds it is worth a special journey.

But Oranienbaum (Lomonosov) is interesting for its history. Prince Menshikov had the palace designed and ordered the German architect Gottfried Schädel to build it. It was finished in 1725, the year Peter the Great died, and looked like an imperial residence. It is a low building in Russian baroque style, facing the sea and Kronstadt. Schädel added long, curving galleries and domed pavilions, probably to make it look more "Russian." Balustraded terraces descend to a canal that leads down to the sea. In 1754 the Empress Elizabeth gave Oranienbaum to her nephew Peter, who built a fortress there and drilled his soldiers; all the early Romanovs liked playing with soldiers, both lead and live. In 1762 Rastrelli was ordered to build a two-story pavilion in the park when Catherine wanted to have some picnics there. Her husband, Peter, told Rinaldi to build a small palace in the garden. Later, Rinaldi created for Catherine a rococo house that became known, for its many chinoiseries, as the Chinese Palace. Several pupils of Tiepolo were summoned from Venice to paint the ceilings. Rinaldi designed the beautiful parquet floors. During the siege of Leningrad, Lomonosov remained in the hands of the Soviets, though for a long time they were completely surrounded by the Germans.

Today the country palaces provide a pompous diadem around the city of Leningrad, and a memory of unrestricted wastefulness on the part of the Czarist rulers, and of the Soviet rulers who ordered the postwar restorations. They were built by serfs in the middle of the Arctic countryside, incongruous structures of exorbitant luxury surrounded by abject poverty, perfect symbols of the extremes that have always been prominent in Russian life and culture.

THE ARTS

THE WRITERS

The early Russian poets wrote in an esoteric language that was used mainly in the church. Slaviansky (Church Slavonic) was not spoken among the Russian people but, rather, was created to talk to the Lord. The Grand Duchess Sophia, the sister of Peter the Great, in her love letters written to Vasily Galitzin at the end of the seventeenth century, didn't use the language of the poets but the idiom of the peasants. Such letters might now be written by uneducated persons, of whom there are not many in the Soviet Union. Peter, the genius reformer, sensed that a reformed Russian language was needed. The common idiom was insufficient in the fields that interested him most—navigation, science, architecture, economics. With unerring instinct he ordered the hidden resources of the spoken language traced rather than go outside of it. Certain terms were taken from Swedish and Dutch —Dutch merchants came with their ships to Peter's new capital— but there is little Latin influence in Russian. French influence was injected later by Catherine II.

The first poets writing in the rejuvenated Russian language were satirists. They were still somewhat clumsy; there was no lucid, simple language yet. Until Peter encouraged the publication of Russian books, Russian literature remained limited to church writing and to annals retelling old legends and fairy tales. Catherine II had little use for Russian, corresponding in French with Diderot and Voltaire, but she continued the search for a reformed Russian language which Peter, her idol, had initiated. In 1783 she founded the Russian Academy. It began work on the first Russian dictionary; the last volume was published in 1794, five years before Pushkin was born.

Alexander Nikolayevich Radishchev and the first generation of Russian writers in the modern sense were well-educated noblemen in touch with ideas abroad, and they had compassion for the depressing social conditions of the Russian people. Radishchev, born in Moscow in 1749 of a family belonging to the landed gentry, was sent to St. Petersburg at thirteen, and became a member of Catherine's exclusive Corps of Pages, securing for himself a brilliant future. He studied at Leipzig, returned to St. Petersburg, and eventually reached the high position of chief of the Custom House in 1790. That year he published *A Journey from St. Petersburg to Moscow*—which was the end of his career.

Radishchev was the first Russian writer deeply concerned with the rights of man. His book, a series of short sketches, was a devastating criticism of the evils of serfdom, which he called brutal and stupid since the peasants had no incentive to work harder. It remains an astonishingly modern work, devoted to the idea that all men are born free, written in a country where no man can truly make that claim. Serfdom, Radishchev wrote, was morally wrong, corrupting both serf and master.

Free men who have committed no crime, and being sold like cattle! Oh law of this land! . . . If only the slaves, weighed down by their heavy bonds, inflamed by despair, were to break down our heads with the iron that hinders their freedom. . . . Soon from their midst would arise great men to replace the slain generation but they would be inspired by a different attitude and have no right to exercise oppression. This is no fancy. My gaze pierces the thick curtain of time which hides the future from our eyes—I see through a whole century to come!

Radishchev didn't incite the serfs to rise. They hadn't learned to read anyway. He addressed himself to Catherine and her court and warned them of a future revolution, as Tolstoy did ninety years later. In Russia, as everywhere, writers were always ahead of their times. Other writers turned Radishchev's ideas into social criticism. Alexander Sumarokov, another alumnus of the Corps of Pages, who had become director of the St. Petersburg Theater, attacked Voltaireanism and cosmopolitanism. Denis Ivanovich Fonvizin, also an aristocrat, criticized the forced westernization of young noblemen in St. Petersburg and continued Radishchev's ideas in *Fragment of a Journey*. ("Oh humanity! You are unknown in these villages. Oh authority! You tyrannize over your fellow men.") Ever since, the best Russian writers have been social critics.

Russia's satirists rejected the Western ways of St. Petersburg, ruled by a court that never tried to find out how the rest of the country lived. The writers resented the vulgar display of luxury at the court; they wanted people to remember their ancestors' simple life in the villages. It was not true that Russia had been "uncivilized" before the time of Peter the Great. The writings of the old annalists proved that the Russians, at least some of them, had used the Cyrillic characters and the Slavonic translation of the Bible in the ninth century. The writers resurrected poetic paraphrases of the Psalms, the civil law code which Yaroslav Vladimirovich gave to the people of Novgorod in 1019, and the beauty of the earliest known icons.

Alexander Sergeyevich Pushkin did more than any other Russian poet for the evolution of style. His contribution came at the right moment; through Pushkin, and after him, modern Russian writing remains intimately associated with St. Petersburg. As a child he listened to his nurse's fairy tales and to the stories told by his father, an aristocrat of whom Pushkin was proud. He knew the old idiom and used it when he wrote his beautiful language; he loved the primitive language of Sophia and her era. Pushkin went back to the past and to the ideas of Peter the Great, whom the poet idolized and of whom he always remained in awe. Pushkin understood Peter—his genius and his brutality, his ruthlessness and high purpose, these very Russian contradictions. Pushkin understood that St. Petersburg was Peter's true beloved child, when he wrote,

> Show your colors, city of Peter
> And stand steadfast like Russia. . . .

Pushkin was educated at the lycée in Tsarskoye Selo and later lived with his parents in their beautiful town house on Fontanka Canal. Life in St. Petersburg was fun, with all its writers, artists, and beautiful women around; occasionally he showed up at the Foreign Ministry, where he had a minor job. But Pushkin was no playboy and soon grew tired of local café society. He became a member of the Green Lamp, a society begun for the discussion of literature and history which soon developed into a secret political association. Many of his friends were later involved in the uprising of the Decembrists. In 1820 he was exiled to the south for expressing views the censors didn't like; they might be called liberal, in the best sense of the word. He was often in trouble with the Czar's censors and secret police after his return. There wasn't enough money and there was the problem of his beautiful wife, Natasha, who liked the high life and the company of "interesting" men. Nicholas I forced Pushkin to become a Gentleman of the Bedchamber, not an enviable position, so that the Czar might see Natasha more easily. Pushkin suffered and died after being wounded in a duel, not unlike some of his romantic characters. His apartment in Moika is now a museum, a shrine.

Pushkin is very much alive in Leningrad today, as a poet and as a man. People sense his passion and compassion, his feeling for beauty, his almost Shakespearean scope of universality. His literary range is enormous, from romantic fairy tale to contemporary satire. He has true feeling and irony, treating his language as Mozart treated his music. Both died much too early: Mozart at thirty-five, Pushkin at thirty-eight. People in Leningrad, even those not literary-minded, talk about him as though he were still around; to them he is what Chopin remains to the people of Warsaw. The Leningraders know where he lived and visit these places, not as tourists but as friends. His romanticism and his humanity appeal to Russians of all social strata. Born rich, he always had a feeling for the poor; he expresses the very soul of Russia. Pushkin's untimely death may have saved him from being persecuted. Nicholas I had found a way of getting rid of uncomfortable intellectuals and writers. They were declared "insane" if their ideas seemed dangerous to the Third Section. The year before Pushkin's death, Peter Chaadayev, the author of *Philosophical Letters,* was declared "mentally unbalanced" and kept "under medical supervision." This happened in 1836. The Czar amused himself reading Pushkin's manuscripts and returning them heavily mutilated.

For nearly a hundred years after the death of Pushkin, the literary cafés on Nevsky Prospekt were haunted by his ghost. Mikhail Lermontov, a fine romantic poet, became famous after writing a poem blaming the court of Czar Nicholas for the death of his friend, and he too was killed in a duel, four years after Pushkin. The Czar read Lermontov's novel *A Hero of Our Time*, after his brother's wife, the Grand Duchess Elena, a German princess from Württemberg, told him about it. She liked music and the arts and kept the semblance of a literary salon. She loved Nikolai Gogol's *Dead Souls* and persuaded the Czar to allow the production of *The Inspector General* at the Alexandrinsky Theater in 1836. The actors, used to stylized drama translated from French and German, didn't understand Gogol's realistic characters. ("What good can Pushkin and Zhukovsky find in it?") They presented the fine play as a vulgar farce for the imperial family and the courtiers who filled the house. Gogol was desperate. "I had made up my mind to collect all the evil things I knew, and then to make fun of them. . . ."

Literary historians speak of a "golden age" of Russian literature, from Pushkin to Gogol, but much of the best was still to come in St. Petersburg—V. G. Belinsky, who wrote brilliantly about the effect of art on society; Nikolai Nekrasov, the poet of peasant life; Ivan Goncharov's masterful portrait of Oblomov, futile and decadent and very true; the great Ivan Turgenev, who spent much of his life in St. Petersburg, restless and often persecuted. In 1852 he wrote a bitter article after the death of Gogol, and was exiled. The Grand Duchess Marie of Hesse-Darmstadt, wife of the Grand Duke Alexander (called by Custine "the finest model of a prince I have ever seen"), greatly admired Turgenev's *Sportsman's Sketches* and protected the author against the Czar. All writers of the era were concerned with the conditions of the serfs, but the Czar wouldn't understand that a work of fiction might influence or even threaten the "real" world. Doubtless Turgenev's *Fathers and Sons* deeply influenced Russian society. The novelist was often in Paris to be near Pauline Viardot, the famous singer whom he loved deeply for forty years.

She was married; the *ménage à trois* remains a cause célèbre in literary history. In St. Petersburg he lived once at 38 Fontanka, where Leo Tolstoy was his guest. Tolstoy was the only great nineteenth-century writer in Russia who remained unaffected by St. Petersburg, though he used the city often as a background, as in *Anna Karenina*. He didn't feel deeply about the place.

Dostoyevsky did. His St. Petersburg is a city of many images: fog and brutality, crime and slums. He lived in the Haymarket district, an area populated with criminals, pimps and prostitutes. "About this place, with its tattered population, its dirty, evil-smelling courtyards and many alleys, Raskolnikov loved to roam in his aimless wanderings," Dostoyevsky wrote in *Crime and Punishment*. In daytime there were small huts and nooks where cheap foodstuffs and secondhand clothes were sold. At night few people went there. Dostoyevsky lived in Kuznechny Perenlok when he wrote *The Brothers Karamazov*. He had come to St. Petersburg as a young man to study at the Military Engineering College but got involved in anti-czarist politics, joining a group that met every Friday evening to discuss the writings of Charles Fourier, the French socialist philosopher.

One day in 1849, the Third Section arrested Dostoyevsky and other members of the group, among them Mikhail Petrashevsky, a young Foreign Ministry official, and the writer M. E. Saltykov. They had talked "subversively" against serfdom, censorship, and despotism. According to the agents of the Third Section, there had been "dangerous arguments about abolishing church, state, and private property." Dostoyevsky had committed the "crime" of reading to his friends Belinsky's "forbidden" letter to Gogol.

Twenty members of the group were taken to Peter and Paul Fortress. (Dostoyevsky's cell is now shown to awed tourists—small, dark, and damp, with a tiny opening high up in one wall; it is inconceivable how a prisoner could live there for eight months.) After a mass trial all defendants were sentenced to be shot in the parade ground. Years later, Dostoyevsky described the scene in *The Idiot*:

"My friend was eighth on the list [says Prince Myshkin], and he would therefore be in the third group to be marched to the posts. The priest went to each of them with the cross. It seemed to him that he had only five minutes to live. He told me those five minutes were like an eternity to him, riches beyond the dreams of avarice. . . ."

The condemned men wore the white gowns of death. They had been split up in groups of three. Each "troika" would be tied to the whipping post, and shot by the squad. Drums rolled and the first three men were blindfolded and bound to the post. With calculated slowness, the officer in charge raised his sabre, gave orders: "Ready . . . take aim." It would be any moment now.

Suddenly a bugle sounded. An officer came galloping across the square, waving a white handkerchief. His Majesty had commuted the sentences to imprisonment in Siberia. A gracious reprieve was read. Nicholas I had arranged the scene as "part of the punishment," and to frighten other political dissenters. One of the convicted men, Grigoryev, became mentally deranged on the spot. Dostoyevsky suffered an epileptic fit. The whole scene was created out of sadism. Petrashevsky was sent to Siberia for life. Dostoyevsky was given four years of hard labor, to be followed by four years of army service as a private. Incredibly, he survived, and wrote *Crime and Punishment*, which in its own way conveys the atmosphere of St. Petersburg as strongly as Pushkin's poetry. From the Haymarket (now absurdly renamed "Square of Peace") it is a short walk to the Summer Garden, where Pushkin loved to stroll, dreaming of Peter the Great. Dostoyevsky too belongs to Leningrad today. In the beautiful park of Pavlovsk, Charles Cameron's noble, classically simple palace, one almost expects Prince Myshkin to step out from under the trees.

An obelisk in the Novaya Derevnya district commemorates the duel in which Pushkin was mortally wounded. Rossi's beautiful Alexandrinsky Theater is now the Pushkin Theater. This is no accident. Neither is it an accident that the inconspicuous tomb of Dostoyevsky in Tikhvin Cemetery is rarely included in guided tours. Dostoyevsky's name can hardly be read on the dark stone. While Pushkin glorified St. Petersburg's beauty, Dostoyevsky stared into the deep abysses of the city's tormented soul. He didn't make it easy for himself or his readers, but he is widely read again in Leningrad and elsewhere by people who identify with his demons and angels. Russia's genius for beauty lives on, and also for subtle characterization and powerful realism.

At the turn of the century, St. Petersburg's literary life revolved around *Apollon,* a monthly magazine that had influence all over Russia. Its editorial offices were in an old palace overlooking the Moika, near the eighteenth-century house where Pushkin had died. A legend claimed that the *Apollon* house, with its elegant staircase and large halls, had been the original scene of Pushkin's *Queen of Spades.* (It is more probable that the house of Princess Galitzin at 10 Gogol Street is the place. Pushkin immortalized her as the Countess in *Queen of Spades.* He also heard Mikhail Glinka play the piano there. St. Petersburg was a small, intimate world.)

Sergei Makovsky, the art historian who called himself a "European," was *Apollon's* publisher. Yevgeny Snosko-Borovsky, a grand master of chess, was editorial secretary, writing out the all-important slips for fees. Mikhail Kuzmin was prose editor, Nikolai Gumilev was in charge of poetry. He was a brilliant man, the great love of Anna Akhmatova, the poetess. They married and founded the neoclassical school of Russian poetry (Acmeism); Gumilev later divorced her. In 1921 he was shot by the Bolsheviks as a White Guard conspirator. Some fine writers contributed to *Apollon*—in St. Petersburg the symbolist poet Alexander Blok, much admired now, and Feodor Sologub, Vyacheslav Ivanov, Alexei Remizov, Vasily Rozanov. Valery Bryusov and Andrei Bely contributed from Moscow; Dmitri Merezhkovsky, Zinaida Hippius, and Konstantin Balmont from Paris. Many were in their thirties. In the afternoon the poets, painters, and theater people would come for tea and arguments—Konstantin Somov, Leon Bakst, Sergei Sudeikin, Vsevolod Meyerhold. *Apollon* reflected local impressions and often generated new ideas.

For a while St. Petersburg was the scene of modernist experiments. Meyerhold produced futuristic drama at the Komisarzhevsky Theater. Anton Chekhov often came to admire the great Vera Komisarzhevskaya. Later Meyerhold went to the Alexandrinsky, where Gogol and Turgenev had seen their plays performed. There was modern French drama at the Mikhailovsky Theater. In the spring, Konstantin Stanislavsky would come there with his celebrated ensemble from Moscow. Maxim Gorky wrote with deep compassion about social outcasts, which didn't make him popular in higher circles. Later, Gorky went to Capri, of all places, where he ran a school for revolutionaries.

Vladimir Mayakovsky, poet, could be heard at the Dog, the literary café in an obscure backyard often frequented by Feodor Chaliapin who came, drank, and sang for nothing. At Bashnia ("The Tower"), the fifth-floor apartment of the poet Ivanov, there was no alcohol, only tea, but the talk was a hundred proof. On Wednesday night the *Apollon* people would come there, and the painters, actors, producers, and philosophers—Berdyayev, Bulgakov, Rozanov, Shestov. To be invited there was the equivalent of being a habitué at the home of Stéphane Mallarmé in Paris, or of Arthur Schnitzler in Vienna. It's hard to realize now that such times existed. Never a dull moment. (At the Leningrad Hotel the poet Yesenin, the husband of Isadora Duncan, later hanged himself.)

The October Revolution finished off the modernist trends but Leningrad still had its poets. Osip Mandelstam died in 1940. During the siege Olga Berggolts wrote there; her husband, Nikolai Molkhanov, planned comparative essays on five great poets who had lived in the city—Pushkin, Lermontov, Nekrasov, Blok, Mayakovsky. Molkhanov died during the siege but the poets live on. There will always be poets in Leningrad. It is that kind of city.

THE COMPOSERS

And there will always be composers. National Russian music began in St. Petersburg when the old folk songs and archaic church melodies were fused, cautiously and reluctantly, with musical techniques imported from Italy, Germany, and France. Echoes of the ancient church songs are often heard in Russian music. Even modern Russian composers still go back to the old idiom. The Church did not permit instrumental music, but the czars and aristocrats imported music and musicians as another luxury, after importing architects, gardeners, and cooks. Even Peter's admirers don't claim that he loved music, but the empresses after him considered musical entertainment a part of court life. In 1731 Empress Anna brought Francesco Araja and his group from Venice to the Winter Palace. Peter's daughter Elizabeth had concerts and early Italian opera at her court.

Catherine II had been taught in her native Germany that music was a basic component of *Kultur*. In 1765, after a large wooden theater had been built in Theater Square, she named Alexander Sumarokov as director. He hired an Italian company and the composer Baldassare Galuppi, a contemporary of the great Domenico Scarlatti. Galuppi wrote opera buffa; Mozart, then eight, had heard some of his operas performed at the King's Theatre in London in 1764. Galuppi gave his and other Italian works in St. Petersburg, at an annual salary of four thousand rubles. His successors were Tommaso Traetta and Giovanni Paisiello, who wrote there his masterpiece *Il Barbiere di Siviglia*

in 1782—thirty-four years before Rossini wrote his more successful version. Paisiello stayed nine years in St. Petersburg, receiving
nine thousand rubles a year. After him came Giuseppe Sarti,
Domenico Cimarosa, and Vincente Martín y Soler whose *Una
Cosa Rara* was more successful in Vienna than Mozart's *Figaro*.

The Italian composers imported Italian prima donnas. Cat-
tarina Gabrielli appeared as a guest star in 1768 and asked for
five thousand ducats, which everybody found outrageous. Catherine II was intrigued by the diva, who was famous for her
beauty and her affairs. The Czarina could claim only affairs.
When she asked the star how she dared ask for more money than
her marshals were getting, Madame Gabrielli is said to have an-
swered, "They do not sing, Your Majesty."

There was no Russian opera, and some aristocrats who were interested in music began asking for some Russian "color" in foreign opera. The Italians, who didn't like to give up their lovely
salaries, complied by incorporating popular Russian songs in
their operas. We don't know how it sounded. The music is lost. In
1772 the exclusive Musical Club was founded. The initiation fee
was thirty rubles; members had to be at least state councilors or
brigade generals. The club soon had eight hundred members and
weekly concerts were arranged, performed by singers and musicians of the czarist chapel.

In 1788 in the Winter Palace Catherine had the Grand Theater
constructed, "largest in Europe" (the Czarina's aim) with three
thousand seats. It burned down a few times and was always
rebuilt. By 1790 St. Petersburg had theaters for Russian, German,
Italian, and French performances. Catherine's son Paul was interested in French opera. Czar Alexander I spent half a million
rubles subsidizing the various theaters.

St. Petersburg's Philharmonic Society was founded in 1802,
predating those in Vienna, New York, and Berlin. Its aims were
"to perform important works" and "to aid the widows and
orphans of deceased musicians." The first aim was nobly fulfilled
with the first St. Petersburg performance of Haydn's *Creation*, on
March 22, 1802. The second was reached four years later when
the society's aid fund reached twenty-five thousand rubles. Musicians joining the society paid annual dues of fifteen rubles, and
their widows would get a life pension of five hundred rubles a

year. It was an early, successful social-security project, undiluted by administrative expenses. The society also bought a concert hall and rented it to artists who had been reluctant to make the long trip to St. Petersburg unless they were sure of a large audience. Noted performers appeared in the city, and were followed by noted teachers. Haydn and Mozart were popular but not Beethoven. ("Your genius is centuries ahead of its time," his friend Prince Galitzin had told him in Vienna.)

Hector Berlioz came in 1847, annoyed with the censorship but delighted with the working conditions when he was told he could have as many rehearsals as he wanted. Giuseppe Verdi came in 1862 to attend the premiere of *La Forza del Destino*, commissioned by the Maryinsky. The opera was no success; people didn't understand the libretto (no one does), and some local musicians said it was silly to pay Verdi twenty-two thousand rubles while a Russian composer might get five hundred. Richard Wagner conducted in 1863 at the Philharmonic, shocking the audience when he turned his back to them and faced the orchestra. The greatest success though was Johann Strauss, who spent twelve summers in St. Petersburg, conducting his waltzes and polkas during the white nights at the Vauxhall establishment in Pavlovsk. His salary—twenty thousand rubles, later twice as much—was paid by the St. Petersburg-Pavlovsk Railroad, Russia's first. The court, the aristocracy, and thousands of music lovers went to Pavlovsk by train. The railroad prospered. Incidentally, Strauss fell in love with a Russian girl but didn't marry her, though the date for the wedding had already been set.

The first important Russian composer was Mikhail Ivanovich Glinka, born in 1804, the son of a wealthy landowner in Smolensk. (Russian music, today quite important in the international repertory, is only a hundred and fifty years old.) As a boy of eight, Glinka saw the Russian soldiers marching off to fight the armies of Napoleon. The experience shaped his life and his music. He studied first in St. Petersburg with German teachers and John Field, the Irish composer, then later in Germany and Italy, where he met Bellini and Donizetti. After his return to St. Petersburg, Glinka joined the circle around Pushkin and began writing an opera on a Russian subject, which no one had attempted before. Musically, *A Life for the Czar* is not a revolutionary effort, just early grand opera with arias, ensembles, and choruses. But the Russian spirit is in it. Glinka harmonized Russian folk melodies on the opera stage and pioneered the way for *the* great Russian music drama, Mussorgsky's *Boris Godunov*.

A Life for the Czar had its successful premiere at St. Petersburg's Bolshoi Theater in 1836. Some aristocratic opera fans were heard to say that Glinka had written "the music of coachmen," unwillingly paying him high tribute: obviously he'd caught the folk tunes that were being hummed by servants and serfs. Musicians said this was what Turgenev had called "the national truth" in music. Later, Alexander Borodin stated that Russian music must not follow Western styles but should be "self-sufficient," bringing the antagonism between Slavophiles and Westerners into music. The antagonism ran deeply through Russian thinking, philosophy, the arts, literature, and criticism.

The literary leaders of the Slavophiles were Konstantin and Ivan Aksakov, the brothers Kireyevsky, and A. S. Khomyakov, cultural isolationists who went back to the roots of Russian thought and feeling in the peasant communes. They quoted Pushkin and spoke vaguely of a Russian renaissance. Inevitably, the Slavophile doctrine was turned into political dogma, supporting czarist despotism under the slogan "Autocracy, orthodoxy, nationalism." Contrarily, the Westerners (Belinsky, Bakunin, Herzen, Turgenev) attacked the Slavophile "anti-intellectuals" for making the mistake, as Alexander Herzen put it, of "imagining that Russia once had an individual culture." He called Slavism "a wounded national feeling, an obscure tradition." Half a century later he might have called it a national inferiority complex. The Westerners wanted a "modern" renaissance—free thought, rationalism, individual liberty. Such arguments divided much of Europe in the early 1840s and eventually led to the events of 1848. The only two countries not directly touched by the wave of revolutions were England, a small island surrounded by the sea, and Russia, a large island surrounded by land. It was no consolation to Russia's Westerners that the Slavophiles were also considered "traitors" by the agents of the Third Section, because of their influence on other Slavs. Nicholas I had not forgotten the rebellion of the Poles in 1830. Eventually the two Russian schools of thought influenced and complemented each other in the field of literature. But not in Russian music, which to this day exhibits schizophrenic traits.

Glinka harmonized the ancient folk songs instinctively rather theoretically in *A Life for the Czar* and again in *Ruslan and Ludmila,* based on the poem by Pushkin, who later inspired other Russian composers. They heard the "inner music" in Pushkin's poetic language, the Russian music: Mussorgsky in *Boris,* Tchaikovsky in *Queen of Spades* and *Eugene Onegin.* This was Turgenev's "national truth" in music, and it was best expressed by a group of Russian composers known as "the Five." All but one were born in the 1830s; all were self-taught dilettantes. (Professional musicians were still considered a sort of higher servants in Russia.)

César Antonovich Cui was an engineer and builder of military fortifications. Alexander Porfirevich Borodin was professor of chemistry at the Naval Academy. Modest Petrovich Mussorgsky was an army officer and later worked in the forestry department. Nikolai Andreyevich Rimsky-Korsakov (the youngest, born in 1844) was a naval officer who wore his uniform even after he became professor at the St. Petersburg Conservatory. (In his autobiography he admitted that at the time of his appointment he had "never written one counterpoint nor heard of the existence of the six-four chord." Only Mili Alexeyevich Balakirev, the intellectual leader of the group, knew something about music—but he was the least gifted of the Five. The best of them, the greatest Russian composer, was Mussorgsky, as Russian as Pushkin and Dostoyevsky; he loved them both, sharing with them the suffering of heart and soul. Paul Henry Lang defines *Boris Godunov* correctly as "the greatest musico-dramatic masterpiece of Eastern Europe . . . the universal tragedy of the Russian people cast in musical folk drama." Living in poverty in St. Petersburg not far from the palaces of the very rich who owned thousands of very poor serfs, Mussorgsky profoundly understood the tragedy of his homeland and had the power to express it in music. No other creative artist in Russia, except for two or three of Russia's greatest writers, combined Mussorgsky's compassion and universality. This genius dilettante was able to express everything in music about nature and nation, children and fools, serfs and masters, soldiers and drunks. The protagonist of *Boris* is not the Czar but the people of Russia. His score was later polished and orchestrated by Rimsky-Korsakov and others, whose intentions were better than their results. Nowadays the best interpreters go back to the lean and powerful original score of Mussorgsky.

The Maryinsky Theater in St. Petersburg first rejected *Boris Godunov*, then performed a revised version in 1874 which was banned by the government after twenty-five performances. To the music bureaucrats of the Czar, *Boris* sounded dangerous; it certainly was perturbing. Mussorgsky became depressed and began drinking. He died in 1881, shortly after the death of Dostoyevsky, with whom he had much in common. *Boris* was revived in Rimsky-Korsakov's version in St. Petersburg in 1896. Rimsky-Korsakov and Alexander Glazunov also doctored and completed Borodin's beautiful *Prince Igor*.

Among the "cosmopolitan" Westerners in Russian music were Alexander Serov, and Anton Rubinstein, who spent many years abroad and was the friend of Mendelssohn, Schumann, and Liszt. After the St. Petersburg Philharmonic Society was dissolved in 1859, Rubinstein founded the Russian Musical Society and in 1862 presided at the opening of the St. Petersburg Conservatory. His first important student was Peter Ilyich Tchaikovsky, Russia's first truly professional composer and the leading Westerner. He studied music in St. Petersburg but in 1866 went as a teacher to Moscow, where the school of music was paradoxically more "international" than St. Petersburg's, dominated by the Five. They never accepted Tchaikovsky. "His music either arouses in us profound pity or simply makes us feel sick," declared Cui. (Today millions of people think of Tchaikovsky's music as *the* Russian music.) Tchaikovsky remains an artist of many contradictions. His early symphonies were rather anti-symphonic, lacking organic development, but his *Pathétique* is one of the most popular works in the international repertory. He always wanted to write opera but he had no sense of drama and didn't understand the importance of the libretto. His finest work, *Eugene Onegin*, remains the beautiful lyrical projection of his own personality. It was a failure at the Moscow premiere in 1879 but a great success at the Maryinsky in St. Petersburg five years later.

Russia's new music also remains connected with the city. Igor

Stravinsky was born in 1882 in nearby Oranienbaum; his father was a bass soloist at the Imperial Chapel. Stravinsky studied law at St. Petersburg University but after meeting Rimsky-Korsakov switched to music. One of his earliest orchestral works, *Feu d'Artifice* (1908), written for the wedding of Rimsky-Korsakov's daughter, attracted the attention of Sergei Diaghilev, who in 1910 commissioned *The Firebird*, the first important discovery of the Ballets Russes. Stravinsky found his new emancipated harmonic language in *Petrouchka* and especially in his 1913 masterpiece, *Le Sacre du Printemps*.

The most important Russian composer of the next generation, Sergei Prokofiev, made his debut in 1911 at the Vauxhall in Pavlovsk, performing his Second Piano Concerto. The critic of the *St. Petersburg Gazette* wrote, "To the devil with this music; we come to Pavlovsk to enjoy ourselves." He missed Johann Strauss. Prokofiev stayed abroad for fifteen years but, unlike Stravinsky, returned to Leningrad, where his opera *War and Peace* was first performed in 1946.

The most recent of the great "local" composers was Dmitri Shostakovich, born in Podolsky Street in 1906, a conservatory student at thirteen. Glazunov was so impressed by his talent that he paid for Shostakovich's scholarship out of his own pocket. In 1926 the Leningrad Philharmonic performed his First Symphony. Ten years later the composer was accused of "modernistic deviationism" and gave up exploration of his new idiom. He might have given us something very new and great but, unlike Stravinsky, he wanted to stay. He loved Leningrad. His heroic Seventh Symphony became the musical epic of the city under siege.

THE BALLET

Until the late seventeenth century, the Russian Church considered all merriment sinful. Czar Alexis was forced to sign a ukase proscribing musical instruments (and outlawing jugglers). It was forbidden to dance, to sing "devilish" songs, to wear masks. Offenders were excommunicated. However, the Church tolerated drunkenness, and M. Krifanic, a Serb traveler, reported, "Men, women, priests, laymen roll about in the streets and drink themselves to death."

Only Count Artamon Matveyev, the Czar's First Minister, dared ignore the Church. He and his wife, a former Miss Hamilton from Scotland, arranged concerts and dance divertissements in their palace for the entertainment of the Czar. The Empress and the children watched from behind a lattice; among them was the little boy who later became Peter the Great and permitted "mixed dancing" at his court. At his daughter's wedding, Peter had two large pies served that contained two dwarves who danced a minuet on the table. That was the Czar's idea of a "ballet."

His widow, Catherine I, was more sophisticated. She often went to the small theater on the site of the later Stroganov Palace, where the first ballets were performed in 1727. The management was German, the dancers were mostly Russians. Under the Empress Anna, the first ball was held in the gallery of the Winter Palace. St. Petersburg was still a frontier town with wooden houses and muddy streets, but the Czarina loved lavish entertaining. In 1737 a Frenchman, Jean Baptiste Landé, who had been hired as a master of ceremonies, asked the Empress for permission "to teach twelve persons of youthful Russian nationality, six boys and six girls who will dance theatrically." Permission was granted. Landé was directed "to teach with sincerity, seriousness, and all the qualities of a good man." On May 4, 1738, the Imperial Ballet School of St. Petersburg was established, to the astonishment of the Muscovites. St. Petersburg was exactly thirty-five years and one day old.

Under Empress Elizabeth the ballet became an established art. Italian groups were brought to St. Petersburg to perform classical dance allegories and interludes between the acts of operas. No one knew what the singers were trying to say but everybody could understand the dancers' pantomime. Giovanni Locatelli gave opera seasons at the Summer Garden. The first prominent foreign ballet master was a Viennese, Franz Hilverding, who introduced the entrechat and the pirouette. By that time St. Petersburg had an audience of regular ballet fans, many wearing small cards with the name of their favorite artist.

Catherine II created the post of Director of the Imperial Theaters. Famous ballet masters were brought from abroad, mostly from France. Charles Le Picq, a pupil of the great Noverre, was in charge of the extravagant ball which Potemkin gave for the Czarina and three thousand guests at his new Taurida Palace. Three hundred musicians performed (some hidden in the chandeliers). Quadrilles and tableaux were danced by young noblemen dresssed in velvet. Sterlet from the Volga, oysters from Riga, pheasants from Bohemia, and grapes from the Crimea were served, on gold plates naturally. The affair cost only half a million rubles, seventy thousand for the candles alone.

Potemkin loved dancing. Once he ordered two army sergeants brought all the way from the Caucasus, and had them dressed up as a couple of peasants, man and woman, performing the *tzigane* for a whole week. Then he promoted the sergeants to majors and sent them back to their regiments. Paul, Catherine's son, danced with other young men of the nobility in Hilverding's ballets, and created some gossip by his preference for female dancers dressed as men. The professional dancers were serfs, selected from the peasant classes and sold to the Imperial Theater. This abominable practice was stopped only in 1824.

Hilverding's successsor was the great Angiolini, who produced the premiere of Gluck's *Don Juan*. After him came Charles Didelot, the pupil of Dauberval and Vestris, a great choreographer who became a great teacher. He was "thin as a skeleton, with a very long red nose who danced with a lyre in his hand." Didelot produced his ballets "with dancers flying about on wires" and other effects. He created the romantic Russian ballet, and trained the first Russian ballerina, Avdotia Istomina. She remains immortalized by Pushkin, an ardent balletomane, in his poem *Eugene Onegin:*

> Suddenly she leaps; then she floats away
> Like some light feather in the west wind's breath.
> She draws herself erect, she turns
> And lightly beats one foot against the other.

After her came Maria Danilova, first to use pointed shoes. She was frail and beautiful, and supposedly died "of a broken heart" at the age of seventeen, "betrayed by a handsome Frenchman." It does sound like Pushkin. Czar Nicholas I loved the ballet (particularly the little dancing girls), often went backstage during intermission, and generously supported the Imperial Ballet, which had moved in 1836 to Rossi's beautiful Theater Street. The school is still there.

The following year Maria Taglioni made her debut at Petersburg's Bolshoi in *La Sylphide*. For the first time, even the women in the audience applauded, breaking established custom. Her successor was the Russian ballerina Elena Andreyevna, who became a star in *Giselle* in 1842. It was common knowledge in the West that the world's greatest ballet was in St. Petersburg. Monday, Wednesday, and Friday were ballet nights at the Bolshoi; evening dress was compulsory. The first four rows were reserved for the nobility and top officials. Bankers, foreigners, and artists sat behind them. Merchants, no matter how nouveau-riche, were placed in the rear. Théophile Gautier, the French writer and librettist of *Giselle*, after a visit to St. Petersburg said that the corps de ballet "has no equal for teamwork, precision, and speed of maneuvre." Carlotta Grisi from Milan and Fanny Elssler from Vienna gave much-admired guest performances.

In 1847 an unknown dancer, Marius Petipa, arrived from Marseilles. After working under Perrot and St. Leon, he became ballet master in 1869, and later a famous choreographer whose style is still alive at the Kirov. His director-manager, Ivan Vsevolozhsky, commissioned Tchaikovsky to write *The Sleeping Beauty*. That took courage; the composer's *Swan Lake* had been a terrible flop in Moscow. *The Sleeping Beauty*, with Petipa's choreography, was a great success at the Maryinsky in 1890, and was followed by *The Nutcracker*. A revised version of *Swan Lake* was produced in 1894, after Tchaikovsky's death, and was a triumph. Petipa, who also created the choreography for Delibes's *Coppélia* and Glazunov's *Raymonda*, remains one of the greatest choreographers. Ironically, in 1903, at the age of eighty-four, after working in St. Petersburg for fifty-six years, he had a flop and was summarily dismissed and forbidden to enter the theater through the stage door.

A new era began in the early years of the century. Sergei Diaghilev, musician, painter, promoter (he organized the first exhibition of Russian portraits at the Taurida Palace in 1904), became interested in the ballet. He worked briefly at the Maryinsky but was soon fired by the bureaucrats. He and his friends—Alexander Benois, Walter Nouvel, Leon Bakst—created a revolutionary new school, a departure from nationalism and realism. Mikhail Fokine, a brilliant dancer and choreographer, brought the new ideas to the stage. He discovered a pale, thin girl among the students of the Imperial Ballet School. Anna Pavlova, twenty-six, made her debut in 1907 in *The Dying Swan*. Kschessinska, Karsavina, Preobrazhenskaya, and Trefilova became famous during the *belle époque* of the St. Petersburg Ballet. Vaslav Nijinsky from Poland "whose leap rose far over the heads of the others" was the great dancer of the era.

Grand Duke Vladimir, president of the Academy of Arts, was very interested in the ballet and subsidized Diaghilev, who took a group of talented artists from the conservative Maryinsky abroad between May and September when the theater was closed in St. Petersburg. Until 1914 Diaghilev created excitement in Paris with his Ballets Russes, blending poetry, music, painting, and dancing as never before, creating a powerful avant-garde force in Europe's musical life. The premiere of *Le Sacre du Printemps*, on May 29, 1913, at the Théâtre des Champs-Élysées in Paris, remains a historical moment in modern music; it caused such a scandal that Stravinsky and Pierre Monteux, the conductor, had to escape through a window from the irate listeners.

After the October Revolution the great ballet company was kept together in Petrograd by Lunacharsky, the able minister of culture, and was renamed in 1935 after Sergei Kirov. However, its character has not changed. "If films had existed when Tchaikovsky's *Swan Lake* was first performed at the end of the last century, the dancers of today's Kirov Ballet could be blended into the old formations and no one would notice the difference," a local expert says. The steps, the techniques, the règlement, originally imported from France and Italy, have remained. This might have created a stilted, artificial system of marionettes, but the classicist style of the Kirov Ballet remains beautifully alive in spite of the strict aesthetic rules. It expresses Russia's eternal tendency toward romanticism. In the country of regulated realism and dialectic materialism, the ballet—only the ballet—continues to live in a romantic world of its own.

The Maryinsky Theater is the perfect frame for the great ballet. In 1935 it was renamed State Academy Kirov Theater for Opera and Ballet; the Leningraders call it simply the Kirov Theater. It is an elegant, beautiful house in white, pale blue, and gold, unchanged from the past, though the imperial seal of the Romanovs above the stage has been replaced by the golden hammer-and-sickle emblem. Old habits die hard though. An American friend of mine was recently told by an Intourist girl, "I got you two good seats in the czars' box." In 1914 a good seat cost thirteen dollars and was hard to get. Today it's three dollars and almost impossible for Leningraders to get. Tourists, members of delegations, officials, and people with good connections are given priority.

Until 1945 almost all important ballet premieres took place in Leningrad. Then Galina Ulanova, the Kirov's prima ballerina, and Agrippina Vaganova, the famous teacher, were summoned to Moscow. A generation later, there were defections of three great Kirov stars—Rudolf Nureyev, Natalia Makarova, and Mikhail

Baryshnikov—who stayed abroad during tours for artistic rather than political reasons, they said. But the artistic reasons were produced by politics. There are other dancers in Leningrad who are unhappy with the "choreographic incest," the rigid classicism, the lack of fresh ideas which may be "dangerous." The Kirov has not recovered from these blows, though it remains the breeding ground of great talents.

No one in Leningrad is quite objective when comparing the Kirov Ballet with Moscow's Bolshoi Ballet. Foreign experts believe that the sources of art and tradition are better preserved in Leningrad than in Moscow. The Bolshoi has representative duties, an almost political significance. It is the theater where the Kremlin leaders take their very important guests. It may be tempted to try perfection for its own sake. "That's impossible in Leningrad," a local balletomane says. "Here the past remains alive. Why, the buttermarket fair that most people know only from Stravinsky's *Petrouchka* was held right here until 1875."

The curriculum of the Kirov Ballet School has not much changed since it was opened in 1738. Classes begin at eight-thirty and may last twelve hours. Four hours a day are devoted to ballet training of the classical technique, the rest is given to academic subjects. The dancers are expected to get a well-rounded education. A few foreigners may be accepted, in exceptional cases, for the eight-year instruction period, but most of the fifteen hundred applicants are from the Soviet Union, where the art of the dance remains a national passion. The physical tests are strict. Eventually not more than ninety new students are selected every year. One out of four will drop out before graduation. The school's four hundred and fifty students are instructed by almost one hundred teachers, but only five or six graduates may be chosen every year to join the Kirov Ballet. The rest find jobs with other ballet groups in Leningrad or elsewhere but it is doubtful whether they will ever make the Kirov or the Bolshoi. Young dancers start with a hundred rubles a month and get a small room, more important even than the money. Leading artists are given good apartments, earn a lot of money, and may be sent abroad. For the great dancing stars the sky is the limit in the Soviet Union.

LENINGRAD TODAY AND TOMORROW

At the end of the Second World War much of Leningrad was a vast pile of ruins and rubble. The industrial districts were destroyed. Only the historical center, the former St. Petersburg, had remained, more or less, owing to its special antiaircraft defenses. But even there many buildings were badly damaged. Outside the city, the beautiful country palaces of the czars—Pushkin, Pavlovsk, Petrodvorets—were burned-out shells.

Reconstruction began right away: first priority was given to the historical center and to the great palaces. In accordance with Lenin's bequest, the continuity of nineteenth-century St. Petersburg with Petrograd, the center of revolutionary Russia, and the present-day Leningrad would be maintained. Russia's former capital was to reflect the history of the nation; the city's architectural continuity would transcend all political eras and changes. This is the official explanation for rebuilding, at immense effort and expense, the palaces of the czars at a time when housing was badly needed for the inhabitants of the fast-growing city. Doubtless much could have been done with all the money spent on preservation and restoration had it been decided to build something new—a modern, functional city, easy to manage, but perhaps as soulless and styleless, sprawling and ugly as Moscow. Lenin was right in preserving what the Marquis de Custine had called a theater set.

By 1965 Leningrad, which had lost over a million and a half people during the war, had again attained its prewar population.

In 1967 there were 3.7 million inhabitants. Today the Leningrad oblast (district) covers an area of almost thirty thousand square miles (a little less than the state of Maine), with almost five million people. In the suburbs new satellite towns have been built, some close to the former imperial palaces and ducal manor houses. Factories and port facilities were built, models of the latest Soviet planning. And all the time housing conditions were distressing, to say the least.

Leningrad's architects in charge of the restoration received strict orders. Within the historical center, the "zone of conservation," everything still standing would be preserved and repaired. All missing parts would be restored after the old plans and blueprints. There would be almost no new construction. In very exceptional cases, some "essential" buildings might be put up—very carefully, to avoid style breaks, but such additions must be "episodical," done only after the most expert scrutiny. Various watchdog committees would make sure "that no one slips something past the artists and architects." They, not the politicians, would make the final decisions. The Leningraders wanted to avoid what had happened in Moscow.

"A barbarian place," a Leningrader says. "A Russian proverb said, 'There is nothing above Moscow except the Kremlin and nothing above the Kremlin except heaven.' Hah! Now there is the twenty-one-floor Intourist Hotel above the Kremlin, and several skyscrapers around it. From certain places one no longer sees the great cathedrals of the Kremlin. Even Stalin had enough sense to put up the university and other atrocious pseudo-Gothic skyscrapers far away from the golden cupolas of the Kremlin."

Despite good intentions and strict controls, mistakes did happen in Leningrad. One cardinal rule said that new structures must always be judged in relation to their vicinity. They must not obstruct the panorama. But one architect damaged the ensemble of several old buildings by putting up a modern structure too close to them. He was demoted to a much lower position. People are unhappy about the modernistic façade of the Hotel Yevropskaya (the former Hotel de L'Europe) at the corner of Nevsky Prospekt and Brodsky Street, which disturbs the serene beauty of Rossi's nearby Arts Square.

"Only a master architect who understands the very soul of Leningrad can work here successfully," Yevgeny Poltoratsky, chief architect of the Atelier of Urbanism, told me. I understood: the master architect should have been born and brought up in Leningrad.

"In this city," said Poltoratsky, "an architect must not go to bed early during the white nights in June and July when the buildings are clearly silhouetted against the pale sky, undisturbed by distorting shadows and sunlight. During the white nights I walk around and meditate."

The city planners drew too large concentric rings around the inner city, the historic center. Within the smaller ring some modern buildings of limited height were permitted "exceptionally." The highest of them, the new Leningrad Hotel, was just at the outside rim of the inner circle—far enough not to interfere with the silhouette. New skyscraper developments would be put up in the outer ring, at least fifteen kilometers from the historic center. They could rise up to thirty floors. Last year, sixty thousand new apartments were built in these developments.

"The first thing we ask ourselves is, 'How will it look as one approaches Leningrad from the sea?' " said Poltoratsky. "I've seen pictures of the World Trade Center's two supertowers in New York's Wall Street district. Couldn't happen here. Our terrain is low. We are allergic to high structures. Admittedly, such thinking demands a high degree of responsibility. Elsewhere they often build first, hoping for the best. Afterwards they are surprised if the ensemble doesn't look good. In Moscow they destroyed a cathedral to make space for a swimming pool. In Leningrad, there are artistic *and* political questions. Our people take a personal interest in their city. When it becomes known that some old buildings must come down to make space for an urban-renewal project, there may be thousands of letters of protest. The new project becomes a sort of referendum. We consider Leningrad an organic development. We want to leave it to our children as it is."

Poltoratsky told me what happened when they were building the metro in Leningrad. The subway will link the peripheral fringes of the large city with the center; a semicircular line will enclose the archipelago. It was necessary to install an escalator underneath an eighteenth-century classicist temple with Doric columns, built by Ruska in Nevsky Prospekt next to Gostiny Dvor. Then strong opposition was expressed against the destruction of the classicist portico. It was removed stone by stone, the escalator was installed underneath, and the portico was put up again.

"*Nous sommes un peu* Tory *en Leningrad,*" said the architect. "When I saw the new skyscrapers they put up all over Paris, I was aghast. Not that we are perfect. In some places here you will notice a sharp style break between *art nouveau* and 1950. There is no connection between the *Jugendstil* features of the Hotel Astoria, anno 1912, and the concrete-and-glass structure of the Hotel Leningrad."

The city was not unprepared for the restoration job. During the First World War, an Office of Conservation and Restoration had been set up where the designs and blueprints of all historical buildings were kept. All details were preserved, down to samples of silk tapestries and the materials used in various rooms. Models of all important buildings and photographs of the façades were filed at the Beaux Arts Academy and the Museum of Ancient St. Petersburg. The city has a long tradition of restoration. Many restorers are local people who were trained in special schools and passed severe tests. They work under strict supervision.

"Leningrad," Poltoratsky said happily, "has the most exacting rules of restoration among all cities of the Soviet Union."

From the window of my room at the Astoria Hotel I looked out on St. Isaac's Square, confusing with its styles and pseudo styles and typical of the city where even "time was copied," as the Marquis de Custine noted in 1839. Klodt's equestrian statue of Czar Nicholas I in the middle of the square is dominated by St. Isaac's Cathedral (named after St. Isaac of Dalmatia), the largest church in Leningrad, a powerful structure. It was designed by a French architect, Richard de Montferrand, in what was then called Imperial Russian style, with a high rotunda and a golden dome conveying the idea of the Pantheon in Rome. To some people it seems clumsy rather than majestic, reminiscent of an enormous, dark elephant. St. Isaac's was built over a period of forty years, between 1818 and 1858, by half a million people, and cost twenty-three million rubles. To put up such a heavy structure—more than 300,000 tons—on marshy ground, whole forests were needed to create the foundations. In the past fifty years additional piles had to be driven into the ground on the Neva side, to keep the cathedral from sliding down. The inner height of the dome, 269 feet from the floor, is less than St. Peter's in Rome (404 feet) but more than St. Paul's in London (225 feet). Everything is heavy and overwhelming—the colonnade with 144 columns of Olonets granite, the bas reliefs and semiprecious stones, the statues and large bronze doors.

The cathedral was "closed for repairs," but I sneaked in with the help of a friendly guard. The icons and marble walls, the mosaics of the saints, the columns of malachite and lapis lazuli, the silver and bronze chandeliers conveyed pomp rather than peace. This was no church for meditation and silent prayer. It must have been impressive during the Easter midnight mass when the dark church, filled with blue incense smoke, was suddenly illuminated as the guns of the fortress boomed. "St. Isaac's had the largest congregation of all the cathedrals," E. M. Almedingen remembers in *My St. Petersburg*. "Particularly on Easter Eve, when women put on their finest jewelery and ball-dresses for the midnight service, the so-called *Zautrenia*. It was little more than a pious social gathering. I shall never forget the sense of shock I had when, once, window-shopping on Nevsky Prospekt, I heard one elegant woman say to another, 'Now that Madame Aline has let me down I can't possibly go to the *Zautrenia*. I have nothing fit to wear.'"

The problem wouldn't arise today: St. Isaac's has been a museum since 1931. So is the Cathedral of Our Lady of Kazan, built between 1801 and 1811, with its colonnade of Corinthian columns copied from St. Peter's in Rome and the central portal copied from the Ghiberti door of the Duomo in Florence. The Kazan Cathedral had some official status; the Te Deum was often attended by the Czar and his dignitaries. The walls and pillars are hung with trophies from the Napoleonic wars. Leningraders say that seen from the air the cathedral resembles the portrait of Napoleon. It is now the Museum of the History of Religion and Atheism, with sections on the history of the papacy, and on the Inquisition.

There is something anomalous about a great church not used for worship which is an "architectural monument" or a museum, with regular visiting hours, tickets, and attendants. (Though even in Italy, the land of churches, many are now closed at night, after so many thefts have occurred there.) Leningrad's largest church open for worship is St. Nicholas Cathedral, once called "the Sailors' Church," near Theater Square. It's beautiful, in blue and gold, with a fine bell tower, and was built by Chevakinsky, a master of the Russian baroque, in the 1750s. Its five gilded domes surmount the lovely park around the church. The Intourist people pretended not to know the hours of service. A foreign resident suggested Saturday evening around six for vespers, "a good time to see the people." I took a taxi. The driver, an elderly man faintly resembling the late Nikita Khrushchev, got out after I paid him and said he might as well go to the service for a while; they had a very good choir. We walked through the gate into the park, behind some women who crossed themselves frequently in the Russian-Orthodox manner, face and shoulders, while they were approaching the cathedral. The main entrance was locked. From a narrow side entrance (only half the door was open and we had to line up behind other people) a narrow staircase went up. On the second landing a glass door led into the main floor of the cathedral. It was locked. Looking through, I saw the interior of the vast, dark, empty church.

The staircase was now jammed with people. Many prayed and crossed themselves, as we walked up slowly, step by step. From inside came the singing voices of the priests and the choir and the powerful sound of the organ. On the third floor, the door was open. Two women were doing a good business selling thin candles. There was a profusion of bright lights and beautiful icons, of gold-colored candlesticks and the sumptuous robes of the priests. The upper room seemed smaller than the empty lower one. It was crowded with worshipers, who seemed oblivious of the presence of other people, praying, singing, crossing themselves. I saw mostly elderly women wearing headkerchiefs, and a few fragile-looking old ladies with old-fashioned hats and clothes that once had been elegant. They wore gloves and carried handbags and seemed to have stepped straight out of a Pushkin or Turgenev novel. There were very few men. Some young people accompanied the elderly women.

The taxi driver had been right: the choir was very good, the powerful Russian voices singing with force and precision. There was no routine about this service. An old woman got down on her knees and everybody moved aside though there was little space. It seemed a scene in a Russian opera—the music and choir, the people crossing themselves, the priests in their robes and high hats—yet in spite of the costumes and lights and the conventional gestures, this was one of the few moments in Leningrad when I did not feel as though I were on a stage set, as I did between the palaces and canals. No, this was life and reality, faith and perhaps a sense of resignation.

I heard German voices behind me, a man and a woman, tourists looking at the people. The man said, "*Das wäre bei uns nicht möglich*"—that couldn't happen back home. He wore East German clothes. I left after a while. People were still coming up the narrow stairway—praying, devout pilgrims in atheist Leningrad.

The taxi was still at the gate; the old man gave me a conspiratorial smile and said, "I thought you would come back. I just turned down a fare. Germans. I didn't like them. East Germans, West Germans, what's the difference? They were all here during the siege. . . ." I got in beside him, and he said, "Where to? Want to look at our synagogue too?"

I said that was a good idea.

"You won't meet many people there now. But it's on the way to the Astoria." He said it almost apologetically. The synagogue was in a quiet side street, large and deserted. The driver told me to walk in through the rear. Inside there was the peculiar scent that brought back memories of the synagogue in my Moravian hometown, where I went on Friday evenings, a mixture of burning candles, wood, old leather. I heard faint voices and walked through a corridor into a small praying chapel. A few men wearing their hats stood in a corner talking. One wore a sports shirt and had a handkerchief over his head, an American tourist who had hoped to attend the service. He said the synagogue was locked but they were trying to get the *schammes* with the keys. An old man wearing an unfashionably long garbardine topcoat and a fedora said they'd just finished the evening prayer. Tonight there had been ten of them; they were lucky.

"It's hard to get ten men these days. The old ones are too tired to come for prayers. And the young ones . . ." He shrugged. "You know what young people are like. Same everywhere, I guess." He said there were not many Jews left in Leningrad, perhaps a thousand. (Later I was told by an official there were over three thousand.) I asked him how life was.

"It isn't good, it isn't bad. It could be worse." He stopped. I noticed that another man had joined us, also a Jew, but there was a sudden silence, an uncomfortable silence. I asked no more questions.

Earlier, I'd heard about Valery Panov, who had been one of the leading dancers of the Kirov Ballet. His wife, Galina Ragozhina, was also an important member of the company. Panov, a great artist, had often been decorated. He had created the choreography for *Queen of Spades* and other classics, and had publicly said that he considered Russian dancing the best, that he considered the training of the Kirov dancers severe but very good. It was also known that certain officials of the Ministry of Culture had asked Panov to make certain changes in his productions for ideological reasons.

In March 1972 Panov and his wife applied for exit visas to Israel. Panov was thirty-four, at the top of his form. Galina was twenty-two, blond, fragile, and pretty.

Panov was at once dismissed by the Kirov Ballet company. His wife was permitted to stay, at the minimum salary paid to the novices of the corps de ballet. She decided to quit.

The Panovs did not get their exit permits. They soon noticed that officially they had become unpersons, and worse. Their telephone was discontinued. Their friends were advised not to see them if they didn't want to get into trouble too. Several times Panov was stopped on the street by heavy-set characters who threatened to beat him up. Once he lost his nerve and got into a fight with a militiaman who had provoked him. Panov was arrested and put in a prison cell for a week with several other men who had been half beaten to death and, as a result, were nearly crippled. That was a message, and part of the threat, of course. Panov had been reminded that he needed a healthy body if he had any hope of continuing his career. A persecuted writer may still write at home (though he won't be able to publish). A persecuted scientist may do work if he has pencil and paper, or a blackboard and a piece of chalk (though his work will not become known outside his room). Panov needed daily exercise but his living room was small and the ceiling too low to practice the leaps that had made him a star at the Kirov Theater. Unless he was either permitted to leave or reinstated, his career as a dancer would be finished. Finally, over two years after asking to leave, the Panovs were allowed to emigrate.

Panov's friends have speculated about why he was punished so severely. He is not a great scientist and knew no valuable secrets, but he was important because his prestige in Russia was very great. The authorities, men and women with an Asiatic mind, felt they might lose face if Panov and his wife left. The loss of face in high circles was the worst part about the defections of Nureyev, Makarova, and Baryshnikov.

This seems also the reason for the instant dismissal of Leonid Tarassuk, the noted curator of European-American arms and armor at the Hermitage Museum, after he applied for a visa to Israel. His application was considered an official slap in the face among Moscow's high bureaucracy. It was denied; instead Tarassuk, an officer in the reserve, was called up for duty. Such delicate subjects are not discussed by the bureaucrats when they sit down to iron out big deals with American executives, and the executives know better than to mention them. They are, after all, "internal Russian affairs," aren't they? Business is business. It has always been like that. Cruelty and inhumanity have remained part of the Russian system since long before the Romanovs came to power. Nothing has changed to this day.

"The similarity between the two Russias, past and present, is startling and depressing," Virginia Cowles writes in *The Russian Dagger*.

Russia has produced many great writers and musicians but very few great rulers. It is impossible to separate government and governed for ever. Why is there always a new tyrant to take the place of the old? Does it spring from the Asiatic streak in the Russian character? Or, as Tolstoy prophesied, is it a natural consequence of the rejection of Christianity?

Someone at the door of the praying chapel said they had found the man with the keys. The synagogue was opened. We were asked to come and take a look.

It is a beautiful synagogue, built some eighty years ago in neo-Renaissance style, with fine columns. There was a sense of harmony and peacefulness about it. They said it was very beautiful when the candles were lit and it was filled with people, on the Sabbath and on the important holidays. A Baron Guensburg, a wealthy St. Petersburg merchant, had paid for it.

The taxi driver nodded, pleased, when I told him I'd seen the synagogue, and he took me to the Astoria and refused a tip. I thanked him and we shook hands.

There was a special parking lot right next to St. Isaac's Cathedral for the foreign guests of the Hotel Astoria, with the metal fence around it guarded day and night. Several young Russians were always looking at the cars, discussing them enthusiastically. The cars were nothing special—a Simca, a Volvo, a Ford. Once a young man said he wished somebody would come to the Astoria in a Ferrari, so he could at last see one. Still talking, the young people would then walk into the small park in front of the cathedral, a round lawn with lilac bushes. Now, early in June, the lilacs were blooming. The colors were more brilliant than in Vienna where I'd seen it weeks earlier, but here it wouldn't last so long, and people appreciated it a great deal more. I often saw them standing in front of the lilacs; even the young boys gazed at them as happily as they had looked at the cars.

Something was always going on in the small park. At six-thirty in the morning a woman would cut the lawn with a hand mower or trim the bushes, or she would clean the paths with a rake. By seven o'clock the sun was already high and many benches were filled with sun-worshipers, sitting back with their eyes closed, enjoying the sweet warmth. The summer is short in Leningrad, and sunshine is a luxury. Around 8:00 A.M. some Russian sailors appeared, looking smart. They kept their caps on and saluted their officers. There were also Swedish sailors, tall and blond, with long hair; they didn't bother to wear caps or salute officers. Many carried triangular packages, having just bought balalaikas at the Astoria's hard-currency Berliozka store. Later they would spend the rest of their good Swedish money at the hotel's currency bar.

St. Isaac's Square is surrounded by palaces. The finest are the Myatlev Palace at No. 9, where Diderot stayed in 1773, and the former Horse Guards Riding School, built by Quarenghi in 1804. Less successful is the pseudobaroque former Ministry of Agriculture, and Marie's Palace (Maryinsky Dvorets), built for the oldest daughter of Czar Nicholas I, now headquarters of the mayor of Leningrad and of the executive committee of the Municipal Council. Its façade is decorated like a soldier's tunic, with the Order of the Red Flag, awarded to the city for its stand against General Yudenich in 1919; and with two Orders of Lenin, one given in 1945 for the heroic defense during the siege, the other commemorating the city's 250th anniversary in 1953. A recently installed light board shows the time and the temperature. Leningraders claim the sign spoils the façade. Who cares about time and temperature anyway?

The worst building in the square is the dark-gray structure formerly known as the Imperial German Embassy, built in 1912 by Peter Behrens, the Berlin architect who had a young assistant named Mies van der Rohe. Judging by the ugly, styleless façade, the assistant had little to do with it. At the beginning of the First World War an angry mob knocked down some of the sculptures along the roof line. During the Second World War the Nazi bombers ruined many fine buildings in Leningrad but missed the former German Embassy. Nearby is the fine late-Empire palace built by Montferrand for Prince Lobanov-Rostovsky; the Carrara marble lions in front of the colonnade are mentioned in Pushkin's *The Bronze Horseman*. St. Isaac's Square is an architectural nutshell of Russian history.

The Astoria Hotel, built in 1912 in *art nouveau* style by Lidval, was long a legend among sophisticated world travelers, who rated it with Raffles' Hotel in Singapore, Shepheard's in Cairo, and the Paris Ritz. Today the Astoria's claim to fame is its *Jugendstil* decorations and chandeliers, and the legend that Hitler had the invitations printed for a great victory banquet to be held there on July 21, 1941, one month after the German invasion of the Soviet Union. No invitations have been found but it is just what Hitler *might* have done.

Anyone willing to climb 262 comfortable steps may reach (daily except Tuesday) the top of the gilded dome of St. Isaac's. The view perfectly conveys the great idea of Peter the Great. On a clear day one sees the delta of the Neva, the flat coastline of the Gulf of Finland, and Kotlin Island with Kronstadt. The city's panorama unfolds, with its geometrically laid out squares—St. Isaac's Square, Decembrists' Square, Palace Square with the 158-foot monolith, impressive even from the top of the 330-foot dome. The gilded spires of Peter and Paul Fortress and the Admiralty, built by Adrian Zakharov. The blue dome of Trinity Cathedral, the Alexander Nevsky Cathedral, Smolny Cathedral. The monumental structures facing the Neva, the Academy of Sciences, the university, Menshikov Palace, the Academy of Fine Arts, built by Kokorinov. (Not everything in the city was built by foreigners; there were great Russian architects.) No Western ruler built such a profusion of enormous palaces.

And water everywhere. The sea, the Neva and its tributaries, the canals. The beautiful, often charming bridges are an important element of the city's architecture. But the water often means terror. When a gale blows from northwest and the waters of the Gulf of Finland turn against the estuary of the Neva, there may be another much feared inundation. The worst occurred in 1824 and again in 1924, when the waters rose three and a half meters above the normal mark.

The city is a magnificent ensemble in the middle of what was once an Arctic wilderness. The view of Leningrad depends on the reflection in the beholder's eyes. It is never dull though for the historian, the artist, the city planner, the student of revolution. Contrarily, Moscow is rarely interesting, except for the politician.

Officially, the rivalry between Moscow and Leningrad does not exist. It is incompatible with the principles of Socialism. But one becomes aware of it soon in Leningrad. The people feel both inferior and superior to Moscow. They admit Moscow is older and larger; they may even admit that Moscow is the "heart" of Russia. But they are sorry for the Muscovites because they cannot live in Leningrad. A young girl told me about a friend who had fallen in love with a Swedish sailor and got permission to marry him and emigrate to Stockholm. The Leningrad girl was sorry for her friend. "Wait a few years. She won't like living in Stockholm. How can one live anywhere else when one was born and brought up here?" A few days later, the Leningrad poet Iosif Brodsky wrote a letter to Leonid Brezhnev before he was ordered to leave his country. ". . . I owe to Russia all I own in this world. . . . I am losing my Soviet citizenship but I remain a Russian poet. I believe I shall return. Poets always return, in person or on paper. . . ."

I met an old couple living in a small dark room, once part of the servants' quarters in a palace along Fontanka, where Pushkin used to walk. The government offered them a small modern flat in the suburbs where they would have sunshine, fresh air, and a bathroom. They said thanks, no. They prefer to remain in the old district where they feel at home. And I met some elderly Jewish people who don't want to go to Israel. They were afraid of being "lost and lonely" there. Life in Leningrad is often hard "but here we are at home."

The Leningraders are convinced they are more "cultured," speak better Russian (though experts admit the best Russian is spoken along the Lower Volga), and have better manners than other Russians. "If someone is rude, trying to push you around, he's probably come from Moscow," a man said. His wife said she wouldn't even want to visit Moscow, except for the Tretyakov Gallery. She was bitter because David Oistrakh hadn't been in Leningrad for years "and it was here that he became famous." Someone else complained that Van Cliburn, very popular in the Soviet Union, on his last trip to Russia had performed in Moscow but not in Leningrad. Western statesmen on official visits to Moscow who come for one day to Leningrad are not popular here.

Some Leningraders claim that "the best thing in Moscow is the Red Arrow train that leaves every night for Leningrad." (My sleeping car compartment, with brass ornaments, mahogany walls, and red plush curtains, looked like a *chambre separée* at Maxim's during the *belle époque*. In the attendant's compartment I saw an old samovar and glasses in silver holders, a telephone, and a black mahogany box on the wall with two rows of flaps such as they had in good European hotels in the early years of the century. As a passenger pushes the button in his compartment, a flap falls down revealing the number. When the train departed, there was martial music from an invisible loudspeaker, and when it arrived in Leningrad at eight in the morning, there were fanfares from the "Leningrad March," written by the Kievan composer R. M. Glière, over the station's loudspeakers.)

Sooner or later every visitor in Leningrad hears the story about the man who gets up in the crowded metro in Moscow and offers his seat to an elderly woman.

She is surprised. "You must be from Leningrad."

"Yes. How did you know?"

She smiles. "Because you offered me your seat."

Now the man smiles. "And you, comrade, must be from Moscow."

"Yes. How did *you* know?"

"Because you didn't say, 'Thank you.'"

Westerners who live in Leningrad must make some adjustments. They are often bewildered by the aura of suspicion surrounding them. After a while they realize there is nothing personal in it. The Russians' suspicion is congenital, atavistic, nonsubjective, perhaps the result of centuries of seclusion and distrust. They rarely invite Westerners into their homes, unless they hold official positions. The neighbors might talk. And "home" may be only a couple of rooms. No person is entitled to more than nine square meters. The director of the Hermitage still lives in the princely apartment which his predecessors were given by the czars—but the apartment was subdivided and he occupies only two rooms.

An American who lived here three years says, "They are beginning to like you when they won't answer certain questions. They remain silent rather than tell you a lie. You may have made a friend—but it takes time." The Leningraders have long memories. "We are just beginning to forget that the Swedes were our enemies in the late seventeenth century," a man says. How long will it take them to forget the siege?

In 1932 the city created a beautiful recreation park on Yelagin Island, named after I. P. Yelagin, a courtier and nobleman at the time of Catherine II. No one in Leningrad calls it by its official name, Kirov Central Park of Culture and Recreation, though everybody goes there on a nice day. The main attraction, a lovely neoclassical palace, was built in 1812 by Rossi for Maria Feodorovna, the widow of Czar Paul I, with a beautiful simple six-columned façade, and a portico on each side. Rossi could do no wrong. Around the palace there is an English-style park with green lawns, oak groves and small lakes, small pavilions and fine statues, all charming and harmonious. From the western tip of his island, Prince Yelagin had a beautiful view of the sea: this was once known as the Strelka Promontory. I spent an afternoon there, walking with D., who appreciates beauty. I saw a music theater and a small summer theater for amateur performances, and there was music from loudspeakers. It was Sunday, and a considerable part of the local population seemed to have come out—citizens, sailors, soldiers, and many pretty girls. Soft drinks and ice cream were sold. People seemed relaxed and happy. Everybody was walking; cars are not permitted on the island.

A car is still a small dream for most Russians. For the Leningraders especially the big dream is a dacha, a second home in the countryside. Leningrad's climate is raw and humid, often the cause of chronic colds. Many parents send their small children to the South for a few weeks every year, if they are lucky and have relatives there. Spring and autumn are often damp. A fine mist rises from the Neva, though it is claimed there is less fog since 1928, when the city's wooden pavements were replaced by asphalt. Summers are short. Late in the fall the statues in the Summer Garden are boarded up, and the wooden landing stages along the Neva are towed upstream. In the public parks the benches are taken away and the open-air dance floors removed. The Leningraders sigh: the long winter is about to begin. Low temperatures will be aggravated by brutal winds from the north. No wonder that during the short summer everybody wants to get out into the lovely countryside that stretches all the way to the Finnish border. A dacha may be anything from a primitive weekend hut to a sumptuous mansion. It is now possible to rent a dacha or to build one on a site leased from the government; it must not have more than six rooms. Certain areas, off limits for hoi polloi, are reserved for the favorites of the regime: technocrats, managers, officials, artists, writers. Even more secluded and closely guarded are the large dachas for Party leaders and foreign diplomats. The favorites of the czarinas had their palaces and country houses around St. Petersburg. The favorites of the present regime have more modest places, but the idea is the same —to keep the rest of the people out.

I spent a Sunday in the dacha of an American diplomat, about an hour's ride from Leningrad, halfway to the border city of Vyborg on the beautiful Karelian isthmus. The countryside was flat and the horizon was wide, extending all the way to the coast of Finland. There was a feeling of Arctic expanse, on this fine day in June, between the beautiful northern woods, pines and birches. The good highway went straight through the woods. Paths led into them, and people were strolling under the trees, enjoying the moment. Elderly women were walking alone. "A luxury we cannot afford any more at home," the wife of the American said later.

There was an idyllic mood about the region. People enjoyed nature and the simple pleasures. Some collected flowers and some were quietly sitting in the sun. Others played featherball, or washed their beloved cars, or went sailing or boating along the coast. People wanted solitude and peacefulness. Everybody formed an invisible little island around himself, protecting his privacy, respecting the other person's. No blaring radio; no noisy togetherness. Some seemed to listen to the song of the birds. Once in a while I saw groups of young children wearing colored caps, "pioneers" hiking through the woods. There were many pioneer homes in the region. On Sundays parents were permitted to visit their kids. It seemed innocent and old-fashioned, and somehow it was moving. Time had stood still here. I was reminded of the summers I spent as a teenager in my cousin Dolek's home in a small place in Poland. Dark pine woods, wild mushrooms, a trout stream, a small lake where I learned to swim, and Uncle Bernard's open Fiat in which I learned to drive. There were horses on the roads, and we often had a flat tire. . . .

The dacha put at the disposal of the American diplomat by the Soviet authorities would cause no excitement around Redding Ridge, Connecticut, where I once lived in Mark Twain's country, but it was comfortable and had a nice garden. Through the trees I saw the sun reflected in the blue sea. As I walked through the gate, I saw a Soviet security guard standing in the bushes. Diplomats are guarded in all countries. But here the guards kept book on who was coming and going, and how long a visitor stayed. It was, after all, a Soviet-style Sunday idyll. Time had not stood still here.

Among my Intourist guides was a young woman who had come as a child from the sunny Crimea to Moscow shortly before World War II. The Leningraders had seemed cool, almost hostile to her. Down South she had heard loud voices and happy laugh-

ter. Everybody was friendly, even strangers would talk to one another. Not in Leningrad, however, where the people have a no-
nonsense attitude toward life. In the Leningrad metro, they are as
reserved as in the London underground. There are a few restaurants, with loud music, but only young people go there. Leningraders meet their friends at home, for long and serious discus-
sions, or to listen to new records. Yet the young woman now
doesn't want to live anywhere but in Leningrad. She was here
during the siege.

"If you lived here at that time, and learned about the decency
and the kindness of the people, who might be dead tomorrow,
you would never be happy in another place. Leningrad is where I
belong." She knows that the cool, reserved people can be relied
upon, that a promise given is a promise kept, that there is respect
for privacy. It is easier to meet people in the South, "but a friend
in Leningrad remains a friend for life."

The Leningraders remain tourists-at-home; they constantly
rediscover their beautiful city. They stroll in Pushkin's Summer
Garden, or along Dostoyevsky's dark canals. They have an instinct for taste and style. "The influence of all the beauty around
you helps to form your judgment," my friend D. says. "You cannot be without a sense of harmony in such surroundings. The
city's architecture, art treasures, parks, the whole atmosphere,
have created a population conditioned to beauty. People here discuss a symphony or a painting with a sense of deep commitment.
Elsewhere—in Moscow, for instance—they talk that way about a
soccer game. Last winter I went to Yalta on a brief vacation. I'd
rented a room by letter. Later the landlady said she had had several offers. She'd taken me sight unseen because I was from
Leningrad. 'Everybody knows that Leningraders are nice and
cultured,' she said. . . . There you are."

The Leningraders' passion for their city was often a political
force. During the siege it became a military force. Soviet historians agree that the people's faith in Leningrad's inviolability
made them, and their city, survive.

"They didn't talk heroically," says D. "They *acted* heroically."

SELECTED BIBLIOGRAPHY

Almedingen, E. M. *My St. Petersburg.*

Apollon. Many issues.

Baedeker, K. *Russland.* Leipzig: 1914.

Cowles, Virginia S. *The Romanovs.* New York: Harper & Row, 1971.

———. *The Russian Dagger.* New York: Harper & Row, 1969.

Custine, Astolphe, Marquis de. *La Russie en 1839.* Paris: 1843.

Descargues, Pierre. *The Hermitage.* London: Thames and Hudson, 1967.

Frederic, Harold. *The New Exodus.* London: William Heinemann, 1892.

Gosling, Nigel, and Jones, Colin. *Leningrad.* London: Studio Vista, 1965.

Heiss, Karl William. *Leningrad.* Pforzheim: Goldstadtverlag, 1963.

Herzen, Alexander I. *My Past and Thoughts.* Translated by Constance Garnett. 6 vols. London: Chatto and Windus, 1924–27.

Lang, Paul Henry. *Music in Western Civilization.* New York: W. W. Norton, 1941.

Lavater-Sloman, Mary. *Katharina und die russische seele.* Zurich: Morgarten-verlag ag., 1941.

Leningradskaya Pravda. Many articles.

Nagel. *Nagel's Moscow and Leningrad.* Geneva and New York: Nagel, 1958.

Paléologue, Georges Maurice. *An Ambassador's Memoirs.* Translated by F. A. Holt. 3 vols. London: Hutchinson, 1923–25.

Radishchev, Alexander N. *A Journey from St. Petersburg to Moscow.* 1790.

Rimsky-Korsakov, Nikolai. *My Musical Life*. New York: Alfred A. Knopf, 1942.

Rumbold, Sir Horace, Bart. *Recollections of a Diplomatist*. 2 vols. London: E. Arnold, 1903.

Salisbury, Harrison E. *The 900 Days*. New York: Harper & Row, 1969.

Schiller, Ulrich. "Auf den Spuren der Revolution," *Merian*, vol. 10/XXIV.

Ségur, Louis Philippe, Comte de. *Mémoires ou souvenirs et anecdotes*. Paris: 1844.

ABOUT THE AUTHOR

JOSEPH WECHSBERG was born in 1907 in Moravia (then Austria-Hungary), and grew up in Czechoslovakia and Europe. He studied in Prague, Vienna, and Paris, traveled all over the world as a ship's musician and writer, and come to America in 1938. During World War II he served in the American Army, and in 1948 he became a foreign correspondent for *The New Yorker*. He speaks several languages, is the author of many books, is interested in many things; friends in Europe, where he spends considerable time, call him "baroque" or "one of the last Renaissance men." Having written about cities before—melancholy Vienna, and mystical, magical Prague—he became fascinated by Leningrad's tragic history and strange beauty, its suffering and greatness. All this he found there—and more.